STUDY GUIDE
VOLUME II: CHAPTERS 15-24

INTERMEDIATE ACCOUNTING
Thirteenth Edition

Douglas W. Kieso, Ph.D., C.P.A.
Aurora University
Aurora, Illinois

Donald E. Kieso, Ph.D., C.P.A.
KPMG Peat Marwick Emeritus Professor of Accounting
Northern Illinois University
DeKalb, Illinois

Jerry J. Weygandt, Ph.D., C.P.A.
Arthur Andersen Alumni Professor of Accounting
University of Wisconsin
Madison, Wisconsin

Terry D. Warfield, Ph.D.
Associate Professor
Director, Andersen Center for Financial Reporting and Control
University of Wisconsin
Madison, Wisconsin

WILEY
JOHN WILEY & SONS, INC.

Cover Photo Credit: Jon Arnold Images/SuperStock, Inc.

To order books or for customer service call 1-800-CALL-WILEY (225-5945).

ISBN-13   9780470380604

Printed in the United States of America

10 9 8 7 6 5 4 3 2 1

Printed and bound by Bind-Rite, Inc.

CONTENTS

NOTE TO STUDENTS

This Study Guide is provided as an aid to your study of *Intermediate Accounting* by Donald E. Kieso, Jerry J. Weygandt, and Terry Warfield. If used wisely, it can supplement and reinforce your understanding of the concepts and techniques presented in the textbook. **Never rely on the Study Guide as a substitute for a thorough reading of the textbook material.** This Study Guide merely highlights the in-depth presentation in the textbook.

An approach that combines use of the Study Guide and textbook material is suggested below.

1. Read the textbook presentation of the chapter.

2. Read the chapter review paragraphs in the Study Guide.

3. Answer the questions and review exercises appearing at the end of the chapter review paragraphs and compare your answers with those found at the end of each chapter. The extent of your success in answering these questions and exercises will indicate your understanding of the chapter. If you were unsuccessful in answering a large percentage of these questions correctly, you should read the textbook again.

4. Work the problems assigned from the textbook.

Solutions to the review questions and exercises are found at the end of each chapter. In addition to identifying the correct answer to each true-false and multiple choice question, an explanation is provided indicating why the answer is false and why a particular alternative (for multiple choice questions) is correct. This approach is designed to aid you in gaining a complete understanding of the material in each chapter.

When preparing for examinations, the Study Guide material may be used to determine your recall of the information presented in specific chapters. Once you have identified those subject areas in need of further review, return to the textbook material for a complete discussion of the subject matter involved. Remember, the Study Guide merely highlights the textbook material; it cannot be relied upon as a comprehensive treatment of a subject area.

In the study of accounting, there is no substitute for hard work and a desire to learn. A proper attitude and a willingness to work will go a long way toward ensuring your success in intermediate accounting.

ACKNOWLEDGEMENTS

We are grateful to James Emig of Villanova University for his accuracy review and constructive comments regarding this edition of the study guide.

Douglas W. Kieso

15

Stockholders' Equity

CHAPTER STUDY OBJECTIVES

1. Discuss the characteristics of the corporate form of organization.

2. Identify the key components of stockholders' equity.

3. Identify the accounting procedures for issuing shares of stock.

4. Explain the accounting for treasury stock.

5. Explain the accounting for and reporting of preferred stock.

6. Describe the policies used in distributing dividends.

7. Identify the various forms of dividend distributions.

8. Explain the accounting for small and large stock dividends, and for stock splits.

9. Indicate how to present and analyze stockholders' equity.

*10. Explain the different types of preferred stock dividends and their effect on book value per share.

CHAPTER REVIEW

1.   Chapter 15 focuses on the stockholders' equity section of the corporate form of business organization. Stockholders' equity represents the amount that was contributed by the shareholders and the portion that was earned and retained by the enterprise. There is a definite distinction between liabilities and stockholders' equity that must be understood if one is to effectively grasp the accounting treatment for equity issues. This chapter addresses the accounting issues related to capital contributed by owners of a business organization, and the means by which profits are distributed through dividends.

The Corporate Form of Entity

2.   (S.O. 1) The corporate form of business organization begins with the submitting of **articles of incorporation** to the state in which incorporation is desired. Assuming the requirements are properly fulfilled, the corporation charter is issued and the corporation is recognized as a legal entity subject to state law. The laws of the state of incorporation that govern owners' equity transactions are normally set out in the state's business corporation act.

3.   Within a given class of stock, each share is exactly equal to every other share. A person's percent of ownership in a corporation is determined by the number of shares he or she possesses in relation to the total number of shares owned by all stockholders. In the absence of restrictive provisions, each share carries the right to participate proportionately in: (a) **profits,** (b) **management,** (c) **corporate assets upon liquidation,** and (d) **any new issues of stock of the same class (preemptive right).**

*   *Note: All asterisked (*) items relate to material contained in the Appendix to the chapter.*

4. The transfer of ownership between individuals in the corporate form of organization is accomplished by one individual selling or transferring his or her shares to another individual. The only requirement in terms of the corporation involved is that it be made aware of the name of the individual owning the stock. A subsidiary ledger of stockholders is maintained by the corporation for the purpose of dividend payments, issuance of stock rights, and voting proxies. Many corporations employ independent **registrars and transfer agents** who specialize in providing services for recording and transferring stock.

5. The basic ownership interest in a corporation is represented by **common stock.** Common stock is guaranteed neither dividends nor assets upon dissolution of the corporation. Thus, common stockholders are considered to hold a residual interest in the corporation. However, common stockholders generally control the management of the corporation and tend to profit most if the company is successful. In the event that a corporation has only one authorized issue of capital stock, that issue is by definition common stock, whether or not it is so designated in the charter.

Corporate Capital

6. (S.O. 2) Owners' equity in a corporation is defined as stockholders' equity, shareholders' equity, or corporate capital. The following categories normally appear as part of stockholders' equity.
   - a. Capital stock.
   - b. Additional paid-in capital.
   - c. Retained earnings.

Stockholders' Equity: Contributed Capital

7. Capital stock and additional paid-in capital constitute contributed (paid-in) capital; retained earnings represents the earned capital of the enterprise (reduced by dividends distributed). Contributed capital (paid-in capital) is the total amount paid in on capital stock. Earned capital is the capital that develops from profitable operations.

8. Stockholders' equity is the difference between the assets and the liabilities of the company—also known as the residual interest. Stockholders' equity is not a claim to specific assets but a claim against a portion of the total assets.

Accounting for the Issuance of Stock

9. (S.O. 3) The par value of a stock has no relationship to its fair market value. At present, the par value associated with most capital stock issues is very low. Low par values help companies avoid contingent liability associated with stock sold below par.

10. When **par value stock** is issued, the Capital Stock (common or preferred) account is credited for an amount equal to par value times the number of shares issued. Any amount received in excess of par value is credited to **additional paid-in capital.** For example, if 200 shares of common stock with a par value of $2 per share are sold for $500, the following journal entry would be made:

Cash	500	
Common Stock		400
Paid-in Capital in Excess of Par		100

Par value stock is always credited at issue date for its par value times the number of shares issued.

11. When **no-par stock** is issued, the Capital Stock account is credited for an amount equal to the value of the consideration received. If no-par stock has a **stated value,** it may be accounted for in the same way as true no-par stock. Alternatively, the stated value may be considered similar to par value with any excess above stated value being accounted for as additional paid-in capital.

Lump Sum Sales

12. More than one class of stock is sometimes issued for a single payment or lump sum amount. Such a transaction requires allocation of the proceeds between the classes of securities involved. The two methods of allocation used are (a) the **proportional method** and (b) the **incremental method.** The former method is used when the fair market value for each class of security is readily determinable, and the latter method is used when only one class's market value is known.

Stock Issued in Noncash Transactions

13. Stock issued for consideration other than cash should be recorded by using the fair market value of the consideration or the fair market value of the stock issued, whichever is more clearly determinable. In cases where the fair market value of both items is not clearly determinable, the board of directors has the authority to establish a value for the transaction.

Costs of Issuing Stock

14. Direct costs incurred to sell stock such as underwriting costs, accounting and legal fees, and printing costs should be debited to Additional Paid-in Capital. Management salaries and other indirect costs related to the stock issue should be expensed as incurred.

Treasury Stock

15. (S.O. 4) **Treasury stock** is a corporation's own stock that **(a)** was outstanding, **(b)** has been reacquired by the corporation, and **(c)** is not retired. Treasury stock is not an asset and should be shown in the balance sheet as a reduction of stockholders' equity. Treasury stock is essentially the same as unissued stock. The reasons corporations purchase their outstanding stock include: **(a)** to provide tax efficient distributions of excess cash to shareholders; **(b)** to increase earnings per share and return on equity; **(c)** to provide stock for employee stock compensation ; **(d)** to contract operations or thwart takeover attempts; and **(e)** to make a market in the stock.

16. Two methods are used in accounting for treasury stock, the **cost method** and the **par value method.** Under the cost method, treasury stock is recorded in the accounts at acquisition cost. When the treasury stock is reissued the Treasury Stock account is credited for the acquisition cost. If treasury stock is reissued for **more** than its acquisition cost, the excess amount is credited to **Paid-in Capital from Treasury Stock.** If treasury stock is reissued for **less** than its acquisition cost, the difference should be debited to any paid-in capital from previous treasury stock transactions. If the balance in this account is insufficient, the remaining difference is charged to retained earnings. The following example shows the accounting for treasury stock under the cost method.

10,000 shares of common stock with a par value of $5 per share were originally issued at $12 per share.

A.   2,000 shares of common stock are reacquired for $20,000.

Entry for Purchase

Treasury Stock	20,000	
Cash		20,000

B.   1,000 shares of treasury stock are resold for $8,000.

Entry for Resale

Cash	8,000	
Retained Earnings	2,000	
Treasury Stock		10,000

17.   The cost of treasury stock is shown in the balance sheet as a deduction from the total of all owners' equity accounts.

Preferred Stock

18.   (S.O. 5) **Preferred stock** is the term used to describe a class of stock that possesses certain preferences or features not possessed by the common stock. The following features are those most often associated with preferred stock issues:

    a.   Preference as to dividends.
    b.   Preference as to assets in the event of liquidation.
    c.   Convertible into common stock.
    d.   Callable at the option of the corporation.
    e.   Nonvoting.

Some features used to distinguish preferred stock from common stock tend to be restrictive. For example, preferred stock may be **nonvoting, noncumulative,** and **nonparticipating.** A corporation may attach whatever preferences or restrictions in whatever combination it desires to a preferred stock issue so long as it does not specifically violate its state incorporation law. The dividend preference of preferred stock is normally stated as a percentage of the preferred stock's par value. For example, 9% preferred stock with a par value of $100 entitles its holder to an annual dividend of $9 per share.

19. Certain terms are used to describe various features of preferred stock. These terms are the following:

a. **Cumulative.** Dividends not paid in any year must be made up in a later year before any profits can be distributed to common stockholders. Unpaid annual dividends on cumulative preferred stock are referred to as **dividends in arrears.**

b. **Participating.** Holders of participating preferred stock share with the common stockholders in any profit distribution beyond a prescribed rate. This participation involves a pro rata distribution based on the total par value of the outstanding preferred and common stock.

c. **Convertible.** Preferred stockholders may, at their option, exchange their preferred shares for common stock on the basis of a predetermined ratio.

d. **Callable.** At the option of the issuing corporation, preferred shares can be redeemed at specified future dates and at stipulated prices.

e   **Redeemable.** The stock has a mandatory redemption period or a redemption feature that the issuer cannot control.

Reporting of Preferred Stock

20. Preferred stock generally has no maturity date and therefore no legal obligation exists to pay preferred stock. As a result, preferred stock is classified as part of stockholder's equity. Mandatory redeemable preferred stock, however, is to be reported as a liability.

Dividends

21. (S.O. 6) Very few companies pay dividends in amounts equal to their legally available retained earnings. The major reasons are: **(a)** agreements with creditors, **(b)** state corporation laws, **(c)** to finance growth or expansion, **(d)** to provide for continuous dividends whether in good or bad years, and **(e)** to build a cushion.

22. Before a dividend is declared, management must consider availability of funds to pay the dividend. Directors must also consider the effect of inflation and replacement costs before making a dividend commitment.

23. The SEC encourages companies to disclose their dividend policy in their annual report. For example, companies that **(a)** have earnings but fail to pay dividends or **(b)** do not expect to pay dividends in the foreseeable future are encouraged to report this information. In addition, companies that have had a consistent pattern of paying dividends are encouraged to indicate whether they intend to continue this practice in the future.

24. (S.O. 7) **Dividends** may be paid in cash (most common means), stock, or some other asset. Dividends other than a stock dividend reduce the stockholders' equity in a corporation through an immediate or promised distribution of assets. When a stock dividend is declared, the corporation does not pay out assets or incur a liability. It issues additional shares of stock to each shareholder and nothing more.

Cash Dividends

25. The accounting for a **cash dividend** requires information concerning three dates: (a) **date of declaration,** (b) **date of record,** and (c) **date of payment.** A liability is established by a charge to retained earnings on the declaration date for the amount of the dividend declared. No accounting entry is required on the date of record. The stockholders who have earned the right to the dividend are determined by whom owns the shares on the date of record. The liability is liquidated on the payment date through a distribution of cash. The following journal entries would be made by a corporation that declared a $50,000 cash dividend on March 10, payable on April 6 to shareholders of record on March 25.

Declaration Date (March 10)

Retained Earnings (or Dividends)	50,000	
Dividends Payable		50,000

Record Date (March 25)

No entry

Payment Date (April 6)

Dividends Payable	50,000	
Cash		50,000

Property Dividends

26. **Property dividends** represent distributions of corporate assets other than cash. A property dividend is a nonreciprocal transfer of nonmonetary assets between an enterprise and its owners. **Such transfers should be recorded at the fair value of the assets transferred.** Fair value is measured by the amount that would be realized in an outright sale near the time of distribution. When the property dividend is declared, fair market value should be recognized in the accounts with the appropriate gain or loss recorded. The fair market value then serves as the basis used in accounting for the property dividend. For example, if a corporation held stock of another company that it intended to distribute to its own stockholders as a property dividend, it would first be required to make sure the carrying amount reflected current market value. If on the date the dividend was declared, the difference between the cost and market value of the stock to be distributed was $75,000, the following additional entry would be made.

Investment in Securities	75,000	
Gain on Appreciation of Securities		75,000

Liquidating Dividends

27.   **Liquidating dividends** represent a return of the stockholders' investment rather than a distribution of profits. In a more general sense, any dividend not based on profits must be a reduction of corporate capital, and to that extent, it is a liquidating dividend.

Stock Dividends

28.   (S.O. 8) A **stock dividend** can be defined as a **capitalization of retained earnings** that results in a reduction in retained earnings and a corresponding increase in certain contributed capital accounts. Total stockholders' equity remains unchanged when a stock dividend is distributed. Also, all stockholders retain their same proportionate share of ownership in the corporation.

29.   When the stock dividend is less than 20-25% of the common shares outstanding at the time of the dividend declaration, generally accepted accounting principles (GAAP) require that the accounting for stock dividends be based on the **fair market value of the stock issued.** When a stock dividend is declared, Retained Earnings is debited at the fair market value of the stock to be distributed. The entry includes a credit to **Common Stock Dividend Distributable** at par value times the number of shares, with any excess credited to **Paid-in Capital in Excess of Par.** Common Stock Dividend Distributable is reported in the stockholders' equity section between the declaration date and date of issuance. For example, consider the following set of facts. Vonesh Corporation, which has 50,000 shares of $10 par value common stock outstanding, declares a 10% stock dividend on December 3. On the date of declaration the stock has a fair market value of $25 per share. The following entry would be made when the stock dividend is declared:

Retained Earnings		
(5,000 x $25)	125,000	
Common Stock Dividend Distributable		50,000
Paid-in Capital in Excess of Par		75,000

When the stock is issued, the entry is:

Common Stock Dividend Distributable	50,000	
Common Stock		50,000

Stock Split

30. A **stock split** results in an increase or decrease in the number of shares outstanding with a corresponding decrease or increase in the par or stated value per share. In general, no accounting entry is required for a stock split as the total dollar amount of all stockholders' equity accounts remains unchanged. A stock split is usually intended to improve the marketability of the shares by reducing the market price of the stock being split. In general, the difference between a stock split and a stock dividend is based upon the size of the distribution. **If the number of shares issued in a stock dividend exceeds 20 or 25% of the shares outstanding, calling it a "stock split" is warranted, and only the par value of the shares issued is transferred from retained earnings.**

Restrictions on Retained Earnings

31. In many corporations restrictions on retained earnings or dividends exist, but no formal journal entries are made. Such restrictions are best disclosed by note.

Stockholders' Equity

32.   (S.O. 9) An example of a comprehensive stockholders' equity section taken from a balance sheet is given in the textbook. A company should disclose the pertinent rights and privileges of the various securities outstanding. Examples of information that should be disclosed are dividend and liquidation preferences, participation rights, call prices, and dates.

33.   Statements of stockholders' equity are frequently presented in the following basic format:

a.   Balance at the beginning of the period.
b.   Additions.
c.   Deductions.
d.   Balance at the end of the period.

34.   Several ratios use stockholders' equity related amounts to evaluate a company's profitability and long-term solvency. The following three ratios are discussed and illustrated in the chapter: (1) rate of return on common stock equity, (2) payout ratio, (3) book value per share.

$$\text{Rate of Return On Common Stock Equity} = \frac{\text{Net income} - \text{Preferred dividends}}{\text{Average common stockholders' equity}}$$

$$\text{Payout Ratio} = \frac{\text{Cash dividends}}{\text{Net income} - \text{Preferred dividends}}$$

$$\text{Book Value Per Share} = \frac{\text{Common stockholders' equity}}{\text{Outstanding shares}}$$

Dividend Preferences

*35.   (S.O. 10) Preferred stock generally has a preference in the receipt of dividends. Preferred stock can also carry features which require consideration at the time a dividend is declared and at the time of payment. These features are (a) the cumulative feature, and (b) the participating feature. The text material includes computational examples of these features in various combinations showing their impact on dividend distributions when both common and preferred stock are involved. When computing book value per share there are additional complications.

GLOSSARY

Additional paid-in capital.	The excess over par value paid in by stockholders in return for the shares issued to them.
Callable preferred stock.	Preferred stock that grants the issuer the right to purchase the stock from stockholders at specified future dates and prices.
Cash dividend.	When a corporation distributes a dividend in cash to the stockholders.
Common stock.	The residual corporate interest that bears the ultimate risks of loss and receives the benefits of success.
Contributed capital.	Capital stock and additional paid-in capital (also called paid-in capital).
Contributed capital (Paid-in capital).	The total amount paid in on capital stock.
Convertible preferred stock.	Preferred stock that provides for the exchange of preferred stock into common stock at a specified ratio.
Cost method.	The Treasury Stock account is debited for the cost of the shares acquired and is credited upon reissuance for this same cost.
Cumulative feature.	A feature of preferred stock entitling the stockholder to receive current and unpaid prior-year dividends before common stockholders receive dividends.

Date of declaration.   The date the board of directors meets and approves the declaration of a dividend.

Date of payment.   The date the board of directors has approved to pay a dividend.

Date of record.   The date on which owners of the stock are entitled to a declared dividend.

Discount on stock.   The amount under par value paid in by stockholders in return for the shares issued to them.

Dividend.   When a corporation distributes assets (or issues additional stock) to the stockholders.

Earned capital.   Capital that develops if the business operates profitably; it consists of all undistributed income that remains invested in the enterprise.

Equity capital.   The contributed capital and earned capital of a corporation.

Large stock dividend.   A stock dividend of more than 20-25% of the number of shares previously outstanding.

Liquidating dividend.   A dividend not based on retained earnings; implying that stockholders are receiving a return of their investment, rather than profits.

No-par stock.   Shares issued with no per-share amount printed on the stock certificate.

Paid-in capital.   Capital stock and additional paid-in capital (also called contributed capital).

Par value stock.   Capital stock that has been assigned a value per share in the corporate charter; it establishes the maximum responsibility of a stockholder in the event of insolvency or other involuntary dissolution.

Participating dividends.   A feature of preferred stock enabling the stockholder to share ratably with common stockholders in any dividends beyond the rate specified on the preferred stock.

Preemptive right.   A stockholder's right to share proportionately in any new issues of stock of the same class.

Preferred stock.   Capital stock that has contractual preferences over common stock in certain areas.

Property dividend.   When a corporation distributes a dividend of an asset other than cash to the stockholders.

Redeemable preferred stock   Preferred stock that has a mandatory redemption period or a redemption feature that the issuer cannot control.

Retained earnings.	Earnings retained for use in the business.
Small (ordinary) stock dividend.	Stock dividends of less than 20-25%.
Stated value.	The amount per share assigned by the board of directors to no-par stock that becomes legal capital per share.
Statement of stockholders' equity.	The disclosure of changes in the separate accounts comprising stockholders' equity.
Stock dividend.	The corporation issues additional stock to its stockholders rather than distributing any assets.
Stock split.	The corporation will issue additional stock to its stockholders; for example, the terms may indicate a split of 2-for-1 which would indicate that for every one share of stock a shareholder owns, they will receive an additional share of stock.
Stockholders'(owners') equity.	The cumulative net contributions by stockholders (owners) plus recorded earnings that have been retained.
Treasury stock.	A corporation's own stock that has been issued, fully paid for, and reacquired by the corporation but not retired.

CHAPTER OUTLINE

Fill in the outline presented below.

(S.O. 1) The Corporate Form

     State Corporate Law

(S.O. 2) Capital Stock

(S.O. 3) Par Value Stock

     No-Par Stock

     Lump Sum Sales

     Stock Issued in Noncash Transactions

     Costs of Issuing Stock

(S.O. 4) Reacquisition of Shares

     Treasury Stock

Chapter Outline *(continued)*

Cost Method

Retirement of Treasury Stock

(S.O. 5) Preferred Stock

Cumulative Preferred Stock

Participating Preferred Stock

Convertible Preferred Stock

Callable Preferred Stock

Redeemable Preferred stock

(S.O. 6) Dividend Policy

Legality of Dividends

Chapter Outline *(continued)*

Financial Condition and Dividend Distributions

(S.O. 7) Types of Dividends

Cash Dividends

Property Dividends

Liquidating Dividends

(S.O. 8) Stock Dividends

Stock Splits

Disclosure of Restrictions on Retained Earnings

(S.O. 9) Presentation and Analysis of Stockholders' Equity

*(S.O. 10) Dividend Preferences

REVIEW QUESTIONS AND EXERCISES

TRUE-FALSE

Indicate whether each of the following is true (T) or false (F) in the space provided.

_____ 1. (S.O. 1) Most corporations are granted their charters directly by the federal government.

_____ 2. (S.O. 1) The preemptive right protects an existing stockholder from involuntary dilution of ownership interest.

_____ 3. (S.O. 3) The par value of a share of common stock usually is a good indication of what the stock is worth on the market.

_____ 4. (S.O. 3) Contributions by shareholders (paid-in capital) and income retained by the corporation represent the two primary sources from which corporate equity is derived.

_____ 5. (S.O. 3) Contributed capital is the capital that develops if the business operates profitably.

_____ 6. (S.O. 4) Under the incremental method, the market value of the securities is used as a basis for those classes that are known and the remainder of the lump sum is allocated to the class for which the market value is not known.

_____ 7. (S.O. 4) When capital stock is issued for noncash assets, the assets received should be recorded at the par value of the stock issued.

_____ 8. (S.O. 4) Management salaries and other indirect costs related to a stock issue should be expensed as incurred.

_____ 9. (S.O. 4) A company might purchase its outstanding stock to provide tax efficient distributions of excess cash to shareholders.

_____ 10. (S.O. 4) Treasury shares are issued shares of the company's own stock that have been reacquired but **not** retired.

_____ 11. (S.O. 4) Treasury stock should be shown as a deduction from total stockholders' equity.

_____ 12. (S.O. 4) Treasury shares represent a reduction in the number of outstanding shares but **not** in the number of issued shares.

_____ 13. (S.O. 4) The gain on the sale of treasury stock should be included in income before extraordinary items on the income statement.

_____ 14. (S.O. 5) Dividends in arrears on preferred stock should be classified on the balance sheet as a liability.

_____ 15. (S.O. 5) Preferred stock does **not** have the voting right unless it possesses the participating feature.

_____ 16. (S.O. 5) The dividend preference related to preferred stock is merely an assurance that the stated dividend rate or amount must be paid before any dividends can be paid on the common stock.

_____ 17. (S.O. 5) A convertible preferred stock issue normally will sell for a lower price than the same issue would without the conversion feature.

_____ 18. (S.O. 6) Very few companies pay dividends in amounts equal to their retained earnings legally available for dividends.

_____ 19. (S.O. 6) The current cash position of a corporation is a prime consideration in deciding whether a cash dividend should be declared.

_____ 20. (S.O. 6) Any dividend other than a stock dividend reduces the stockholders' equity in the corporation.

_____ 21. (S.O. 6) All things being equal, growth companies tend to pay larger dividends than well-established companies, because growth companies have to provide an extra incentive for potential investors.

_____ 22. (S.O. 7) A declared cash dividend is **not** a liability because the board of directors can simply undeclare the dividend.

_____ 23. (S.O. 7) A corporation must pay cash dividends on treasury stock.

_____ 24. (S.O. 7) A property dividend is a nonreciprocal transfer of nonmonetary assets between an enterprise and its owners.

_____ 25. (S.O. 7) The distribution of a nonmonetary asset as an ordinary dividend may be regarded as equivalent to an exchange with owners and, therefore, recorded at the book value of the nonmonetary asset distributed.

_____ 26. (S.O. 7) Any dividend **not** based on profits must be a reduction of corporate capital, and to that extent, it is a liquidating dividend.

_____ 27. (S.O. 7) A stock dividend results in a capitalization of retained earnings with no corresponding decrease in total stockholders' equity.

_____ 28. (S.O. 8) When a stock dividend is less than 20-25% of the common shares outstanding at the time of the dividend declaration, the par value of the stock issued should be transferred from retained earnings.

_____ 29. (S.O. 8) One of the major distinctions between a stock split and a stock dividend is the fact that a stock split alters the par or stated value of the stock issue involved, while a stock dividend does **not** affect par or stated value.

_____ 30. (S.O. 8) From an accounting standpoint, no entry is recorded for a stock split.

_____ 31. (S.O. 8) If a stock dividend is large (more than 20-25%), the distribution should be referred to as a stock split.

_____ 32. (S.O. 8) The rate of return on common stock equity is computed by dividing sales by average common stockholders' equity.

MULTIPLE CHOICE

Select the best answer for each of the following items and enter the corresponding letter in the space provided.

_____ 1.   (S.O. 1) In a corporate form of business organization legal capital is best defined as:

A.   the amount of capital the state of incorporation allows the company to accumulate over its existence.
B.   the par value of all capital stock issued.
C.   the amount of capital the federal government allows a corporation to generate.
D.   the total capital raised by a corporation within the limits set by the Securities and Exchange Commission.

_____ 2.   (S.O. 2) Stockholders of a business enterprise are said to be the residual owners. The term residual owner means that shareholders:

A.   are entitled to a dividend every year in which the business earns a profit.
B.   have the rights to specific assets of the business.
C.   bear the ultimate risks and uncertainties and receive the benefits of enterprise ownership.
D.   can negotiate individual contracts on behalf of the enterprise.

_____ 3.   (S.O. 3) When accountants refer to capital of a corporate organization they mean:

A.   the cash held by the organization at the point in time when the reference to capital is made.
B.   the assets of a business organization that are durable and last a long period of time.
C.   money borrowed to finance the operations of the organization.
D.   stockholders' equity or owners' equity.

_____ 4.   (S.O. 3) When a corporation sells stock to investors, the transaction will increase

	Contributed Capital	Earned Capital
A.	Yes	No
B.	Yes	Yes
C.	No	Yes
D.	No	No

_____ 5.   (S.O. 3) The accounting for stockholders' equity is governed by:

A.   the corporation's board of directors.
B.   the Securities and Exchange Commission.
C.   the American Institute of CPAs.
D.   the business corporation act of the state of incorporation.

_____ 6.   (S.O. 3) Normally, stock issued by a corporation has certain rights and privileges that can be restricted only by special contracts at the time the shares are issued. In the absence of restrictive provisions, each share carries all of the following rights **except**:
A.   to share proportionately in profits and losses.
B.   to share proportionately in corporate assets upon liquidation.
C.   to share proportionately in any new issue of stocks or bonds by the corporation.
D.   to share proportionately in management of the corporation.

_____ 7.   (S.O. 3) Stock that has a fixed per-share amount printed on each stock certificate is called:

    A.   share value stock.
    B.   fixed value stock.
    C.   uniform value stock.
    D.○   par value stock.

_____ 8.   (S.O. 3) When stock is purchased by shareholders at a price below par value:

    A.   a liability should be recorded in the financial statements, classified as long-term, and payable upon dissolution of the company to creditors not fully reimbursed.
    B.   a contingent liability exists that is an obligation to the corporation's creditors.
    C.•   a contingent liability exists that is an obligation to the corporation.
    D.   the difference between purchase price and par value must be paid by the original shareholder to the corporation before they may sell the stock to another party.

_____ 9.   (S.O. 3) Which of the following is **not** a legal restriction related to profit distributions by a corporation?

    A.   The amount distributed to owners must be in compliance with the state laws governing corporations.
    B.•   The amount distributed in any one year can never exceed the net income reported for that year.
    C.   Profit distributions must be formally approved by the board of directors.
    D.   Dividends must be in full agreement with the capital stock contracts as to preferences and participation.

_____ 10.   (S.O. 3) When common stock is sold by a corporation a journal entry is prepared which includes a debit to cash and a credit to the common stock account. If the debit to cash is greater than the credit to the common stock account then it can be assumed that:

    A.   the common stock is worth more than its current market value.
    B.•   a gain on the sale of stock is a part of the transaction.
    C.   the common stock was sold at a discount
    D.   the stated value of the common stock is less than the per share price investors were willing to pay.

_____ 11.   (S.O. 3) Aguirre Company issues 500 shares of its $5 par value common stock having a market value of $25 per share and 750 shares of its $15 par value preferred stock having a market value of $20 per share for a lump sum of $24,000. How would the proceeds be allocated between the common and preferred stock?

	Common Stock	Preferred Stock
A.	$ 2,500	$21,500
B.	$10,909	$13,091
C.•	$12,500	$15,000
D.	$12,750	$11,250

_____ 12.   (S.O. 3) The general rule to be applied when stock is issued for services or property other than cash is that the property or services be recorded at:

A. ٭   the fair market value of the stock issued.
B.   the fair market value of the noncash consideration received.
C.   either the fair market value of the stock issued or the fair market value of the noncash consideration received, whichever is more clearly determinable.
D.   a value that clearly reflects the intentions of the parties entering into the transaction and provides a relevant basis for recording.

_____ 13.   (S.O. 4) Treasury stock is:

A.   canceled as soon as it is acquired.
B.   a current asset.
C.   stock owned by the Treasurer of the company.
D.٭   included in issued shares.

_____ 14.   (S.O. 4) In January 2010 Castro Corporation, a newly formed company, issued 10,000 shares of its $10 par common stock for $15 per share. On July 1, 2010, Castro Corporation reacquired 1,000 shares of its outstanding stock for $12 per share. The acquisition of these treasury shares:

A.   decreased total stockholders' equity.
B.   increased total stockholders' equity.
C.   did not change total stockholders' equity.
D.٭   decreased the number of issued shares.

_____ 15.   (S.O. 4) Crawford Company acquired treasury stock for cash at a price in excess of its par value. Three months later the treasury stock was sold at a price that exceeded its acquisition price. Assume that Crawford Company uses the cost method to account for treasury stock transactions. What effect would the resale of the treasury stock have on the following items?

	Additional Paid-in Capital	Retained Earnings	Total Stockholders' Equity
A.	Increase	No Effect	Increase
B.	Decrease	No Effect	Decrease
C.	Increase	Increase	Increase
D.	No Effect	No Effect	No Effect

_____ 16.   (S.O. 4) On February 1, 2010, Martin Company reacquired 8,000 shares of its $30 par value common stock for $32 per share. Martin uses the cost method to account for treasury stock. What journal entry should Martin make to record the acquisition of treasury stock?

		Debit	Credit
A.	Treasury stock	240,000	
	Additional paid-in capital	16,000	
	Cash		256,000
B.	Treasury stock	240,000	
	Retained earnings	16,000	
	Cash		256,000
C.	Retained earnings	256,000	
	Cash		256,000
D.	Treasury stock	256,000	
	Cash		256,000

_____ 17.   *(S.O. 5) Many corporations issue preferred stock in addition to common stock to finance operations. While the preferences given to preferred stock may vary in many situations, the most common preference is:

A.*   they are assured a dividend, usually at a stated rate, before any amount may be distributed to common shareholders.
B.   preferred shareholders receive a larger dividend than do common shareholders because they have given up the right to vote.
C.   receipt of dividends every time a common stock dividend is declared.
D.   the right to convert shares of preferred for shares of common on a basis determined in the preferred stock indenture.

_____ 18.   (S.O. 5) Cumulative preferred dividends in arrears should be shown in a corporation's balance sheet as:

A.ª   an increase in current liabilities.
B.   an increase in stockholders' equity.
C.   a footnote.
D.   an increase in current liabilities for the current portion and long-term liabilities for the long-term portion.

_____ 19.   (S.O. 6) Which of the following is **not** one of the primary considerations management must make before a cash dividend is declared?

A.   The availability of funds to pay the dividend.
B.   The legal permissibility of the dividend.
C.   The effect of inflation on the company and alternative uses of the cash to be paid for dividends.
D.*   The tax impact on stockholders of the receipt of the dividends.

20. (S.O. 7) How does the declaration of a cash dividend affect the following account balances?

	Retained Earnings	Current Liabilities	Cash Account
A.	Decrease	No Effect	Decrease
B.	Increase	Decrease	No Effect
C.	Decrease	Increase	No Effect
D.	Decrease	No Effect	Increase

21. (S.O. 7) Tillie Corporation has a current ratio (Current Assets/Current Liabilities) of 2:1. How will the payment of a cash dividend declared two weeks ago affect the following?

	Current Ratio	Working Capital
A.	Increase	No Effect
B.	Decrease	Decrease
C.	Increase	Increase
D.	No Effect	Decrease

22. (S.O. 7) Two alternatives exist once a credit balance in retained earnings is recorded. It can be left intact and the offsetting assets used in the operations of the business or it can be:

   A.   reduced by a distribution of assets to the stockholders.
   B.   increased as a result of a sale of common stock above par value.
   C.   increased as a result of a sale of treasury stock at an amount in excess of par value.
   D.   reduced by a distribution of assets to creditors.

23. (S.O. 7) When a corporation declares a property dividend, the corporation should:

   A.   divide the property equally among all stockholders.
   B.   record the dividend by debiting retained earnings for an amount equal to the fair value of the property to be distributed.
   C.   record the dividend by debiting retained earnings for an amount equal to the book value of the property to be distributed.
   D.   record the dividend on its books at the carrying value of the property distributed and inform stockholders as to the fair value of the property so they may individually recognize a gain or loss.

24. (S.O. 7) Mildred Corporation owned 2,000 shares of Lester Corporation. These shares were purchased in 2006 for $18,000. On October 15, 2010, Mildred declared a property dividend of one share of Lester for every ten shares of Mildred held by a stockholder. On that date, when the market price of Lester was $14 per share, there were 18,000 shares of Mildred outstanding. What gain and net reduction in retained earnings would result from this property dividend?

	Gain	Net Reduction in Retained Earnings
A.	$0	$16,200
B.	$0	$25,200
C.	$9,000	$ 7,200
D.	$9,000	$16,200

_____ 25. (S.O. 8) A feature common to both stock dividends and stock splits is:

A.   a reduction in total stockholders' equity of a corporation.
B.   a transfer from retained earnings to additional paid-in capital.
C.   a reduction in par value.
D.   a change in the number of shares of stock outstanding.

_____ 26. (S.O. 8) Total stockholders' equity will increase as a result of a:

	Stock Dividend	Stock Split
A.	Yes	Yes
B.	No	No
C.	Yes	No
D.	No	Yes

_____ 27. (S.O. 8) Foerch Corporation declared a stock dividend of 4,000 shares when the par value was $1 per share, and the market value was $5 per share. How does the entry to record this declaration affect total stockholders' equity?

A.   No effect.
B. $ 4,000 increase.
C. $ 4,000 decrease.
D. $20,000 decrease.

_____ 28. (S.O. 8) Unlike a stock split, a stock dividend requires a formal journal entry in the financial accounting records because:

A.   stock dividends are payable on the date they are declared.
B.   stock dividends represent a transfer from retained earnings to capital stock.
C.   stock dividends increase the relative book value of an individual's stock holdings.
D.   stock splits increase the relative book value of an individual's stock holdings.

_____ 29. (S.O. 8) What is the most likely effect of a stock split on the par value per share and the number of shares outstanding?

	Par Value Per Share	Number of Shares Outstanding
A.	Decrease	Increase
B.	Decrease	No effect
C.	Increase	Increase
D.	No effect	No effect

_____ 30. (S.O. 8) At the beginning of 2010, M.R. Magoo Company had retained earnings of $100,000. During the year M.R. Magoo reported net income of $50,000, sold treasury stock at a gain of $18,000, declared a cash dividend of $30,000, and declared and issued a small stock dividend of 1,500 shares ($10 par value) when the market value of the stock was $20 per share. The amount of retained earnings available for dividends at the end of 2010 was:

A. $ 90,000.
B. $105,000.
C. $108,000.
D. $123,000.

_____ 31. (S.O. 8) M. Wauboosie Company has 280,000 shares of $10 par value common stock outstanding. During the year M. Wauboosie declared a 5% stock dividend when the market price of the stock was $24 per share. Two months later M. Wauboosie declared a $.60 per share cash dividend. As a result of the dividends declared during the year, retained earnings decreased by:

    A. $168,000.
    B. $176,400.
    C. $336,000.
    D. $512,400.

Answers to questions 32 and 33 are based on the following information.

Bodhi Corporation had the following information in its financial statements for the years ended 2009 and 2010:

Cash Dividends for the year 2010	$ 5,000
Net Income for the year ended 2010	62,000
Market price of stock, 12/31/09	10
Market price of stock, 12/31/10	12
Common stockholders' equity, 12/31/09	1,100,000
Common stockholders' equity, 12/31/10	1,200,000
Outstanding shares, 12/31/10	120,000
Preferred dividends for the year ended 2010	10,000

_____ 32. (S.O. 8) What is the Rate of Return on Common Stock Equity and the Payout Ratio for Bodhi Corporation for the year ended 2010?

	Rate of Return on Common Stock Equity	**Payout Ratio**
A.	5.1%	8.1%
B.	4.5%	9.6%
C.	5.6%	8.1%
D.	5.1%	24.2%

_____ 33. (S.O. 8) What is the Price Earnings Ratio and Book Value Per Share for Bodhi Corporation for the year ended 2010?

	Price Earnings Ratio	**Book Value Per Share**
A.	21.3	$ 9.58
B.	21.3	$10.00
C.	27.7	$ 9.58
D.	27.7	$10.00

REVIEW EXERCISES

1. (S.0. 3 and 4) Spangler Corporation entered into the following stock transactions during the past year:

   (1)   Received a charter allowing it to issue 15,000 shares of $100 par value preferred stock and 18,000 shares of $20 par value common stock.

   (2)   Issued 11,000 shares of common stock to the corporate founders in exchange for land and a building valued by the board of directors at $70,000 and $215,000 respectively.

   (3)   Sold 9,000 shares of preferred stock for $115 per share.

   (4)   Sold 1,000 shares of preferred stock at par value and 800 shares of common stock at $50 per share to an investor.

   (5)   Purchased 500 shares of preferred stock for $108 per share.

   (6)   Purchased 700 shares of common stock for $72 per share.

   (7)   Sold 300 shares of the preferred stock held as treasury stock for $110 per share.

   (8)   Resold 400 shares of common stock held as treasury stock for $65 per share.

Instructions:

   a.   Prepare journal entries for the transactions noted above. No other transactions have affected the stock accounts. Record all treasury stock transactions using the cost method.

   b.   Assuming that Spangler Corporation had retained earnings of $187,000 (not including the above transactions), prepare the stockholders' equity section of its balance sheet based on the above transaction.

a.

	General Journal		J1
Date	**Account Title**	**Debit**	**Credit**

b.

2.   (S.0. 4) Marks Corporation's stockholders' equity at December 31, 2010, is as follows:

Common stock, $10, par (10,000 shares)......................	$100,000
Paid-in capital in excess of par.......................................	3,000
	103,000
Retained earnings	197,000
Total stockholders' equity.....................................	$300,000

The following treasury stock transactions occurred during 2011.

Jan. 2 — Purchased at $12 per share, 1,000 shares of Marks Corporation common stock.

Feb. 4 — Sold 500 shares of treasury stock at $13 per share.

May 10 — Sold 500 shares of treasury stock at $8 per share.

Instructions:
Prepare journal entries to record the treasury stock transactions in 2011 under the cost method.

General Journal

J1

Date	Account Title	Debit	Credit

3.   (S.O. 7) Cole Corporation has 100,000 shares of common stock outstanding. The corporation also owns 100,000 shares of William Company common stock purchased 5 years ago at $10 per share. Cole decided to distribute the William Company stock as a property dividend on the basis of one share of William stock for each share of Cole stock owned. The William stock has a current market value of $25 per share and has been accounted for using the cost method since the date of acquisition.

Instructions:
Prepare the journal entries Cole Corporation would make for the declaration and payment of the dividend.

	General Journal		J1
Date	**Account Title**	**Debit**	**Credit**

4. (S.O. 7 and 8) The Courtney Corporation has the following accounts in its stockholders' equity section at the beginning of 2010:

Preferred Stock, $100 par value, 7% cumulative and nonparticipating, 5,000 shares authorized, 4,000 shares issued and outstanding (one year's dividends in arrears)	$ 400,000
Common Stock, $5 par value, 35,000 shares authorized, 15,000 shares issued and outstanding	75,000
Paid-in Capital in Excess of Par—Common	300,000
Retained Earnings	$1,080,000

During 2010, Courtney Corporation declared and distributed the following dividends in the order shown:

1. The arrears dividend and the current dividend on preferred and a $3 per share common dividend.
2. A 15% stock dividend on common stock, current market price is $28 per share.
3. A $2 per share dividend on common stock outstanding.

Instructions:
 a. Prepare journal entries for the declaration and distribution of each dividend. (Assume each dividend is distributed prior to the declaration of the subsequent dividend.)
 b. By what amount did these transactions change (increase or decrease) the total stockholders' equity section of Courtney Corporation?

a.

	General Journal		J1
Date	Account Title	Debit	Credit

b.

5.   (S.O. 7) On January 1, 2010, the Frank Company burned to the ground and all of the company's accounting records were destroyed. Because the company must pay income taxes for the year 2009, the board of directors has come to you for assistance in arriving at a reasonable estimate of the company's 2009 net income before income taxes. Though the company has no documents to substantiate the following, the company's bookkeeper does remember a few balances and transactions that took place during 2009.

Unappropriated Retained Earnings balance, January 1, 2009	$65,900
Unappropriated Retained Earnings balance, December 31, 2009	66,900
Cash in bank, December 31, 2009	7,965
Stock dividend declared and distributed during 2009	4,000
Issued 100 shares of $100 par value common stock at $103	10,300
Declared and paid a cash dividend during 2009	5,000
Accounts payable, December 31, 2009	8,000

Instructions:

Using the pertinent data from above prepare a statement estimating Frank Company's 2009 net income before income taxes.

SOLUTIONS TO REVIEW QUESTIONS AND EXERCISES

TRUE-FALSE

1. (F) Anyone who wishes to establish a corporation must submit articles of incorporation to the proper department of the government of the state in which incorporation is desired. The federal government does not grant corporate charters.

2. (T)

3. (F) The par value of a stock issued has no relationship to the fair market value of the stock. Par value has but one real significance; it establishes the maximum responsibility of a stockholder in the event of corporate insolvency or other involuntary dissolution.

4. (T)

5. (F) Contributed capital (paid-in capital) is the term used to describe the total amount paid in on capital stock at any given time. Earned capital is the capital that develops if the business operates profitably.

6. (T)

7. (F) The general rule to be applied when stock is issued for assets other than cash is that the noncash assets be recorded at either their fair market value or the fair market value of the stock issued, whichever is more clearly determinable.

8. (T)

9. (T)

10. (T)

11. (T)

12. (T)

13. (F) If treasury stock is reissued at a price in excess of the acquisition cost, the excess is credited to an account titled Paid-in Capital from Treasury Stock. This account is shown in the equity section of the balance sheet. A corporation cannot report a "gain" or a "loss" from dealing in its own stock.

14. (F) No liability exists for preferred dividends in arrears. The only time a liability exists for dividends is after they are declared by the board of directors. Any dividends in arrears on preferred stock should be disclosed in a footnote to the financial statements.

15. (F) The participating feature of preferred stock refers to the right of preferred shareholders to share ratably with the common stockholders in any profit distribution beyond the prescribed rate. Preferred stock is normally nonvoting stock.

16. (T)

17.   (F)   The shareholder who owns convertible preferred stock not only enjoys the preferred claim on dividends, but also has the option of converting into a common shareholder. Because of the attractiveness of this feature, convertible preferred stock will normally sell for a higher price than the same issue would without the conversion feature.

18.   (T)

19.   (T)

20.   (T)

21.   (F)   This statement is generally false. Growth companies need all the capital they can generate either through operations (net income) or outside financing (investors or creditors). People investing in such companies generally recognize this fact and hope they generate a positive increase in the value of their stock holdings.

22.   (F)   A declared cash dividend is a liability.

23.   (F)   Cash dividends are not declared and paid on treasury stock.

24.   (T)

25.   (F)   A property dividend is a nonreciprocal transfer of nonmonetary assets between an enterprise and its owners. A transfer of a nonmonetary asset to a stockholder or to another entity in a nonreciprocal transfer should be recorded at the fair value of the asset transferred, and a gain or loss should be recognized on the disposition of the asset.

26.   (T)

27.   (T)

28.   (F)   When a stock dividend is less than 20-25% of the common shares outstanding at the time of the dividend declaration, the fair market value of the stock issued should be transferred from retained earnings.

29.   (T)

30.   (T)

31.   (T)

32.   (F)   The rate of return on common stock equity is comptued by dividing net income less preferred dividends by average common stockholders' equity.

MULTIPLE CHOICE

1.   (B)   In law, capital is considered that portion of stockholders' equity that is required by statute to be retained in the business for the protection of creditors. Generally, legal capital is the par value of all capital stock issued.

2.   (C)   As residual owners, shareholders have the risks and rewards of ownership. The interests of stockholders is measured by the difference between the assets and liabilities of the enterprise. Dividends may be paid by the entity but are not guaranteed even if earnings occur. Shareholders do not have rights to specific assets; they have a claim against a portion of total assets. Shareholders are not allowed to negotiate individual contracts. Such negotiations are a function of the entity's board of directors and officers.

3.   (D)   Capital of a corporation, as referred to by accountants, represents the stockholders' equity. This is the net capital or net equity of a business and is represented by the difference between total assets and total liabilities. Thus, accountants define capital more narrowly than total assets but more broadly than legal capital.

4.   (A)   Contributed capital is the term used to describe the total amount paid in on capital stock at any given time. It is the amount advanced by the stockholders to the corporation for use in the business. Earned capital is the capital that develops if the business operates profitably. It consists of all undistributed income that remains invested in the enterprise.

5.   (D)   When it comes to accounting for stockholders' equity, the business corporation act of the state of incorporation governs. Some of these laws are quite uniform; others vary considerably, which means that permissible transactions may vary from state to state and that accounting must reflect these differences. State laws usually prescribe the requirements for issuing stock, the treatment of proceeds of issued stock, the distributions permitted to stockholders, the effects of retiring stock, the regulations for and restrictions on acquiring treasury stock, as well as other procedures and restrictions.

6.   (C)   Shareholders are allowed to share proportionately in any new issue of stock. This is referred to as the preemptive right of shareholders. The other alternatives (A, B, and D) reflect the rights of shareholders.

7.   (D)   Stock that has a fixed per-share amount printed on each stock certificate is known as par value stock. Par value has but one real significance; it establishes the maximum responsibility of a stockholder in the event of insolvency or other involuntarily dissolution. Par value establishes the nominal value per share and is the minimum amount that must be paid in by each stockholder if the stock is to be fully paid when issued.

8.   (B)   The purchase of stock below par value results in a contingent liability. This contingency would only become a real liability if the amount below par must be collected in order to pay creditors upon dissolution of the company. The contingency, if realized, is an obligation to creditors as the amount of legal capital is less than it should have been   because of the discount.

9.	(B)	Alternatives A, C, and D represent legal restrictions related to profit distribution by a corporation. Alternative B is not a legal restriction. Even though corporations may not pay dividends in excess of total earnings, they can distribute a dividend in a particular year that exceeds the earnings for that year as long as they have undistributed earnings from prior years.
10.	(D)	If stock is sold and the debit to cash exceeds the credit to common stock, then the stock was either par value or stated value stock which was sold for more than the par or stated value. The information about the transaction gives no concrete evidence about market value of the stock. Also, a corporation cannot make a gain or loss when selling its own stock.

11.   (B)

Fair market value of common (500 X $25)	$12,500
Fair market value of preferred (750 X $20)	15,000
Aggregate fair market value	$27,500
Allocated to Common: ($12,500/$27,500) X $24,000 = $10,909	
Allocated to Preferred: ($15,000/$27,500) X $24,000 = $13,091	
Total Allocation	$24,000

12.	(C)	When stock is issued for services or property other than cash, the transaction should be valued at the fair market value of the item that is more clearly determinable. If the value of the stock and noncash consideration are both readily determinable and the transaction is the result of an arm's-length exchange, there will probably be little difference in the fair market values of each item.
13.	(D)	Treasury stock is a company's own stock that has been reacquired after having been issued and fully paid. In order for stock to be classified as treasury stock, it must remain uncanceled in the corporate treasury. Thus, treasury stock is considered to be issued but not outstanding.
14.	(A)	Total stockholders' equity is reduced by the carrying amount of treasury stock. Under the cost method, treasury stock is subtracted from the total of capital stock, additional paid-in capital, and retained earnings. The total stockholders' equity is the same even though the components are different in amount.
15.	(A)	Under the cost method treasury stock is debited for the cash price paid when it is acquired. At the time the treasury stock is reissued it is credited at its acquisition cost and any excess over the original purchase price is credited to Additional Paid-in Capital. Thus, the resale transaction would cause Additional Paid-in Capital and Total Stockholders' Equity to increase with no effect on Retained Earnings.
16.	(D)	Martin Company should make the following journal entry to record the acquisition of its treasury stock using the cost method:

Treasury Stock (8,000 shares x $32)	256,000	
Cash		256,000

17.   (A)   Preferred shareholders are normally assured a dividend before any amount may be distributed to common shareholders. This does not mean that preferred shareholders will receive a dividend every year. If common shareholders do not receive a dividend, one does not need to be distributed to preferred shareholders. The size of the preferred dividend is normally based on a stated percentage rate of the preferred stock's par value. The amount of the dividend has no relationship to the amount distributed to common. The only way preferred shareholders receive a dividend every time a common stock dividend is declared is if the preferred stock is fully participating. Conversion of preferred shares into shares of common is a right that is specifically stated in the documentation describing the preferred stock issue and is not a normal preference.

18.   (C)   Preferred dividends only become a liability when they are declared by the board of directors. Therefore, preferred dividends in arrears are not recorded as a liability. However, they should be disclosed in a footnote to the financial statements.

19.   (D)   While the receipt of a cash dividend may result in an increase in tax liability for stockholders, this is not one of the major considerations management makes prior to declaring a cash dividend. The other three alternatives represent primary considerations management must make before a cash dividend is declared.

20.   (C)   The declaration of a cash dividend is recorded by a debit to Retained Earnings and a credit to Dividends Payable. Thus, the Retained Earnings account will decrease and Current Liabilities will increase. The cash account is unaffected by the declaration of a cash dividend. Cash will decrease when the dividend is paid.

21.   (A)   The payment of a cash dividend, previously declared, will cause the current ratio to increase because current assets (Cash) and current liabilities (Dividends Payable) decrease by the same amount. For example, if current assets were $100,000 and current liabilities were $50,000, the current ratio would be 2:1 and working capital would be $50,000 ($100,000 - $50,000). If a previously declared $10,000 cash dividend was paid, current assets would drop to $90,000 and current liabilities would drop to $40,000. Thus, after the payment of the dividend, the current ratio would be 2.25:1 ($90,000/$40,000), but working capital would still be $50,000 ($90,000 - $40,000).

22.   (A)   The credit balance in retained earnings serves as the basis for distributions of assets to stockholders (dividends). The sale of common stock or treasury stock would not result in an increase in retained earnings, and the payment to a creditor is merely a decrease in both assets and liabilities.

23.   (B)   The accounting profession requires that property dividends be recorded at the fair value of the assets transferred with a gain or loss being recognized on the disposal by the company.

24. (D) A transfer of a nonmonetary asset to a stockholder or to another entity in a nonreciprocal transfer should be recorded at fair value of the asset transferred, and a gain or loss should be recognized on the disposition of the asset. On the date of declaration (10/15/10), Mildred Corporation will make the following journal entries for the 1,800 shares of Lester Corporation stock it will distribute (18,000 shares/10 shares = 1,800 shares).

Investment in Lester Stock	9,000	
Gain on Appreciation of Securities		9,000
Retained Earnings (1,800 x $14)	25,200	
Property Dividends Payable		25,200

In the first entry, a gain on the appreciation of stock of $9,000 is recorded and is computed by taking the difference between the fair value of the stock at $14 and its cost of $9 ($18,000/2,000 shares) and multiplying the difference by the number of shares to be distributed. ($14 - $9 = $5 x 1,800 shares = $9,000). A gain of $9,000 is recorded.

In the second entry, retained earnings is debited for $25,200 which is the fair value of the stock to be distributed ($14 x 1,800 shares = $25,200). Retained earnings is decreased by $25,200, but this is partially offset when the gain of $9,000 on appreciation of stock is closed to retained earnings. Therefore, the net reduction in retained earnings is $16,200 ($25,200 - $9,000).

25. (D) The only feature listed that is common to both stock dividends and stock splits is the fact that the number of shares outstanding will change. Total stockholders' equity is not affected by a stock dividend or stock split. No transfer is made from retained earnings for a stock split, and there is no reduction in par value for a stock dividend.

26. (B) Total stockholders' equity is unaffected by a stock dividend or a stock split. A stock dividend is a capitalization of retained earnings. No assets are distributed, and each stockholder has exactly the same proportionate interest in the corporation and the same book value after the stock dividend was issued as before it was declared. A stock split is a device to reduce the market value of a company's stock so greater trading may take place. From an accounting standpoint, no entry is recorded for a stock split; a memorandum note is made indicating that the par value of the shares has changed and the number of shares has increased.

27. (A) The declaration of a stock dividend has no effect on total stockholders' equity. No assets are distributed, and each shareholder has the same proportionate equity interest and the same total book value after the stock dividend was issued as before. A stock dividend is recorded by debiting retained earnings for either the par value or market value of the shares to be distributed and crediting common stock and additional paid-in capital. Therefore, total stockholders' equity does not change, only its composition.

28. (B) A stock split does not alter any of the amounts comprising stockholders' equity because no formal journal entry is made. The number of shares and the par value of each share is adjusted to reflect the stock split but the amounts appearing in the capital stock account remain unchanged. In contrast, a stock dividend requires a formal entry transferring an amount from retained earnings to capital stock. Total stockholders' equity is not affected by either stock splits or stock dividends.

29. (A)   The most likely effect of a stock split is to decrease the par value per share and increase the number of shares outstanding. No formal journal entries are made for a stock split.

30. (A)

Retained Earnings

Cash Dividend	30,000	100,000	Beginning Bal.
Stock Dividend	30,000*	50,000	Net Income
		90,000	Ending Bal.

*(1,500 x $20 =$30,000)

31. (D)   Stock dividend:
    280,000 x .05 = 14,000 x $24 .... $336,000
    Cash dividend:
    280,000 + 14,000 = 294,000 x $.60   176,400
    Decrease in retained earnings....................... $512,400

32. (B)   The Rate of Return on Stockholders' Equity is computed by dividing net income less preferred dividends ($62,000 - $10,000 = $52,000) by average common stockholders' equity [$1,100,000 + $1,200,000)/2 = $1,150,000]; therefore it is 4.5% or ($52,000/$1,150,000). The Payout Ratio is computed by dividing cash dividends by net income less preferred dividends ($5,000/$52,000 = 9.6%).

33. (D)   The Price Earnings Ratio is computed by dividing the market price of the stock by the earnings per share [$12/($52,000/120,000) = 27.7]. The Book Value Per Share is computed by dividing common stockholders' equity by outstanding shares ($1,200,000/120,000 = $10.00).

REVIEW EXERCISES

1. a. **Journal Entries:**

    (1) No entry necessary.

    (2)

Land..	70,000	
Building...	215,000	
Common Stock		220,000
Paid-in-Capital in Excess of Par--Common stock...		65,000

    (3)

Cash..	1,035,000	
Preferred stock		900,000
Paid-in-Capital in Excess of Par--Preferred Stock .		135,000

    (4)

Cash..	140,000	
Common Stock		16,000
Paid-in-Capital in Excess of Par--Common Stock .		24,000
Preferred Stock		100,000

    (5)

Treasury Stock--Preferred...	54,000	
Cash		54,000

    (6)

Treasury Stock--Common..	50,400	
Cash		50,400

    (7)

Cash..	33,000	
Treasury Stock--Preferred (108 x 300)...................		32,400
Paid-in-Capital from Treasury Stock--Preferred		600

    (8)

Cash..	26,000	
Retained Earnings	2,800	
Treasury Stock--Common ($72 x 400)...................		28,800

b.

Spangler Corporation
Stockholders' Equity Section

Preferred Stock-Par value $100 per share;
    Authorized 15,000 shares; issued 10,000 shares...................... $1,000,000
Additional Paid-in Capital-Preferred Stock 135,000
                                                     $1,135,000

Common Stock-Par value $20 per share;
    Authorized 18,000 shares; issued 11,800 shares...................... 236,000
Additional Paid-in Capital-Common Stock 89,000
                                                     325,000
Additional Paid-in Capital from Treasury Stock--Preferred 600
Total Paid-in Capital 1,460,600
Retained Earnings.. 184,200
    Total Paid-in Capital and Retained Earnings $1,644,800
Less Cost of Treasury Stock ($21,600 Preferred +
  $21,600 Common).. (43,200)
                                                     $1,601,600

2.   Jan. 2   Treasury Stock (1,000 x 12)........................... 12,000
                       Cash.. 12,000

       Feb. 4   Cash (500 x 13)... 6,500
                       Treasury Stock (500 x 12)...................... 6,000
                       Paid-in Capital from Treasury Stock....... 500

       May 10   Cash (500 x 8)... 4,000
                       Paid-in Capital from Treasury Stock 500
                       Retained Earnings 1,500
                       Treasury Stock (500 x 12)...................... 6,000

3.   Declaration of Dividend:
      Investment in Securities... 1,500,000
         Gain on Appreciation of Securities.................................... 1,500,000

      Retained Earnings 2,500,000
         Property Dividend Payable 2,500,000

   Payment of Dividend:
      Property Dividend Payable 2,500,000
         Investment in Securities...................................... 2,500,000

---

4. a. 1. Retained Earnings 101,000

            Dividend Payable - Preferred.. 56,000[a]

            Dividend Payable - Common... 45,000

    [a](400,000 x .07 x 2 = $56,000)

        Dividend Payable - Preferred... 56,000

        Dividend Payable - Common... 45,000

            Cash 101,000

    2. Retained Earnings 63,000

            Stock Dividend Distributable - Common .... 11,250[b]

            Paid-in Capital in Excess of Par - Common 51,750

    [b](15,000 x .15 x $5 = $11,250)

        Stock Dividend Distributable - Common................................ 11,250

            Common Stock 11,250

    3. Retained Earnings 34,500

            Dividend Payable - Common... 34,500[c]

    [c](15,000 + 2,250 x $2 = $34,500)

        Dividend Payable - Common... 34,500

            Cash 34,500

  b. Decrease: $135,500 ($101,000 + $34,500 = $135,500)

      A stock dividend has no effect on total stockholders' equity.

5. Retained Earnings,
    December 31, 2009 .... $66,900
    Add:
        Stock Dividend .... $ 4,000
        Cash Dividend 5,000   9,000
                                                                                                            $75,900
    Less:
    Retained Earnings
        January 1, 2009.. 65,900
        Estimated 2009 Net Income before Income Taxes........................ $10,000

16

Dilutive Securities and Earnings per Share

CHAPTER STUDY OBJECTIVES

1. Describe the accounting for the issuance, conversion and retirement of convertible securities.

2. Explain the accounting for convertible preferred stock.

3. Contrast the accounting for stock warrants and stock warrants issued with other securities.

4. Describe the accounting for stock compensation plans under generally accepted accounting principles.

5. Discuss the controversy involving stock compensation plans.

6. Compute earnings per share in a simple capital structure.

7. Compute earnings per share in a complex capital structure.

*8. Explain the accounting for stock appreciation rights.

*9. Compute earnings per share in a complex situation.

CHAPTER REVIEW

1. Chapter 16 examines the issues related to accounting for dilutive securities at date of issuance and at time of conversion. Also, the impact of the computation of earnings per share is presented. The significance attached to the earnings per share figure by stockholders and potential investors has caused the accounting profession to direct a great deal of attention to the calculation and presentation of earnings per share.

Dilutive Securities

2. (S.O. 1) **Dilutive securities** are defined as securities that are not common stock in form but that enable their holders to obtain common stock upon exercise or conversion. The most notable examples include convertible bonds, convertible preferred stocks, warrants, and contingent shares.

Convertible Bonds

3. In the case of **convertible bonds,** the conversion feature allows the corporation an opportunity to obtain equity capital without giving up more ownership control than necessary. Also, the conversion feature entices the investor to accept a lower interest rate than he or she would normally accept on a straight debt issue. Accounting for convertible bonds on the date of issuance follows the procedures used to account for straight debt issues.

*Note: All asterisked (*) items relate to material contained in the Appendix to the chapter.

4.   If bonds are converted into other securities, the issue price of the stock is based upon **the book value of the bonds**. No gain or loss is recorded as the issue price of the stock is recorded at the book value of the bonds. For example, assume that Irvine Corporation has convertible bonds with a book value of $3,200 ($3,000 plus $200 unamortized premium) convertible into 120 shares of common stock ($10 par value) with a current market value of $35 per share. The journal entry to be made is as follows:

Bonds Payable	3,000	
Premium on Bonds Payable	200	
Common Stock		1,200
Paid-in Capital in Excess of Par		2,000

5.   When an issuer wishes to induce prompt conversion of its convertible debt to equity securities, the issues may offer some form of additional consideration ("sweetener"). The sweetener should be reported as an expense of the current period at an amount equal to the fair value of the additional consideration given.

6.   Convertible debt that is retired without exercise of the conversion feature should be accounted for as though it were a straight debt issue. Any difference between the cash acquisition price of the debt and its carrying amount should be reflected currently in income as a gain or loss.

Convertible Preferred Stock

7.   (S.O. 2) **Convertible preferred stock** is accounted for in the same manner as nonconvertible preferred stock at date of issuance. When conversion takes place, the book value method is used. Preferred Stock, along with any related Additional Paid-in Capital, is debited; Common Stock and Additional Paid-in Capital (if an excess exists) are credited. If the par value of the common stock issued exceeds the book value of the preferred stock, Retained Earnings is debited for the difference.

Stock Warrants

8.   (S.O. 3) **Stock warrants** are certificates entitling the holder to acquire shares of stock at a certain price within a stated period. Warrants are potentially dilutive as are convertible securities. However, when stock warrants are exercised, the holder must pay a certain amount of money to obtain the shares. Also, when stock warrants are attached to debt, the debt remains after the warrants are exercised.

9.   When detachable stock warrants are attached to debt, the proceeds from the sale should be allocated between the two securities. This treatment is in accordance with GAAP, and is based on the fact that the stock warrants can be traded separately from the debt. Allocation of the proceeds between the two securities is normally made on the basis of their fair market values at the date of issuance. The amount allocated to the warrants is credited to **Paid-in Capital--Stock Warrants.** The two methods of allocation available are (a) **the proportional method** and (b) **the incremental method.**

10.   To value the warrants under the proportional method, a value must be placed on the bonds without the warrants and then on the warrants. For example, assume that Pontell Corporation issued 1,000, $500 bonds with warrants attached for par ($500,000). Each bond has one warrant attached. It is estimated that the bonds would sell for 98 without the warrants and the value of the warrants in the market is $25,000. The allocation between the bonds and the warrants would be made as follows:

Fair market value of bonds
   (without warrants) ($500,000 x .98) $490,000
Fair market value of warrants   25,000
Aggregate fair market value $515,000

Allocated to bonds: $\dfrac{\$490,000}{\$515,000}$ x $500,000 = $475,728

Allocated to warrants: $\dfrac{\$25,000}{\$515,000}$ x $500,000 = $ 24,272

The journal entry for the issuance of the bonds is:

Cash (1,000 x $500)	500,000	
Discount on Bonds Payable	24,272	
Bonds Payable		500,000
Paid-in Capital-Stock Warrants		24,272

11.   When detachable warrants are exercised, Cash is debited for the exercise price and Paid-in Capital-Stock Warrants is debited for the amount assigned to the warrants. The credit portion of the entry includes Common Stock and Additional Paid-in Capital. If detachable warrants are never exercised, Paid-in Capital Stock Warrants is debited and Paid-in Capital from Expired Warrants is credited. If all the warrants described in paragraph 10 above are exercised under the following terms, for $15 cash and one warrant the holder will receive one share of $5 par value common stock, the journal entry to record the transaction would be the following:

Cash (1,000 x $15)	15,000	
Paid-in Capital--Stock Warrants	24,272	
Common Stock (1,000 x $5)		5,000
Paid-in Capital in Excess of Par		34,272

12.   Where the fair value of either the warrants or the bonds is not determinable, the incremental method may be used. That is, the security for which the market value is determinable is used and the remainder of the purchase price is allocated to the security for which the market value is not known.

Stock Rights

13.   **Stock rights** are issued to existing stockholders when a corporation's directors decide to issue new shares of stock. Each share owned normally entitles the stockholders to one stock right. This privilege allows each stockholder the right to maintain his or her percentage ownership in the corporation. Only a memorandum entry is required **when rights are issued to existing stockholders.**

Stock Compensation Plans

14.   (S.O. 4) A **stock option** is another form of warrant that arises in stock compensation plans used to pay and motivate employees. This type of warrant gives selected employees the option to purchase common stock at a given price over an extended period of time.

15.   In the past, the FASB gave companies a choice in the method of recognizing the cost of compensation under a stock option plan. The two choices were:
    a.   the fair value method, and
    b.   the intrinsic value method.

The FASB now requires the use of the fair value method.

The Fair Value Method

16.   Using the fair value method, total compensation expense is computed based on the fair value of the options expected to vest on the date the options are granted to the employees. Fair value for public companies is to be estimated use an option pricing model, with some adjustments for the unique factors of employee stock options. No adjustments are made after the grant date in response to subsequent changes in the stock price—either up or down.

Allocating Compensation Expense

17.   In general, compensation expense is recognized in the periods in which the employee performs the service—the **service period.** Unless otherwise specified, the service period is the vesting period—the time between the grant and the vesting date.

18.   To illustrate the accounting for a stock option plan, assume that on September 16, 2009, the stockholders of Jesilow Company approve a plan that grants the company's three executives options to purchase 4,000 shares each of the company's $1 par value common stock. The options are granted on January 1, 2010, and may be exercised at any time within the next five years. The option price per share is $30, and the market price of the stock at the date of grant is $40 per share.

Using the fair value method, total compensation expense is computed by applying an acceptable fair value option pricing model. We will assume that the fair value option pricing model determines total compensation expense to be $180,000.

Assuming the expected period of benefit is 3 years (starting with the grant date), the journal entries for each of the next three years are as follows:

Compensation Expense	60,000	
Paid-in Capital--Stock Options		60,000

If all of the options are exercised on July 1, 2014, the journal entries are as follows:

Cash (12,000 x $30)	360,000	
Paid-in Capital--Stock Options	180,000	
Common Stock (12,000 x $1)		12,000
Paid-in Capital in Excess of Par		528,000

Employee Stock Purchase Plans

19. Employee stock purchase plans (ESPPs) general, permit all employees to purchase stock at a discounted price for a short period at time. Compensation expense is not reported if:
   a.   Substantially all full-time employees may participate on an equitable basis;
   b.   The discount from market is small; and
   c.   The plan offers no substantive option feature.

Restricted Stock

20. **Restricted-stock plans** transfer shares of stock to employees, subject to an agreement that the shares cannot be sold, transferred or pledged until vesting occurs. These shares are subject to forfeiture if the conditions for vesting are not met.

21.   Major advantages of restricted-stock plans are:
   a.   Restricted stock never becomes completely worthless.
   b.   Restricted stock generally results in less dilution to existing stockholders.
   c.   Restricted stock better aligns the employee incentives with the companies' incentives.

22. The accounting for restricted stock follows the same general principles as accounting for stock options at the date of grant. That is, the company determines the fair value of the restricted stock at the date of grant (usually the fair value of a share of stock) and then expenses that amount over the service period.

23. To illustrate the accounting for restricted-stock plans, assume that on January 1, 2010, Lindsey Company issues 2,000 shares of restricted stock to its President, Amy Carlson. Lindsey's stock has a fair value of $12 per share on January 1, 2010. Additional information is as follows:
   a. The service period related to the restricted stock is four years.
   b. Vesting occurs if Carlson stays with the company for a four-year period.
   c. The par value of the stock is $1 per share.
   Lindsey makes the following entry on the grant date(January 1, 2010):

Unearned Compensation	24,000	
Common Stock (2,000 x $1)		2,000
Paid in Capital in Excess of Par (2,000 x $11)		22,000

Unearned compensation represents the cost of services yet to be performed, which is not an asset. Thus, the company reports unearned compensation in stockholder's equity in the balance sheet, as a contra-equity account. At December 31, 2010, Lindsey records compensation expense of $ 6,000 (2,000 shares x $12 x 25%) and the same amount for the following three years.

Debate Over Stock Option Accounting

24.   (S.O. 5) Companies tried to avoid showing stock compensation as an expense, however, due to the pressure to have transparent financial reporting, many companies changed their attitudes and allowed the FASB to require recognition of stock–based expense.

Earnings Per Share

25.   (S.O. 6) **Earnings per share** indicates the income earned by each share of common stock. Generally, earnings per share information is reported below net income in the income statement. When the income statement contains intermediate components of income (e.g., income from continuing operations), earnings per share should be disclosed for each component.

Simple Capital Structure

26.   (S.O. 6) A corporation's capital structure is **simple** if it consists only of common stock or includes no potentially dilutive convertible securities, options, warrants, or other rights that upon conversion or exercise could in the aggregate dilute earnings per common share. The formula for computing earnings per share is as follows:

$$\frac{\text{Net Income - Preferred Dividends}}{\text{Weighted Average Number of Shares Outstanding}} = \text{Earnings per share}$$

If the preferred stock is cumulative and the dividend is not declared in the current year, an amount equal to the dividend that should have been declared for the current year only should be subtracted from net income or added to the net loss.

Weighted Average Number of Shares Outstanding

27.   The weighted average number of shares outstanding during the period constitutes the basis for the per share amounts reported. Shares issued or purchased during the period affect the number of outstanding shares and must be weighted by the fraction of the period they are outstanding. When stock dividends or stock splits occur, computation of the weighted average number of shares requires restatement of the shares outstanding before the stock dividend or split (they are assumed to have been outstanding since the beginning of the year). If a stock dividend or stock split occurs after the end of the year, but before the financial statements are issued, the weighted average number of shares outstanding for the year (and any other years presented in comparative form) must be restated.

Complex Capital Structure

28.   (S.O. 7) A capital structure is complex if it includes securities that could have a dilutive effect on earnings per common share. A complex capital structure requires a dual presentation of earnings per share, each with equal prominence on the face of the income statement. The dual presentation consists of **basic EPS** and **diluted EPS.** Companies with complex capital structures will not report diluted EPS if the securities in their capital structure are antidilutive (increase EPS).

Diluted EPS--Convertible Securities

29.   The **if-converted** method is used to measure the dilutive effects of potential conversion on EPS. The if-converted method for a convertible bond assumes (a) the conversion of convertible securities at the beginning of the period (or at the time of the issuance of the security, if issued during the period) and (2) the elimination of related interest, net of tax or preferred dividend. Thus the denominator is increased by the additional shares assumed converted and the numerator is increased by the amount of interest expense, net of tax or preferred dividend associated with those potential common shares.

Dilutive EPS-Options and Warrants

30.   Stock options and warrants outstanding are included in diluted earnings per share unless they are antidilutive. If the exercise price of the option or warrant is lower than the market price of the stock, dilution occurs. If the exercise price of the option or warrant is higher than the market price of the stock, common shares are reduced. In this case, the options or warrants are antidilutive because their assumed exercise leads to an increase in earnings per share.

Treasury Stock Method

31.   The treasury stock method is used in determining the dilutive effect of options and warrants. This method assumes that the proceeds from the exercise of options and warrants are used to purchase common stock for the treasury. To illustrate the treasury stock method, assume 2,000 options are outstanding with an exercise price of $25 per common share. If the market price of the common stock is $60 per share, computation of the incremental shares using the treasury stock method would be:

Proceeds from exercise of 2,000 options	
(2,000 x $25)	$50,000
Shares issued upon exercise of options	2,000
Treasury shares purchasable with proceeds ($50,000/$60)	833
Incremental shares outstanding (potential common shares)	1,167

32.   For both options and warrants, exercise is not assumed unless the average market price of the stock is above the exercise price during the period being reported. As a practical matter, a simple average of the weekly or monthly prices is adequate, so long as the prices do not fluctuate significantly.

Stock Appreciation Rights

*33. (S.O. 8) **Stock appreciation rights** are a form of employee compensation that avoids some of the cash flow problems recipients of nonqualified stock option plans face. Under a stock appreciation rights plan, an employee is given the right to receive **share appreciation,** which is defined as the excess of the market price of the stock at the date of exercise over a pre established price. This share appreciation may be received in cash, shares of stock, or a combination of both. Compensation cost for the plan at any interim period is the difference between the current market price of the stock and the option price multiplied by the number of stock appreciation rights. The measurement date is the date of exercise.

Appendix 16-B

*34. (S.O. 9) **Appendix 16-B** is a comprehensive illustration of the computations involved in presenting earnings per share. This appendix is an outstanding demonstration of the various steps involved in arriving at diluted earnings per share. Students are encouraged to study this illustration prior to working the problems at the end of the chapter.

GLOSSARY

Antidilutive securities.	Securities which upon conversion or exercise increase earnings per share (or reduce the loss per share).
Book value approach.	A method used for determining the issue price of stock when bonds are converted into stock which records the stock issued using the book value of the bonds at the issue date.
Complex capital structure.	When a corporation's capital structure includes securities that could have a dilutive effect on earnings per common share.
Convertible bonds.	A security that combines the benefits of a bond with the privilege of exchanging it for stock at the holder's option.

Convertible preferred stock.	Preferred stock which is convertible into common stock at the holder's option.
Detachable stock warrants.	Warrants that can be sold separately from their bonds.
Diluted earnings per share.	Earnings per share based on the number of common shares outstanding plus all contingent issuances of common stock that could reduce earnings per share.
Dilutive securities.	Securities that are not common stock in form, but enable their holders to obtain common stock upon exercise or conversion. Examples include convertible bonds, convertible preferred stocks, stock warrants, and contingent shares.
Earnings per share.	The income earned by each share of common stock.
Grant date.	The date someone receives stock options.
If-converted method.	The method used to measure the dilutive effect of convertible securities which assumes (1) the conversion of the convertible securities at the beginning of the period (or at the time of issuance of the security, if issued during the period), and (2) the elimination of interest, net of tax or preferred dividend.
Induced conversion.	When an issuer wishes to induce prompt conversion of its convertible debt to equity securities, the issuer may offer some form of additional consideration (such as cash or common stock).
Market value approach.	A method used for determining the issue price of stock when bonds are converted into stock which records the stock issued using its market price at the issue date.
Measurement date.	The first date on which are known both (1) the number of shares that an individual employee is entitled to receive and (2) the option or purchase price.
Nondetachable stock warrants.	Warrants that cannot be sold separately from their bonds.
Restricted-stock plans	Stock plans that transfer shares of stock to employees, subject to an agreement that the shares cannot be sold, transferred or pledged until vesting occurs.
Service period.	The period in which the employee performs the service for which he or she is being compensated.
Simple capital structure.	When a corporation's capital structure consists only of common stock or includes no potentially dilutive convertible securities, options, warrants, or other rights that upon conversion or exercise could in the aggregate dilute earnings per common share.

*Stock appreciation rights (SARs).	Similar to a stock option plan except executives do not have to purchase the stock but instead are given a right to receive the excess of the market price of the stock at the date of exercise over a pre-established price.
Stock option.	A warrant which gives selected employees the option to purchase common stock at a given price over an extended period of time.
Stock option plans.	Long-term compensation plans which attempt to develop in executives a strong loyalty toward the company by giving them an equity interest based on changes in long-term measures such as increases in earnings per share, revenues, stock price, or market share.
Stock rights.	Existing stockholders have the right (preemptive privilege) to purchase newly issued shares in proportion to their holdings.
Stock warrants.	Certificates entitling the holder to acquire shares of stock at a certain price within a stated period.
Sweetener.	The additional consideration offered by an issuer that wishes to set up an induced conversion.
Treasury stock method.	The method used to measure the dilutive effect of options and warrants which assumes (1) the options or warrants are exercised at the beginning of the year (or date of issue if later), and (2) the proceeds from the exercise of options and warrants are used to purchase common stock for the treasury.
Weighted average number of shares outstanding.	The basis for the per share amounts reported which reflects shares issued or purchased during the period by calculating the number of shares outstanding by the fraction of the period they are outstanding.

CHAPTER OUTLINE

Fill in the outline presented below.

    (S.O. 1) Convertible Debt

        Conversions

            Book value approach

        Induced Conversions

Chapter Outline *(continued)*

Retirement of Convertible Debt

(S.O. 2) Convertible Preferred Stock

(S.O. 3) Stock Warrants

Proportional Method

Incremental Method

(S.O. 4) Stock Compensation Plans

Accounting for Stock Compensation

Employee Stock Purchase Plans

Restricted Stock

(S.O. 5) Debate over Stock Option Accounting

(S.O. 6) Earnings per Share

Chapter Outline *(continued)*

Simple Capital Structure

Weighted Average Number of Shares Outstanding

(S.O. 7) Complex Capital Structure

Diluted EPS--Convertible Securities

If-converted method

Diluted EPS--Options and Warrants

Treasury stock method

Earnings per Share Presentations and Disclosures

*(S.O. 8) Stock Appreciation Rights

*(S.O. 9) Comprehensive Earnings per Share Illustration

DEMONSTRATION PROBLEM (S.O. 3)

Petersilia Company issued $200,000 face value of bonds with a coupon rate of 9%. To make the bonds more attractive, the company issued detachable stock warrants at the rate of one warrant for each $100 bond sold. The bonds sold at issuance for 97.5. The value of the bonds without the warrants is considered to be $175,000, and the value of the warrants in the market is $35,000.

Instructions:
Prepare the journal entry for the issuance of the bonds and warrants.

Solution:
Value of bonds and warrants formulas:

(1) $\dfrac{\text{Value of bonds without warrants}}{\text{Value of bonds without warrants} + \text{value of warrants}} \times \text{Purchase Price} = \begin{array}{c}\text{Value assigned}\\ \text{to bonds}\end{array}$

(2) $\dfrac{\text{Value of warrants}}{\text{Value of bonds without warrants} + \text{value of warrants}} \times \text{Purchase Price} = \begin{array}{c}\text{Value assigned}\\ \text{to warrants}\end{array}$

(1) $\dfrac{\$175,000}{\$175,000 + \$35,000} \times \$195,000^* = \$162,500$

(2) $\dfrac{\$35,000}{\$175,000 + \$35,000} \times \$195,000^* = \$32,500$

Journal Entry:

Cash...	195,000	
Discount on Bonds Payable...............................	37,500	
Bonds Payable		200,000
Paid-in Capital-Stock Warrants...............................		32,500

*($200,000 x .975)

REVIEW QUESTIONS AND EXERCISES

TRUE-FALSE

Indicate whether each of the following is true (T) or false (F) in the space provided.

_____ 1.   (S.O. 1) One of the primary reasons for issuing convertible debt is the desire to raise equity capital that, assuming conversion, will arise when the original debt is converted.

_____ 2.   (S.O. 1) Current authoritative pronouncements require that a portion of the proceeds received from the issuance of convertible debt be accounted for as being attributable to the conversion feature.

_____ 3.   (S.O. 2) When convertible preferred stock is converted into common stock and the par value of the common stock issued exceeds the book value of the preferred stock, then retained earnings is usually debited for the difference.

_____ 4.   (S.O. 3) The proceeds from the sale of debt with nondetachable stock warrants should be allocated between the two securities.

_____ 5.   (S.O. 3) Nondetachable warrants do **not** require an allocation of the proceeds between the bonds and the warrants.

_____ 6.   (S.O. 4) The FASB requires recognition of compensation cost using the fair value method.

_____ 7.   (S.O. 4) Using the fair value method, total compensation expense is computed based on the fair value of the options expected to vest on the date the options are granted to the employees.

_____ 8.   (S.O. 4) Under the fair value method, total compensation cost is computed as the excess of the market price of the stock over the option price on the measurement date.

_____ 9.   (S.O. 4) The measurement date for stock options granted to employees is the first date on which are known both (a) the number of shares that an individual employee is entitled to receive and (b) the market value of the stock.

_____ 10.   (S.O. 4) Under the fair value method, compensation expense is recognized as of the measurement date.

_____ 11.   (S.O. 4) A major advantage of a restricted–stock plan is that restricted stock never becomes completely worthless.

_____ 12.   (S.O. 4) When accounting for restricted stock, a company determines the fair value of the restricted stock at the date of grant and then expenses that amount over the service period.

_____ 13.   (S.O. 4) When accounting for restricted stock, Unearned Compensation represents the cost of services yet to be performed, which is **not** an asset.

_____ 14.   (S.O. 5) Accounting for stock options is a classic example of the ease the FASB has in issuing an accounting standard.

_____ 15.   (S.O. 6) A corporation's capital structure is simple if it includes securities that could have a dilutive effect on earnings per common share.

_____ 16.   (S.O. 6) In computing earnings per share, if a stock dividend occurs after the end of the year, but before the financial statements are issued, the weighted-average number of shares outstanding for the prior year (and any other years presented in comparative form) must be restated.

_____ 17.   (S.O. 6) When stock dividends or stock splits occur, computation of the weighted average number of shares requires restatement of the shares outstanding before the stock dividend or split.

_____ 18   (S.O.7) Diluted earnings per share indicates the dilution of earnings per share that would have occurred if all contingent issuances of common stock that would have reduced earnings per share had taken place.

_____ 19.   (S.O. 7) Antidilutive securities are securities, which upon their conversion or exercise decrease earnings per share (or increase the loss per share).

_____ 20.   (S.O. 7) The if-converted method for a convertible bond assumes (1) the conversion of the convertible securities at the beginning of the period (or at the time of issuance of the security, if issued during the period), and (2) the elimination of related interest, net of tax or preferred dividend.

_____ 21.   (S.O. 7) The treasury stock method assumes that the options or warrants are exercised at the grant date and the proceeds from the exercise of options and warrants are used to sell treasury stock.

_____ 22.   (S.O. 7) Antidilutive securities should be ignored in all calculations and should **not** be considered in computing diluted earnings per share.

_____ 23.   (S.O. 7) The treasury stock method will increase the number of shares outstanding whenever the exercise price of an option or warrant is below the market price of the common stock.

_____ 24.   (S.O. 7) Earnings per share data are required for each of the following: (a) income from continuing operations, (b) income before extraordinary items, and (c) net income.

_____ *25.   (S.O. 8) In accounting for stock appreciation rights granted to key executives, compensation is measured at the date of grant as the difference between the market price and book value of the stock involved.

MULTIPLE CHOICE

Select the best response for each of the following items and enter the corresponding letter in the space provided.

_____ 1.   (S.O. 1) Corporations issue convertible debt for two main reasons. One is the desire to raise equity capital that, assuming conversion, will arise when the original debt is converted. The other is:

      A.   the ease with which convertible debt is sold even if the company has a poor credit rating.
      B.   the fact that equity capital has issue costs that convertible debt does not.
      C.   that many corporations can obtain financing at lower rates.
      D.   that convertible bonds will always sell at a premium.

_____ 2.   (S.O. 1) Binder Corporation issued at a premium of $50 a $1,000 bond convertible into 200 shares of common stock (par value $3). At the time of the conversion the unamortized premium is $40, the market value of the bond is $1,200, and the stock is quoted on the market at $6. If the bond is converted into common, what is the amount of the gain or loss to be recorded on redemption of the bonds payable?

      A. $240
      B. $200
      C. $160
      D. $0

_____ 3.   (S.O. 1) Calavita Company has outstanding $500,000 par value convertible bonds convertible into 50,000 shares of $1 par value common stock. Calavita wishes to reduce its annual interest cost. To do so, the company agrees to pay the holders of its convertible bonds an additional $45,000 if they will convert. Assuming conversion occurs, which of the following journal entries would be correct?

A. Bonds Payable	500,000	
Loss on Redemption of Bonds Payable	45,000	
Common Stock		50,000
Paid-in Capital in Excess of Par		450,000
Cash		45,000
B. Bonds Payable	500,000	
Common Stock		50,000
Paid-in Capital in Excess of Par		405,000
Cash		45,000
C. Bonds Payable	500,000	
Premium on Bonds	45,000	
Common Stock		50,000
Paid-in Capital in Excess of Par		450,000
Cash		45,000
D. Bonds Payable	500,000	
Debt Conversion Expense	45,000	
Common Stock		50,000
Paid-in Capital in Excess of Par		450,000
Cash		45,000

_____ 4. (S.O. 1) When convertible debt is retired by the issuer, any material difference between the cash acquisition price and the carrying amount of the debt should be:

     A. reflected currently in income, but not as an extraordinary item.
     B. reflected currently in income as an extraordinary item.
     C. treated as a prior period adjustment.
     D. treated as an adjustment of additional paid-in capital.

_____ 5. (S.O. 2) Tierra Linda Co. issued 5,000 shares of common stock (par value $2) upon conversion of 5,000 shares of preferred stock (par value $1) that was originally issued for a $400 premium. The entry would include a debit to retained earnings for:

     A. $5,400.
     B. $5,000.
     C. $4,600.
     D. -0-

_____ 6. (S.O. 2) The conversion of preferred stock into common requires that any excess of the par value of the common shares issued over the carrying amount of the preferred being converted should be:

     A. reflected currently in income, but not as an extraordinary item.
     B. reflected currently in income as an extraordinary item.
     C. treated as a prior period adjustment.
     D. treated as a direct reduction of retained earnings.

_____ 7. (S.O. 3) The major difference between convertible debt and stock warrants is that upon exercise of the warrants:

     A. the stock is held by the company for a defined period of time before they are issued to the warrant holder.
     B. the holder has to pay a certain amount of cash to obtain the shares.
     C. the stock involved is restricted and can only be sold by the recipient after a set period of time.
     D. no paid-in capital in excess of par can be a part of the transaction.

_____ 8. (S.O. 3) Schieble Corporation offered detachable 5-year warrants to buy one share of common stock (par value $2) at $30 (at a time when a share was selling for approximately $45). The price paid for 2,000, $1,000 bonds with the warrants attached was par, or $200,000. Assuming the market price of the Schieble bonds was known to be $180,000, but the market price of the warrants without the bonds cannot be determined, what are the amounts that should be allocated to the warrants and the bonds?

	Warrants	Bonds
A.	$20,000	$180,000
B.	$0	$200,000
C.	$20,000	$200,000
D.	$0	$180,000

9. (S.O. 4) On July 1, 2010, Dombrink Company granted Gil Geis, an employee, an option to buy 400 shares of Dombrink Co. stock for $20 per share, the option exercisable for 5 years from date of grant. Using a fair value option pricing model, total compensation expense is determined to be $1,200. Geis exercised his option on October 1, 2010 and sold his 400 shares on December 1, 2010. Quoted market prices of Dombrink Co. stock during 2010 were:

July 1	$20 per share
October 1	$24 per share
December 1	$27 per share

   The service period is for three years beginning January 1, 2010. As a result of the option granted to Geis, using the fair value method, Dombrink should recognize compensation expense for 2010 on its books in the amount of:

   A. $ 0.
   B. $300.
   C. $400.
   D. $1,200.

10. (S.O. 4) On January 1, 2010, Perry Company granted Bill Thompson, an employee, an option to buy 100 shares of Perry Co. stock for $20 per share, the option exercisable for 5 years from date of grant. Using a fair value option pricing model, total compensation expense is determined to be $600. Thompson exercised his option on September 1, 2010, and sold his 100 shares on December 1, 2010. Quoted market prices of Perry Co. stock during 2010 were:

July 1	$20 per share
September 1	$24 per share
December 1	$27 per share

    The service period is for two years beginning January 1, 2010. As a result of the option granted to Thompson, using the fair value method, Perry should recognize compensation expense for 2010 on its books in the amount of:

    A. $ 0.
    B. $300.
    C. $600.
    D. $700.

11. (S.O. 4) On December 31, 2010, the Granados Company granted some of its executives options to purchase 100,000 shares of the company's $10 par common stock at an option price of $50 per share. The Black-Scholes option pricing model determines total compensation expense to be $400,000. The options become exercisable on January 1, 2011, and represent compensation for executives' services over a two-year period beginning January 1, 2011. At December 31, 2011 none of the executives had exercised their options. What is the impact on Granados' net income for the year ended December 31, 2011 as a result of this transaction under the fair value method?

    A. $400,000 decrease.
    B. $200,000 decrease.
    C. $0.
    D. $200,000 increase.

_____   12.   (S.O. 4) Which of the following is **not** a characteristic of a noncompensatory stock option plan?

      A.   Substantially all full-time employees may participate on an equitable basis.
      B.   The plan offers no substantive option feature.
      C.   Unlimited time period permitted for exercise of an option as long as the holder is still employed by the company.
      D.   Discount from the market price of the stock no greater than would be reasonable in an offer of stock to stockholders or others.

_____   13.   (S.O. 4) On June 30, 2010, Vila Corporation granted compensatory stock options for 10,000 shares of its $24 par value common stock to certain of its key employees. The market price of the common stock on that date was $31 per share and the option price was $28. Using a fair value option pricing model, total compensation expense is determined to be $32,000. The options are exercisable beginning January 1, 2012, providing those key employees are still in the employ of the company at the time the options are exercised. The options expire on June 30, 2013.

On January 4, 2012, when the market price of the stock was $36 per share, all options for the 10,000 shares were exercised.

The service period is for two years beginning January 1, 2010. Using the fair value method, what should be the amount of compensation expense recorded by Vila Corporation for these options on December 31, 2010 ?

      A. $ 0.
      B. $ 7,500.
      C. $16,000.
      D. $32,000.

_____   14.   (S.O. 4) Which of the following is **not** an advantage of restricted stock plans.

A. Restricted stock better aligns the employee incentives with the companies' incentives.
B. Restricted stock can be sold before vesting occurs.
C. Restricted stock never becomes completely worthless.
D. Restricted stock generally results in less dilution to existing stockholders.

_____   15.   (S.O. 6) Due to the importance of earnings per share information, it is required to be reported by all:

	Public Companies	**Nonpublic Companies**
A.	Yes	Yes
B.	Yes	No
C.	No	No
D.	No	Yes

16.   (S.O. 6) On January 1, 2010, Kihnley Corporation had 25,000 shares of its $5 par value common stock outstanding. On March 1, the Corporation sold an additional 50,000 shares on the open market at $25 per share. The Corporation issued a 20% stock dividend on May 1. On August 1, the Corporation purchased 28,000 shares and immediately retired the stock. On November 1, 40,000 shares were sold for $30 per share. What is the weighted average number of shares outstanding for 2010?

    A.   51,667
    B.   71,667
    C.   75,000
    D.   102,000

17.   Kasravi Co. had net income for 2010 of $200,000. The average number of shares outstanding for the period was 100,000 shares. The average number of shares under outstanding options (although not exercisable at this time), at an option price of $30 per share is 6,000 shares. The average market price of the common stock during the year was $36. What should Kasravi Co. report for earnings per share for the year ended 2010?

	Basic Earnings Per Share	Diluted Earnings Per Share
A.	$2.00	$1.98
B.	$2.00	$1.88
C.	$1.90	$1.88
D.	$1.92	$1.90

18.   (S.O. 7) On January 2, 2010, Terry Co. issued at par $500,000 of 7% convertible bonds. Each $1,000 bond is convertible into 10 shares of common stock. No bonds were converted during 2010. Terry had 50,000 shares of common stock outstanding during 2010. Terry's 2010 net income was $600,000 and the income tax rate was 30%. Terry's diluted earnings per share for 2010 would be (rounded to the nearest penny):

    A. $12.49.
    B. $12.00.
    C. $11.35.
    D. $10.46.

19.   (S.O. 7) Warrant's exercisable at $25 each to obtain 30,000 shares of common stock were outstanding during a period when the average market price of the common stock was $30. Application of the treasury stock method for the assumed exercise of these warrants in computing diluted earnings per share will increase the weighted average number of outstanding shares by:

    A.   30,000.
    B.   25,000.
    C.   5,000.
    D.   0.

_____   20.   (S.O. 7) Warrants exercisable at $20 each to obtain 10,000 shares of common stock were outstanding during a period when the average market price of the common stock was $25. Application of the treasury stock method for the assumed exercise of these warrants in computing diluted earnings per share will increase the weighted average number of outstanding common shares by:

    A.   10,000.
    B.   1,667.
    C.   2,000.
    D.   8,000.

_____   21.   (S.O. 7) During 2010 Clark Company had a net income of $50,000 (no extraordinary items) and 50,000 shares of common stock and 10,000 shares of preferred stock outstanding. Clark declared and paid dividends of $.50 per share to common and $6.00 per share to preferred. For 2010 Clark Company should report diluted earnings (loss) per share of:

    A. $.83-1/3.
    B. $1.00.
    C.   ($.20).
    D. $.50.

_____   22.   (S.O. 7) Mohamed Corporation has net income for the year of $360,000 and a weighted average number of common shares outstanding during the period of 125,000 shares. The company has a convertible debenture bond issue outstanding. The bonds were issued two years ago at par ($1,500,000), carry a 7% interest rate, and are convertible into 25,000 shares of common stock. The company has a 40% tax rate. Diluted earnings per share are:

    A. $3.10.
    B. $2.82.
    C. $2.68.
    D. $2.42.

_____   23.   (S.O. 7) Wiebe Inc. purchased Mobley Co. and agreed to give stockholders of Mobley Co. 10,000 additional shares in 2011 if Mobley Co.'s net income in 2010 is $300,000; in 2009 Mobley Co.'s net income is $290,000. Wiebe Inc. has net income for 2009 of $100,000 and has an average number of common shares outstanding for 2009 of 100,000 shares. What should Wiebe report as earnings per share for 2009?

	Basic Earnings Per Share	Diluted Earnings Per Share
A.	$1.00	$1.00
B.	$ .91	$1.00
C.	$1.00	$ .91
D.	$ .91	$ .91

_____ *24. (S.O. 8) With respect to stock appreciation rights, the measurement date for measuring compensation is the date:
      A.   of grant.
      B.   the stock appreciates above a predetermined amount.
      C.   the rights mature.
      D.   of exercise.

_____ *25. (S.O. 8) At the beginning of 2010 Bradley Company established a stock appreciation rights (SAR) program where executives receive cash at the date of exercise (any time in the next 3 years) for the difference between the market price of the stock and the pre established price of $15 on 5,000 SARs. The market price of the stock on December 31, 2010 is $20 per share. The service period runs for 2 years (2010-2011). If the market price of the stock on December 31, 2011 is $17 per share, the journal entry to be made for 2011 by Bradley Company for the SARs is:

A.	Liability Under Stock Appreciation Plan	2,500		
	Compensation Expense		2,500	
B.	Compensation Expense	10,000		
	Liability Under Stock Appreciation Plan		10,000	
C.	Liability Under Stock Appreciation Plan	10,000		
	Compensation Expense		10,000	
D.	Compensation Expense	12,500		
	Liability Under Stock Appreciation Plan		12,500	

REVIEW EXERCISES

1. (S.O. 3) Anteater Company issued 100 bonds, each with a face amount of $1,000, with detachable stock warrants at 101. Each warrant entitled its holder to acquire one share of $100 par common stock for $120 per share. Through discussion with investment bankers, it is determined that the bonds would sell for 97 without the warrants. The market value of each warrant is $50.

    Instructions:

      a. Record the issuance of the bonds.
      b. Record the subsequent exercise of all of the warrants.
      c. Record the entry necessary if all of the warrants expire before being exercised.

a.

	General Journal		J1
Date	**Account Title**	**Debit**	**Credit**

b.

	General Journal		J1
Date	**Account Title**	**Debit**	**Credit**

c.

General Journal			J1
Date	Account Title	Debit	Credit

2.   (S. O. 6) Richman Company had 100,000 shares of common stock outstanding as of January 1, 2010. The following common stock transactions occurred during 2010.

March 1--Issued 20,000 shares for cash.
June 1--Issued a 10% stock dividend.
September 1--Reacquired 10,000 shares as treasury shares.
November 1--Sold the 10,000 treasury shares for cash.

Instructions:
Compute the weighted-average common shares for 2010.

3.   (S. 0. 6) Turk Company had net income of $1,792,000 for the year ended December 31, 2010. The Company has 25,000 shares of $100 par value, 10% preferred stock outstanding. The preferred stock is cumulative, but not convertible. On January 1, 2010 Turk had 275,000 shares of common stock outstanding. On April 1, the Company sold 80,000 additional shares of common. The Turk Company board of directors issued a 3 for 1 stock split on June 1, and on October 1 the board purchased 165,000 shares of its common stock on the open market.

Instructions:
Compute earnings per share for 2010.

_____

_____

_____

_____

_____

_____

_____

_____

_____

4.   (S.0.7) The following information relates to UCI Company for 2010:

Common shares outstanding l/l/10 100,000
Common shares issued 7/1/10 upon conversion of bonds
    having a face amount of $200,000 10,000
Net income--2010 .... $200,000
Income tax rate 40%

4%, 10-year convertible bonds issued 1/1/10 at 100:

    Face amount $200,000
    Conversion terms--50 shares of common for each $1,000 bond (all of the bonds
    were converted on 7/1/10.)

10%, $10 par, convertible, cumulative preferred stock issued 1/1/09 at $11:
    Par value $500,000
    Conversion terms--2 shares of common for each share of preferred.

Instructions:
a.   Compute the basic earnings per share for UCI at the end of 2010.
b.   Compute diluted earnings per share for UCI at the end of 2010.

a.

b.

SOLUTIONS TO REVIEW QUESTIONS AND EXERCISES

TRUE-FALSE

1. (T)

2. (F)   At the time of issuance, convertible debt is recorded like a straight debt issue. Any discount or premium that results from the issuance of convertible debt is amortized assuming the bonds will be held to maturity date because it is difficult to predict when, if at all, conversion will occur.

3. (T)

4. (F)   Nondetachable warrants must be sold with the security as a complete package; thus, no allocation is permitted.

5. (T)

6. (T)

7. (T)

8. (F)   Under the fair value method, total compensation cost is computed based on the fair value of the options expected to vest on the date the options are granted to the employees.

9. (F)   The measurement date is the first date on which are known both (1) the number of shares that an individual employee is entitled to receive and (2) the option or purchase price, if any.

10. (F)   In general, under the fair value method, compensation expense is recognized in the periods in which the employee performs the service--the service period.

11. (T)

12. (T)

13. (T)

14. (F)   The stock option saga is a classic example of the difficulty the FASB faces in issuing an accounting standard.

15. (F)   A corporation's capital structure is simple if it consists only of common stock or includes no potentially dilutive convertible securities, options, warrants, or other rights that upon conversion or exercise could in the aggregate dilute earnings per common share.

16   (T)

17. (T)

18. (T)

19.   (F)   Antidilutive securities are securities, which upon their conversion or exercise increase earnings per share (or decrease the loss per share).

20.   (T)

21.   (F)   The treasury stock method assumes that the options or warrants are exercised at the beginning of the year (or date of issue if later) and the proceeds from the exercise of options and warrants are used to purchase common stock for the treasury.

22.   (T)

23.   (T)

24.   (T)

*25.   (F)   With respect to stock appreciation rights, compensation is measured at the date of exercise rather than the date of grant. Also, the compensation is defined as the excess of the market price of the stock at the date of exercise over a preestablished price.

MULTIPLE CHOICE

1.   (C)   The conversion privilege entices the investor to accept a lower interest rate then would normally be the case on a straight debt issue. A conversion feature will not normally override a poor credit rating and the issue costs of convertible debt and equity capital. Also, it is not an assurance that convertible debt will sell at a premium.

2.   (D)   The entry to record the conversion of the bond into common stock would be as follows:

Bonds Payable	1,000	
Premium on Bonds Payable	40	
Common Stock ($3 x 200)		600
Paid-in Capital in Excess of Par		440

And no gain or loss is recorded.

3.   (D)   The additional $45,000 is recorded as an expense of the period in which the conversion takes place and not as a reduction in equity. The $45,000 is not a loss because the company voluntarily offered the inducement to cause conversion. Alternative C which includes a debit to Premium on Bonds is incorrect as no premium was involved in this bond issue.

4.   (B)   The method used to record the issuance of convertible debt follows that used in recording straight debt issues. Although theoretical objections can be raised to using straight debt accounting when convertible debt is retired, to be consistent, a gain or loss on retiring convertible debt needs to be recognized in the same way as a gain or loss on retiring debt that is not convertible.

5.   (C)   The entry to record the conversion would be:

Convertible Preferred Stock	5,000	
Paid-In Capital in Excess of Par	400	
Retained Earnings	4,600	
Common Stock		10,000

6.   (D)   Convertible preferred stock is considered to be a part of stockholders' equity prior to the time it is converted. Thus, when convertible preferred stocks are exercised, there is no theoretical justification for recognition of a gain or loss. Therefore, any excess of the par value of common shares issued over the carrying amount of the preferred being   converted is treated as a direct reduction of retained earnings. The rationale for this treatment is that the preferred shareholders are offered an additional return to facilitate the conversion of their shares to common stock.

7.   (B)   Warrants are certificates entitling the holder to acquire shares of stock at a certain price within a stated period. Warrants are similar to convertible securities because, if exercised, they become common stock. The major difference is the fact that warrants require the holder to pay a certain amount of cash to obtain the shares.

8.   (A)   In instances where the fair value of either the warrants or the bonds is not determinable, the incremental method used in lump sum security purchases may be used. That is, the security for which the market value is determinable is used and the remainder of the purchase price is allocated to the security for which the market value is not known. Therefore, the amount allocated to the warrants and the bonds would be as follows:

Lump sum receipt	$200,000
Allocated to the bonds	180,000
Balance allocated to warrants	$ 20,000

9.   (C)   Under the fair value method, total compensation expense is computed based on the fair value of the option expected to vest on the date the options are granted to the employees. Once total compensation cost is determined, it must be allocated to the periods in which the employee performs the service. Dombrink should recognize $400 ($1,200/3) is the compensation expense for the year ended 2010.

10.   (B)   Under the fair value method, total compensation expense is computed based on the fair value of the option expected to vest on the date the options are granted to the employees. Once the total compensation cost is determined, it must be allocated to the periods in which the employee performs the service. Perry should recognize $300 ($600/2) as the compensation expense for the year ended 2010.

11.   (B)   Granados will make the following journal entry:

Compensation Expense	200,000	
Paid-in Capital--Stock Options		200,000
($400,000/2)		

Therefore, because of the debit to compensation expense, there is a $200,000 decrease in net income.

12.   (C)   The time permitted for exercise must be limited to a reasonable period of time. The other three alternatives represent appropriate characteristics that the options must possess. If the options do not possess these characteristics they are classified as compensatory.

13.   (C)   Total compensation cost must be allocated to the periods in which the employees perform the service. Compensation expense should be recognized for $16,000 ($32,000/2) for the year ended December 31, 2010.

14.   (B)   Restricted stock cannot be sold before vesting occurs. All the other items are advantages of a restricted-stock plan.

15.   (B)   Companies whose debt and equity securities are traded in a public market are required to report earnings per share information on the face of the income statement. Nonpublic companies are not required to report earnings per share information because of cost/benefit considerations. In most instances, nonpublic companies do not have a large enough number of shares outstanding to make the computation and reporting of earnings per share data meaningful.

16.   (C)

Dates Outstanding	Shares Outstanding	Restatement	Fraction of Year	Weighted Shares
1/1 - 3/1	25,000	1.2	2/12	5,000
3/1 - 8/1	75,000	1.2	5/12	37,500
8/1 - 11/1	62,000		3/12	15,500
11/1 - 12/31	102,000		2/12	17,000
Weighted Average Number of Shares Outstanding				75,000

17.   (A)   Basic earnings per share--ignoring all dilutive securities--is $2.00 ($200,000/100,000). The computation of diluted earnings per share is as follows:

	Diluted Earnings Per Share
Average number of shares under options outstanding	6,000
Option price per share	x $30
Proceeds upon exercise of options	$180,000
Average market price of common stock	$36
Treasury shares that could be repurchased with proceeds ($180,000/$36)	5,000
Excess of shares under option over treasury shares that could be repurchased (6,000 - 5,000)	1,000
Average number of common shares outstanding	100,000
Total average number of common and common equivalent shares	101,000
Net income for the year	$200,000
Earnings per share	$ 1.98

18.   (C)   The if-converted method for a convertible bond assumes (1) the conversion of the convertible securities at the beginning of the period (or at the time of issuance of the security, if issued during the period), and (2) the elimination of related interest, net of tax or preferred dividend. The conversion of the bonds will increase common stock by 5,000 shares [($500,000/$1,000) x 10]. The elimination of the related interest will increase net income by $24,500 [($500,000 x .07) x (1 - .30)]. Therefore, diluted earnings per share is $11.35 ($624,500/55,000).

19.   (C)   The treasury stock method assumes that the options or warrants are exercised at the beginning of the year (or date of issue if later) and the proceeds from the exercise of options and warrants are used to purchase common stock for the treasury. Therefore, exercise of the warrants would receive $750,000 ($25 x 30,000), which could then be used to purchase 25,000 treasury shares ($750,000/$30). The difference between 30,000 and 25,000 is an increase in 5,000 shares.

20.   (C)

Proceeds from exercise of options (10,000 x $20)	$200,000
Shares issued upon exercise	10,000
Treasury shares purchased ($200,000 ÷ $25)	(8,000)
Incremental shares outstanding	2,000

21. (C)   Net Income .... $ 50,000
            Preferred Dividend ....   (60,000)
            Difference.. $(10,000)
            ($10,000) ÷ 50,000 = ($.20) Net loss per share

The preferred stock is antidilutive because conversion would create an increase in earnings per share. The increase would result from the fact that preferred dividends would be eliminated. The reduction of preferred dividends ($60,000) causes a percentage increase in income available to common shareholders (numerator) greater than the percentage increase in common stock shares caused by conversion of the preferred stock.

22. (B)   Net income for the year $360,000
            Add: Adjustment for interest (net of tax) on 7% debentures   63,000
            Adjusted net income $423,000
            Average number of shares outstanding   125,000
            Add: shares assumed to be issued upon conversion of bonds   25,000

            Average number of common & equivalent shares   150,000

            Primary Earnings Per Share: $423,000 ÷ 150,000 = $2.82

23. (A)   In a business combination, when the acquirer promises to issue additional shares (contingent shares), only upon the attainment of increased earnings above the present level should the additional shares be considered as outstanding for the purpose of computing diluted earnings per share. Therefore, both basic earnings per share   and diluted earnings per share would be reported at $1.00 ($100,000/100,000).

*24. (D)   With stock appreciation rights, the final amount of cash or shares (or a combination of the two) to be distributed is not known until the date of exercise--the measurement date—and therefore total compensation cannot be measured until this date.

*25. (A)   At the end of 2010 Bradley Company would make the following journal entry:

            Compensation Expense   12,500
                Liability Under Stock Appreciation Plan   12,500

            *[($20 - $15) x 5,000] x 50%

At the end of 2011 the cumulative liability would be the difference between the market price of the stock ($17) and the pre-established price ($15). This $2 difference multiplied by the 5,000 SARs would require a liability balance of $10,000 at the end of 2011. Thus, the Liability account would be debited and the Compensation Expense credited for $2,500.

REVIEW EXERCISES

1.   a.   Cash 101,000

           Discount on Bonds Payable... 3,951

               Bonds Payable 100,000

               Paid-in Capital--Stock Warrants............................. 4,951

           Total proceeds = $100,000 x 1.01 = $101,000

           Market value of warrants = 100 warrants x $50 = $5,000

           Market value of bonds w/o warrants = $100,000 x .97 = $97,000

           Proceeds allocated to warrants:

$$\frac{\$5,000}{\$5,000 + \$97,000} \text{ x } \$101,000 \quad = \quad 4,951$$

           Proceeds allocated to bonds:

$$\frac{\$97,000}{\$5,000 + \$97,000} \text{ x } \$101,000 \quad = \quad \underline{96,049}$$

$$\underline{\underline{\$101,000}}$$

    b.   Cash 12,000

           Paid-in Capital--Stock Warrants...................................... 4,951

               Common Stock... 10,000

               Paid-in Capital in Excess of Par............................... 6,951

    c.   Paid-in Capital--Stock Warrants....................................... 4,951

               Paid-in Capital from Expired Warrants.................... 4,951

2.

Shares Outstanding	Restatement	Fraction of Year	Weighted Shares
100,000	1.10	2/12	18,333
120,000	1.10	6/12	66,000
122,000*		2/12	20,333
132,000		2/12	22,000
			126,666 shares

*(120,000 x 1.10) - 10,000

3.

Dates Outstanding	Shares Outstanding	Restatement	Fraction of Year	Weighted Shares
1/1 - 4/1	275,000	3	3/12	206,250
4/1 - 10/1	355,000	3	6/12	532,500
10/1 - 12/31	900,000		3/12	225,000
Weighted Average Number of Shares Outstanding				963,750

Earnings Per Share:

Net Income	1,792,000	
Preferred Dividend		
25,000 x $100 x 10%	(250,000)	
	$1,542,000	

$1,542,000/963,750 = $1.60

4. a.

Net income	$200,000
Less: 10% preferred stock dividend requirement	50,000
Income applicable to common stockholders	$150,000
Weighted average number of common shares outstanding [(100,000 x 1/2) + (110,000 x 1/2)]	105,000
Earnings per common share	$ 1.43

b. Per share effect of 4% convertible bonds

Interest expense for the 1/2 year avoided	
(4% x $200,000 x 1/2)	$4,000
Income tax reduction due to interest	
(40% x $4,000)	1,600
Interest expense avoided (net of tax)	2,400
Number of shares assumed converted as of the beginning of year [(($200,000/$1,000) x 50) x 1/2]	5,000

Per share effect:

$$\frac{\text{Incremental Numerator Effect}}{\text{Incremental Denominator Effect}} \quad \frac{\$2,400}{5,000} = \$0.48$$

Per share effect of 10% convertible preferred stock:
Dividend requirement avoided $ 50,000

Number of shares assumed converted as of the
beginning of year [($500,000/$10) x 2]   100,000

Per share effect:

$$\frac{\text{Incremental Numerator Effect}}{\text{Incremental Denominator Effect}} \quad \frac{\$50,000}{100,000} = \quad \$\ 0.50$$

Recomputation of EPS Using Incremental Effect of 4% Convertible Bonds

Income applicable to common stockholders	$150,000
Add: Interest expense avoided (net of tax)	2,400
Total	$152,400

Weighted average number of common shares outstanding	105,000
Add: Number of additional common shares assumed issued upon conversion of bonds	5,000
Total	110,000

Re computed earnings per share ($152,400/110,000) $ 1.39

Recomputation of EPS Using Incremental Effect of 10% Convertible Preferred

Numerator from previous calculation	$152,400
Add: Dividend requirement avoided	50,000
Total	$202,400

Denominator from previous calculation (shares)	110,000
Add: Number of common shares assumed issued upon conversion of preferred stock	100,000
Total	210,000
Recomputed earnings per share ($202,400/210,000)	$ 0.96

17

Investments

CHAPTER STUDY OBJECTIVES

1. Identify the three categories of debt securities and describe the accounting and reporting treatment for each category.

2. Understand the procedures for discount and premium amortization on bond investments.

3. Identify the categories of equity securities and describe the accounting and reporting treatment for each category.

4. Explain the equity method of accounting and compare it to the fair value method for equity securities.

5. Describe the accounting for the fair value option.

6. Discuss the accounting for impairments of debt and equity investments.

7. Explain why companies report reclassification adjustments.

8. Describe the accounting for transfer of investment securities between categories.

*9. Explain who uses derivatives and why.

*10. Understand the basic guidelines for accounting for derivatives.

*11. Describe the accounting for derivative financial instruments.

*12. Explain how to account for a fair value hedge.

*13. Explain how to account for a cash flow hedge.

*14. Identify special reporting issues related to derivative financial instruments that cause unique accounting problems.

*15. Describe the accounting for variable-interest entities.

CHAPTER REVIEW

1. The problems of accounting for investments involve measurement, recognition, and disclosure. Investments are generally classified as either debt securities or equity securities. Chapter 17 covers both temporary and long-term investments. The first section presents accounting for debt securities; the second section covers accounting for equity securities; and the remainder of the chapter presents the equity method of accounting, disclosure requirements, impairments, and accounting for the transfer of investment securities between categories.

Debt Securities

2. (S.O. 1) **Debt Securities** are instruments representing a creditor relationship with an enterprise. Debt securities include U.S. government securities, municipal securities, corporate bonds, convertible debt, commercial paper, and all securitized debt instruments.

Note: All asterisked (*) items relate to material contained in the Appendix to the chapter.

3.   Debt securities are grouped into the following three separate categories:

   a.   **Held-to-maturity:** Debt securities that the enterprise has the positive intent and ability to hold to maturity.

   b.   **Trading:** Debt securities bought and held primarily for sale in the near term to generate income on short-term price differences.

   c.   **Available-for-sale:** Debt securities not classified as held-to-maturity or trading securities.

Amortization on Bond Investments

4.   (S.O. 2) The effective-interest method is required to amortize premium or discount unless some other method—such as the straight-line method—yields a similar result. The effective-interest method is applied to bond investments in a fashion similar to that described for bonds payable. The effective-interest rate or yield is computed at the time of investment and is applied to its beginning carrying amount (book value) for each interest period to compute interest revenue. The investment carrying amount is increased by the amortized discount or decreased by the amortized premium in each period.

Held-to-Maturity Debt Securities

5.   Held-to-maturity debt securities are accounted for at amortized cost, not fair value. A Held-to Maturity Securities account is used to indicate the type of debt security purchased

Available-for-Sale Debt Securities

6.   Available-for-sale debt securities are reported at fair value. The unrealized gains and losses related to changes in the fair value of available-for-sale debt securities are recorded in an unrealized holding gain or loss account. This account is reported as other comprehensive income and as a separate component of stockholders' equity until realized. A valuation account called "Securities Fair Value Adjustment (Available-for-Sale)" is used instead of debiting or crediting the Available-for-Sale Securities account to enable the company to maintain a record of its amortized cost.

7.   The realized gain or loss is reported in the Other Revenues and Gains section or the Other Expenses and Losses section of the income statement.

Trading Securities

8   Trading securities are reported at fair value, with unrealized holding gains and losses reported as part of net income. Any discount or premium is not amortized. A holding gain or loss is the net change in the fair value of a security from one period to another, exclusive of dividend or interest revenue recognized but not received. A valuation account called "Securities Fair Value Adjustment (Trading)" is used instead of debiting or crediting the Trading Securities account.

Equity Securities

9.   (S.O. 3) **Equity securities** are described as securities representing ownership interest such as common, preferred, or other capital stock. They also include rights to acquire or dispose of ownership interests at an agreed upon or determinable price such as warrants, rights, and call options or put options.

10. The degree to which one corporation **(investor)** acquires an interest in the common stock of another corporation **(investee)** generally determines the accounting treatment for the investment subsequent to acquisition. Investments by one corporation in the common stock of another and the accounting method to be used can be classified according to the percentage of the voting stock of the investee held by the investor:

<u>Holding Method</u>

a.	Less than 20%	Fair Value Method
b.	Between 20% and 50%	Equity Method
c.	More than 50%	Consolidated Statements

Fair Value Method

11. When an investor has an interest of less than 20%, it is presumed that the investor has little or no influence over the investee. If market prices are available, the investment is valued and reported subsequent to acquisition using the **fair value method.** The fair value method requires that companies classify equity securities at acquisition as **available-for-sale securities** or **trading securities.**

12. When acquired, available-for-sale equity securities are recorded at cost. Net income earned by the investee is **not** considered a proper basis for recognizing income from the investment by the investor. Therefore, net income is not considered earned by the investor until cash dividends are declared by the investee. The net unrealized gains and losses related to changes in the fair value are recorded in an Unrealized Holding Gain or Loss-Equity account that is reported as a part of other comprehensive income and as a separate component of stockholders' equity until realized. The offsetting portion of the entry is debited or credited to the valuation account, Securities Fair Value Adjustment (Available for Sale).

13. The accounting entries to record trading equity securities are the same as for available-for-sale equity securities except for recording the unrealized holding gain or loss. For trading equity securities, the unrealized holding gain or loss is reported as part of net income.

Equity Method

14. (S.O. 4) When an investor has a holding interest of between 20% and 50% in an investee corporation, the investor is generally deemed to exercise significant influence over operating and financial policies of the investee. The FASB has also listed other factors to consider in determining whether an investor can exercise "significant influence" over an investee. In instances of "significant influence," the investor is required to account for the investment using the **equity method.**

15. Under the **equity method** the investment's carrying amount is periodically increased (decreased) by the investor's proportionate share of the earnings (losses) of the investee and decreased by all dividends received by the investor from the investee. The investor must record as separate components the amount of ordinary and extraordinary income as reported by the investee.

16. Under the equity method, if an investor's share of the investee's losses exceeds the carrying amount of the investment, the investor should discontinue applying the equity method and not recognize additional losses (unless the investor's loss is not limited or if return to profitability appears to be assured).

17. The following transactions illustrate the journal entries for an investment accounted for under the equity method.

a.   On 1/3/10 Workowski Corporation purchased 55,000 shares (26%) of Wendy Company at a cost of $8 per share.

Investment in Wendy Company.............................	440,000	
Cash		440,000

b.   At the end of 2010 Wendy Company reported net income of $350,000 (all ordinary). Workowski's share is $91,000 ($350,000 x .26).

Investment in Wendy Company.............................	91,000	
Revenue from Investment.................................		91,000

c.   In early 2011, Wendy Company paid a $75,000 dividend. Workowski's share is $19,500 ($75,000 x .26).

Cash	19,500	
Investment in Wendy Company		19,500

d.   Wendy Company reported a $215,000 net loss (all ordinary) in 2011. Workowski's share is $55,900.

Loss on Investment..	55,900	
Investment in Wendy Company		55,900

Consolidated Financial Statements

18. When one corporation (the parent) acquires a voting interest of more than 50% in another corporation (the subsidiary), the investor corporation is deemed to have a **controlling interest.** When the parent treats the subsidiary as an investment, **consolidated financial statements** are generally prepared in addition to separate financial statements for the parent and the subsidiary. The subject of when and how to prepare consolidated financial statements is discussed extensively in advanced accounting. If the parent and the subsidiary prepare separate financial statements, the investment in the common stock of the subsidiary is presented as a long-term investment on the financial statements of the parent under the equity method.

Fair Value Option

19. (S.O. 5) Companies have the option to report most financial instruments at fair value, with all gains and losses related to changes in fair value reported in the income statement. This option is applied on an instrument-by-instrument basis. The fair value option is generally available only at the time a company first purchases the financial asset or incurs a financial liability. If a company chooses the fair value option, it must use this method until the company no longer has ownership.

20. Companies may also use the fair value option for investments that would follow the equity method of accounting and their own debt instruments.

Impaired Investments

21. (S.O. 6) Each period every investment must be evaluated to determine if it has suffered a loss in value that is other than temporary (an **impairment**). If an investment is deemed impaired, the cost basis of the individual security is written down to a new cost basis. The amount of the writedown is accounted for as a realized loss and, therefore, included in net income.

Reclassification Adjustments

22. (S.O. 7) As indicated, unrealized holding gains and losses related to available-for-sale securities are reported as part of other comprehensive income. The reporting of changes in unrealized gains or losses in comprehensive income is straightforward unless securities are sold during the year--then a **reclassification adjustment** is necessary.

Transfers Between Categories

23. (S.O. 8) Transfers between any of the investment categories are accounted for at fair value. The text gives an illustration of measurement basis and how Stockholders' Equity and Net Income are impacted upon a transfer between investment categories.

Accounting for Derivative Instruments

*24.   (S.O. 9) In general derivatives are a product that has been developed to manage the risks due to changes in market prices and include such things as interest-rate swaps and options and current futures and options, stock-index future and options, cap, floors, commodity futures, swaptions, leaps, and collaterized mortgage obligations. They are called derivatives because their value is derived from values of other assets (for example stock, bonds, or commodities) or is related to a market-determined indicator (for example, interest rates or the Standard and Poor's stock composite index).

*25.   Any individual or company that wants to insure against different types of business risks often can use derivative contracts to achieve this objective. Producers and consumers both find derivatives useful so they can hedge their positions to ensure an acceptable financial result. A speculator is betting that the change in the derivative value will go a certain way and therefore makes the purchase with the purpose of gaining earnings based on their prediction. An arbitrageur purchases and sells derivatives in an attempt to exploit inefficiencies in various derivative markets.

Basic Principles in Accounting for Derivatives

*26.   (S.O. 10) Derivatives should be recognized in the financial statements as assets and liabilities and should be reported in the balance sheet at fair value. On the income statement, any unrealized gain or loss should be recognized in income if the derivative is used for speculation purposes. If the derivative is used for hedging purposes, the accounting for any gain or loss depends on the type of hedge used.

*27.   (S.O. 11) When distinguishing between the differences of traditional and derivative financial instruments, a derivative financial instrument has the following three basic characteristics:
   a.   The instrument has (1) one or more underlyings and (2) an identified payment provision (an underlying is a specified interest rate, security price, commodity price, index of prices or rates, or other market-related variable).

   b.   The instrument requires little or no investment at the inception of the contract.

   c.   The instrument requires or permits net settlement (for example, a profit can be realized without an actual purchase and sale of the underlying item).

Derivatives Used for Hedging—Fair Value Hedge

*28.   (S.O. 12) In a **fair value hedge**, a derivative is used to hedge (offset) the exposure to changes in the fair value of a recognized asset or liability or of an unrecognized commitment. In accounting for fair value hedges, the derivative should be presented at its fair value on the balance sheet with any gains and losses recorded in income.

Derivatives Used for Hedging—Cash Flow Hedge

*29.   (S.O. 13) **Cash flow hedges** are used to hedge exposures to cash flow risk, which is exposure to the variability in cash flows. In accounting for cash flow hedges, the derivative should be presented at fair value on the balance sheet, but gains or losses are recorded in equity as a part of other comprehensive income.

Other Reporting Issues

*30.   (S.O. 14) **Hybrid securities** have characteristics of both debt and equity and often are a combination of traditional and derivative financial instruments. In some cases, a host security is combined with an **embedded derivative**. When this occurs, the embedded derivative should be separated from the host security and accounted for using the accounting for derivatives. This separation process is referred to as **bifurcation**.

*31.   For the special accounting of hedges to occur, certain criteria must first be met. The general criteria relate to the following areas:

        a.   Designation, documentation, and risk management.
        b.   Effectiveness of the hedging relationship.
        c.   Effect on reported earnings of changes in fair value or cash flows.

Variable-Interest Entities

*32.   In order to prevent companies like Enron from hiding debt and risk in special purpose entities, the FASB created a **risk-and-reward model** to be used in situations where voting interests are unclear. A **variable-interest entity** (VIE) is an entity that has (1) insufficient equity investment at risk, (2) stockholders lack decision-making rights, or (3) stockholders do not absorb the losses or receive the benefits of a normal stockholder.

GLOSSARY

Amortized cost.
The acquisition cost adjusted for the amortization of discount or premium, if appropriate.

Available-for-sale securities.
Securities not classified as held-to-maturity or trading securities.

*Bifurcation
The process of separating the host security from the embedded derivative in a hybrid security for accounting purposes.

*Call option
A call option is a derivative that gives the holder the right, but not the obligation, to buy shares at a preset price.

*Cash flow hedge
Cash flow hedges are derivatives used to hedge exposures to cash flow risk, which is exposure to the variability in cash flows.

Consolidated financial statements.
Financial statements which disregard the distinction between separate legal entities and treat the parent and subsidiary corporations as a single economic entity.

Controlling interest.
When one corporation acquires a voting interest of more than 50% in another corporation.

Debt securities.
Instruments representing a creditor relationship with an enterprise and including U.S. government securities, municipal securities, corporate bonds, convertible debt, commercial paper, and all securitized debt instruments.

*Derivative financial instruments.
Innovative financial instruments that derive their value from the value of some underlying asset (i.e., stocks, bonds, or commodities) or are tied to a basic indicator (i.e., interest rates, Dow-Jones averages).

*Embedded derivative.
When a hybrid security is comprised of a host security and a derivative, the part associated with the derivative is called an embedded derivative.

Equity method.
A method of valuing securities whereby the investment's carrying amount is periodically increased (decreased) by the investor's proportionate share of the earnings (losses) of the investee and decreased by all dividends received by the investor from the investee.

Equity securities.
Securities representing ownership interest such as common, preferred, or other capital stock.

Fair value.
The amount at which a financial instrument could be exchanged in a current transaction between willing partners, other than in a forced or liquidation sale.

*Fair value hedge.	A derivative used to hedge or offset the exposure to changes in the fair value of a recognized asset or liability or of an unrecognized firm commitment.
*Futures contract.	A firm contractual agreement between a buyer and seller for a specified asset on a fixed date in the future.
*Hedging.	The action taken to offset risk.
Held-to-maturity securities.	Securities that the enterprise has the positive intent and ability to hold to maturity.
Holding gain or loss.	The net change in the fair value of a security from one period to another, exclusive of dividend or interest revenue recognized but not received.
Impairment.	A loss in value that is other than temporary.
*Interest rate swap.	A transaction between two parties who swap interest payments based on fixed or floating rates.
*Intrinsic value.	The difference between the market price and the preset strike price at any point in time.
Parent.	A corporation that has acquired a controlling interest in another corporation (the subsidiary).
*Put option.	The option to sell shares at a preset price which increases in value when the underlying asset decreases in value.
Security.	A share, participation, or other interest in property or in an enterprise of the issuer or an obligation of the issuer that: (a) is represented by an instrument or is registered by the issuer, (b) is commonly traded, and (c) is divisible into a distinct class or interest.
Subsidiary.	The corporation that has been acquired by a parent corporation.
*Time value.	Refers to the option's value over and above its intrinsic value.
Trading securities.	Securities bought and held primarily for sale in the near term to generate income on short-term price differences.
*Underlying.	A specified interest rate, security price, commodity price, index or prices or rates, or other market-related variable.
*Variable-interest entity	An entity that has one of the following characteristics: (1) insufficient equity investment at risk, (2) stockholders lack decision-making rights, or (3) stockholders do not absorb the losses or receive the benefits of a normal stockholders.

*Warrant.	A certificate presenting stock rights which states the number of shares that the holder of the right may purchase and also the price at which they may be purchased.

CHAPTER OUTLINE

Fill in the outline presented below.

(S.O. 1) Investments in Debt Securities

Held-to-Maturity Debt Securities

Available-for-Sale Debt Securities

Trading Debt Securities

(S.O. 2) Amortization on Bond Investments

(S.O. 3) Investments in Equity Securities

Holdings of Less Than 20%

Available-for-Sale Equity Securities

Trading Equity Securities

Holdings Between 20% and 50%

(S.O. 4) Equity Method

Chapter Outline *(continued)*

Holdings of More Than 50%

(S.O. 5) Fair Value Option

(S.O. 6) Impairments of Debt and Equity Investments

(S.O. 7)   Reclassification Adjustments

(S.O. 8) Transfers Between Categories

*(S.O. 9) Understanding Derivatives

Who Uses Derivatives

Why Use Derivatives?

Chapter Outline *(continued)*

*(S.O. 10) Basic Principles in Accounting for Derivatives

*(S.O. 11) Differences between Traditional and Derivative Financial Instruments

Derivatives Used for Hedging

*(S.O. 12) Fair Value Hedge

*(S.O. 13) Cash Flow Hedge

*(S.O. 14) Other Reporting Issues

Embedded Derivatives

Qualifying Hedge Criteria

*(S.O. 15) Variable-Interest Entities

REVIEW QUESTIONS AND EXERCISES

Indicate whether each of the following is true (T) or false (F) in the space provided.

_____ 1.   (S.O. 1) Held-to-maturity securities are securities that the enterprise has the positive intent and ability to hold to maturity.

_____ 2.   (S.O. 1) Available-for-sale securities are securities that are bought and held primarily for sale in the near term to generate income on short-term price differences.

_____ 3.   (S.O. 1) Both debt securities and equity securities can be classified as held-to-maturity.

_____ 4.   (S.O. 1) Held-to-maturity securities are accounted for at fair value.

_____ 5.   (S.O. 1) Unrealized gains and losses related to changes in the fair value of available-for-sale debt securities are recorded in an unrealized holding gain or loss account which is reported as a part of net income.

_____ 6.   (S.O. 1) Trading securities are reported at fair value, with unrealized holding gains and losses reported as part of net income.

_____ 7.   (S.O. 2) Amortization of discount or premium on available-for-sale debt securities is debited or credited to the Available-for-Sale Securities account.

_____ 8.   (S.O. 2) Amortization of discount or premium on trading debt securities is debited or credited to the Securities Fair Value Adjustment (Trading) account.

_____ 9.   (S.O. 2) If one corporation acquires an interest of less than 20% in another corporation, that investor is generally deemed to have little influence over the investee and will account for the investment under the equity method.

_____ 10.   (S.O. 3) The fair value method requires that companies classify equity securities at acquisition as held-to-maturity securities or available-for-sale securities.

_____ 11.   (S.O. 3) When an investor has holdings of less than 20% in an investee and the securities are classified as trading securities, unrealized holding gains or losses are reported as part of net income.

_____ 12.   (S.O. 4) In instances of "significant influence" (generally an investment of 20% or more), the investor is required to account for the investment using the equity method.

_____ 13.   (S.O. 4) The equity method gives recognition to the fact that investee earnings increase investee net assets that underlie the investment and investee losses and dividends decrease the net assets.

_____ 14.   (S.O. 4) Under the equity method, if the investee's net income includes extraordinary items, the investor treats a proportionate share of the extraordinary items as an extraordinary item, rather than as ordinary investment revenue before extraordinary items.

_____ 15. (S.O. 4) Whenever an investment in equity securities does **not** qualify for equity method treatment or for the use of consolidated financial statements, the investor is required to use the fair value method in accounting for the investment.

_____ 16. (S.O. 4) If the decline in value of securities is judged to be other than temporary, the cost basis of the individual security is written down to a new cost basis.

_____ 17. (S.O. 4) Once the equity method is adopted by an investor, the method must continue in use until the investment to which it has been applied is sold or liquidated by some other means.

_____ 18. (S.O. 5) Companies can choose the fair value option at any time they are holding a financial instrument.

_____ 19. (S.O. 5) Companies may also use the fair value option for their own debt instruments.

_____ 20. (S.O. 6) For debt securities, the impairment test is to determine whether "it is probable that the investor will be unable to collect all amounts due according to the contractual terms."

_____ *21 (S.O. 10) Derivatives should be reported in the balance sheet at historical cost.

_____ *22. (S.O. 10) Gains and losses resulting from the speculation of derivatives should **not** be recognized immediately in income.

_____ *23. (S.O. 11) A call option increases in value when the underlying asset decreases in value.

_____ *24. (S.O. 13) With a cash flow hedge, gains or losses are to be recorded in equity as a part of other comprehensive income.

_____ *25. (S.O. 14) Embedded derivatives should be recorded in the same manner as the host security.

MULTIPLE CHOICE

Select the best answer for each of the following items and enter the corresponding letter in the space provided.

_____ 1. (S.O. 1) Debt securities bought and held primarily for sale in the near term to generate income on short-term price differences are:

        A.   held-to-maturity debt securities.
        B. • trading debt securities.
        C.   available-for-sale debt securities.
        D.   never-sell debt securities.

_____ 2. (S.O. 1) Debt securities that are accounted for at amortized cost, **not** fair value are:

        A. ø held-to-maturity debt securities. •
        B.   trading debt securities.
        C.   available-for-sale debt securities.
        D.   never-sell debt securities.

_____   3.   (S.O. 1) Debt securities from which there is no recognized unrealized holding gains or losses in net income nor included as other comprehensive income are:

A. held-to-maturity debt securities.
B. trading debt securities.
C. available-for-sale debt securities.
D. never-sell debt securities.

_____   4.   (S.O. 1) Debt securities acquired by a corporation which are accounted for by recognizing unrealized holding gains or losses and are included as other comprehensive income and as a separate component of stockholders' equity are:

A. held-to-maturity debt securities.
B. trading debt securities.
C. available-for-sale debt securities.
D. never-sell debt securities.

_____   5.   (S.O. 1) On August 1, 2010, the McCellen Company acquired $100,000, 8% bonds of Lankford Co. for $104,000. The bonds were dated August 1, 2010, and mature on July 31, 2015, with interest payable each January 31 and July 31. McCellen plans on holding the bonds till their maturity.

What entry should McCellen make to record the purchase of the bonds on August 1, 2010?

A.	Held-to-Maturity Debt Securities	104,000	
	Interest Receivable	2,000	
	Cash		106,000
B.	Held-to-Maturity Debt Securities	104,000	
	Cash		104,000
C.	Held-to-Maturity Debt Securities	106,000	
	Accrued Interest Receivable		2,000
	Cash		104,000
D.	Held-to-Maturity Debt Securities	100,000	
	Premium on Debt Securities	6,000	
	Cash		106,000

_____ 6.   (S.O. 1) On January 1, 2010, Alton Co. purchased $100,000 of 10%, Olson, Inc. bonds with interest payable on July 1 and January 1 for $107,000. On February 1, 2010, Alton purchased $100,000 of 12%, Ehrlich Co. bonds with interest payable on August 1 and February 1 for $95,000. Alton classifies the Olson and Ehrlich bonds as trading debt securities. On December 31, 2010, the fair value of the Olson and Ehrlich bonds are $110,000 and $94,000, respectively. At December, 2010, what adjusting entry should be made by Alton?

A.   No entry should be made.

B.   Securities Fair Value
        Adjustment (Trading)   3,000
          Unrealized Holding Gain or
          Loss--Income   3,000

C.   Securities Fair Value
        Adjustment (Trading)   2,000
          Unrealized Holding Gain or
          Loss--Income   2,000

D.   Unrealized Holding Gain or Loss--
        Income   1,000
          Securities Fair Value
          Adjustment (Trading)   1,000

Questions 7 and 8 are based on the following information:

Sharon Company purchased $100,000 of 10% bonds of Livingston Co. on January 1, 2010, paying $94,025. The bonds mature January 1, 2020; interest is payable each July 1 and January 1. The discount of $5,975 provides an effective yield of 11%. Sharon Company uses the effective interest method and plans to hold these bonds to maturity.

_____ 7.   (S.O. 2) On July 1, 2010, Sharon Company should increase its Held-to-Maturity Debt Securities account for the Livingston Co. bonds by:

        A. $171.
        B. $299.
        C. $342.
        D. $598.

_____ 8.   (S.O. 2) For the year ended December 31, 2010, Sharon Company should report interest revenue from the Livingston Co. bonds at:

        A. $10,000.
        B. $10,342.
        C. $10,352.
        D. $10,598.

Questions 9 and 10 are based on the following information:

Kennedy Co. purchased $100,000 of 8%, 5-year bonds from Ekberg, Inc. on January 1, 2010, with interest payable on July 1 and January 1. The bonds sold for $104,158 at an effective interest rate of 7%. Using the effective interest method, Kennedy Co. decreased the Available-for-Sale Debt Securities account for the Ekberg, Inc. bonds on July 1, 2010 and December 31, 2010 by the amortized premiums of $354 and $366, respectively.

_____   9.   (S.O. 2) At December 31, 2010, the fair value of the Ekberg, Inc. bonds was $106,000. What should Kennedy Co. report as other comprehensive income and as a separate component of stockholders' equity?

A.   No entry should be made.
B. $ 720.
C. $1,842.
D. $2,562.

_____   10.   (S.O. 2) At February 1, 2011, Kennedy Co. sold the Ekberg bonds for $103,000. After accruing for interest, the carrying value of the Ekberg bonds on February 1, 2011 was $103,375. Assuming Kennedy Co. has a portfolio of Available-for-Sale Debt Securities, what should Kennedy Co. report as a gain (or loss) on the bonds?

A. $ 0.
B.   ($ 375).
C.   ($2,187).
D.   ($2,937).

_____   11.   (S.O. 2) Use of the effective interest method in amortizing bond premiums and discounts results in:

A.   a greater amount of interest income over the life of the bond issue than would result from use of the straight-line method.
B.   a varying amount being recorded as interest income from period to period.
C.   a variable rate of return on the book value of the investment.
D.   a smaller amount of interest income over the life of the bond issue than would result from use of the straight-line method.

_____   12.   (S.O. 3) If a company has acquired a 20% to 50% interest in another corporation, this generally results in:
A.   an insignificant level of influence.
B.   a passive level of influence.
C.   a significant level of influence.
D.   a controlling level of influence.

_____   13.   (S.O. 3) When a company has acquired a "passive interest" in another corporation, the acquiring company should account for the investment:

A.   by using the equity method.
B.   by using the fair value method.
C.   by using the effective interest method.
D.   by consolidation.

_____   14.   (S.O. 3) On January 3, 2010, Slezak Company purchased 22% of Urban Corporation's common stock for $250,000. Shortly after the purchase, Slezak Company executives tried to obtain representation on Urban Corporation's board of directors and failed. During 2010 Urban reported net income of $150,000 and paid cash dividends of $80,000 on the common stock. The balance in Slezak Company's Investment in Urban Corporation account at December 31, 2010, should be:
A. $265,400.
B. $234,600.
C. $250,000.
D. $300,600.

15. (S.O. 3) Equity securities acquired by a corporation which are accounted for by recognizing unrealized holding gains or losses as other comprehensive income and as a separate component of stockholders' equity are:

  A. available-for-sale securities where a company has holdings of less than 20%.
  B. trading securities where a company has holdings of less than 20%.
  C securities where a company has holdings of between 20% and 50%.
  D. securities where a company has holdings of more than 50%.

16. (S.O. 4) McCoy Corporation purchased 7,400 shares of Chudzick Company's common stock. The purchase price was $362,600, which is equal to 50% of Chudzick Company's retained earnings balance. Chudzick Company's 46,000 shares of common stock are actively traded, and each share has a par value of $10. McCoy Corporation should account for this long-term investment using the:

  A. fair value method.
  B. equity method.
  C. consolidation method.
  D. amortized cost method.

17. (S.O. 4) Bista Corporation declares and distributes a cash dividend that is a result of current earnings. How will the receipt of those dividends affect the investment account of the investor under each of the following accounting methods?

	Fair Value Method	Equity Method
A.	No Effect	Decrease
B.	Increase	Decrease
C.	No Effect	No Effect
D.	Decrease	No Effect

Use the following information for questions 18 and 19.

Silverman Co. owns 8,000 of the 20,000 outstanding shares of DeFano, Inc. common stock. During 2010, DeFano earns $100,000 and pays cash dividends of $80,000.

18. (S.O. 4) If the beginning balance in the investment account was $200,000, the balance at December 31, 2010 should be:

  A. $200,000.
  B. $208,000.
  C. $220,000.
  D. $240,000.

19. (S.O. 4) Silverman should report investment revenue for 2010 of:

  A. $ 0.
  B. $ 8,000.
  C. $32,000.
  D. $40,000.

_____   20.   (S.O. 8) Transfers of investments between any of the categories should be accounted for at:

        A.   original cost.
        B.   book value.
        C.   equity value.
        D.   fair value.

REVIEW EXERCISES

1.   (S.O. 1 and 2) Schmidt Corporation purchased $100,000 of 10%, 10-year bonds on January 1, 2010, with interest payable on July 1, and January 1. The bonds are to be classified as available-for-sale securities. The bonds sell for $88,530 which results in a bond discount of $11,470 and an effective interest rate of 12%. At December 31, 2010, the fair value and the carrying amount of the bonds are equal.

Instructions:

a.   Prepare the entry to record the purchase of the bonds on January 1, 2010.
b.   Prepare a schedule of interest revenue and bond discount amortization--effective interest method for the periods 1/1/10, 7/1/10, 1/1/11 and 7/1/11.
c.   Prepare the journal entries to record interest revenue on July 1, 2010 and December 31, 2010.
d.   On July 1, 2011, Schmidt Corporation sells the bonds for $88,000. Prepare the journal entry recording interest revenue on that date and another entry to record the sale.

a.

General Journal			J1
Date	**Account Title**	**Debit**	**Credit**

b.

Schmidt Corporation
Schedule of Interest Revenue and Bond Discount Amortization

Date	Cash Received	Interest Revenue	Bond Premium Amortization	Carrying Amount of Bonds
1/1/10				
7/1/10				
1/1/11				
7/1/11				

c.

	General Journal		J1
Date	**Account Title**	**Debit**	**Credit**

d.

	General Journal		J1
Date	Account Title	Debit	Credit

2.   (S.O. 3)   Funk Company has the following securities in its investment portfolio on December 31, 2009 (all securities were purchased in 2009): (1) 5,000 shares of Beem Co. common stock which cost $55,000, (2) 30,000 shares of Lenard Co. common stock which cost $150,000, and (3) 4,000 shares of Taylor Co. common stock which cost $120,000. The Securities Fair Value Adjustment account shows a credit of $8,500 at the end of 2009.

In 2010 Funk completed the following securities transactions:
(a)   On March 15, sold 2,000 shares of Beem's common stock at $10 per share less fees of $150.
(b)   On June 1, purchased 10,000 shares of Chong Co. common stock at $12 per share plus fees of $200.

On December 31, 2010, the market values per share of these securities were: Beem $8, Lenard $10, Taylor $28, and Chong $15.   In addition, the Treasurer of Funk told you that, even though all these securities have readily determinable fair values, Funk will not actively trade these securities because the company plans to hold them for more than one year.

Instructions:

(a)   Prepare the entry for the security sale on March 15, 2010.
(b)   Prepare the journal entry to record the security purchase on June 1, 2010.
(c)   Compute the unrealized gains or losses and prepare the adjusting entry for Beem on December 31, 2010.

a.

General Journal			
			J1
Date	**Account Title**	**Debit**	**Credit**

b.

	General Journal		J1
Date	Account Title	Debit	Credit

c.

Date	Account Title	Debit	Credit
General Journal			J1

3.   (S.O. 6) Perez Corporation has municipal bonds classified as available-for-sale at December 31, 2009. These bonds have a par value of $1,600,000, an amortized cost of $1,400,000, and a fair value of $1,150,000. The unrealized loss of $250,000 previously recognized as other comprehensive income and as a separate component of stockholders' equity is now determined to be other than temporary. That is, the company believes that these bonds should be recorded as impaired.

Instructions:

a.   Prepare the journal entry to recognize the impairment.
b.   What is the new cost basis of the municipal bonds? Given that the maturity value of the bonds is $1,600,000, should Perez accrete the difference between the carrying amount and the maturity value over the life of the bonds?
c.   At December 31, 2010, the fair value of the municipal bonds is $1,275,000. Prepare the entry (if any) to record the information.

a.

	General Journal		J1
Date	**Account Title**	**Debit**	**Credit**

b. _____

_____

_____

_____

_____

_____

c.

General Journal			J1
Date	Account Title	Debit	Credit

SOLUTIONS TO REVIEW QUESTIONS AND EXERCISES

TRUE-FALSE

1. (T)

2. (F) Available-for-sale securities are securities not classified as held-to-maturity or trading securities. Trading securities are securities bought and held primarily for sale in the near term to generate income on short-term price differences.

3. (F) Only debt securities can be classified as held-to-maturity because, by definition, equity securities have no maturity date.

4. (F) Held-to-maturity securities are accounted for at amortized cost, not fair value. Amortized cost is the acquisition cost adjusted for the amortization of discount or premium, if appropriate.

5. (F) Unrealized gains and losses related to changes in the fair value of available-for-sale debt securities are recorded in an unrealized holding gain or loss account which is reported as other comprehensive income and as a separate component of stockholders' equity until realized.

6. (T)

7.   (T)

8.   (F)   Discounts or premiums are not amortized for trading securities.

9.   (F)   If one corporation acquires an interest of less than 20% in another corporation, that investor is generally deemed to have little influence over the investee and will account for the investment under the fair value method.

10.   (F)   The fair value method requires that companies classify equity securities at acquisition as available-for-sale securities or trading securities. Because equity securities have no maturity date, they cannot be classified as held-to-maturity.

11.   (T)

12.   (T)

13.   (T)

14.   (T)

15.   (T)

16.   (T)

17.   (F)   If an investor's level of influence or ownership falls below that necessary for continued use of the equity method, a change must be made to the fair value method. If the investor's level of influence or ownership increases to 50% or more, a change to the consolidated method must be made.

18.   (F)   The fair value option is generally available only at the time a company first purchases the financial asset or incurs a financial liability.

19.   (T)

*20.   (T)

*21.   (F)   Derivatives should be reported in the balance sheet at fair value.

*22.   (F)   Gains and losses on derivatives resulting from the speculation of derivatives should be recognized immediately in income.

*23.   (F)   A call option increases in value when the underlying asset also increases in value. A put option increases in value when the underlying asset decreases in value.

*24.   (T)

*25.   (F)   Embedded derivatives should be bifurcated from the host security and recorded separately as a derivative instrument.

MULTIPLE CHOICE

1. (B) Debt securities bought and held primarily for sale in the near term to generate income on short-term price differences are trading debt securities. (A) Debt securities that the enterprise has the positive intent and ability to hold to maturity are held-to-maturity securities. (C) Debt securities not classified as held-to-maturity or trading securities are available-for-sale securities.

2. (A) Held-to-maturity securities are accounted for at amortized cost, not fair value. (B) Trading securities and (C) available-for-sale securities are accounted for at fair value. (D) Generally accepted accounting principles do not recognize "never-sell" debt securities.

3. (A) When accounting for held-to-maturity debt securities, there is no recognized unrealized holding gains or losses in net income. (B) When accounting for trading debt securities, unrealized holding gains or losses are recognized in net income. (C) When accounting for available-for-sale debt securities, unrealized holding gains or losses are recognized but they are included as other comprehensive income and as a separate component of stockholders' equity. (D) Generally accepted accounting principles do not recognize "never-sell" debt securities.

4. (C) When accounting for available-for-sale debt securities, unrealized holding gains or losses are recognized and included as other comprehensive income and as a separate component of stockholders' equity. (A) When accounting for held-to-maturity debt securities, there is no recognized unrealized holding gains or losses. (B) When accounting for trading debt securities, unrealized holding gains or losses are recognized in net income. (D) Generally accepted accounting principles do not recognize "never-sell" debt securities.

5. (B) The requirement is to determine the journal entry to make when a bond investment is acquired at a premium. It is common to combine the par value of the bonds ($100,000) and the premium on bond investment ($4,000) into one account and debit the total of $104,000 to the account Held-to-Maturity Debt Securities. The entry made by McCellen Company to record the purchase of bonds on August 1, 2010, would be:

Held-to-Maturity Debt Securities	104,000	
Cash		104,000

6. (C) The total cost of Alton's trading portfolio is $202,000. The fair value of the trading portfolio at December 31, 2010 is $204,000. An adjusting entry made to the valuation account of $2,000 should therefore be made so the fair value of the trading portfolio is recognized on the balance sheet.

7. (A) The effective interest rate (11%) is applied to the beginning carrying amount (book value = $94,025) for each interest period (1/2 a year) to compute interest revenue of $5,171 (11% of $94,025 x 1/2). The investment carrying amount is then increased by the amortized discount which equals the difference between the interest revenue and cash received of $171 ($5,171 - $5,000).

8.   (C)   The amount of amortized discount for the period from January 1, 2010 to July 1, 2010 is equal to $171 (see answer to Problem 7). To compute the amortized discount for the period from July 1, 2010 to December 31, 2010, the new carrying amount of the bonds of $94,196 ($94,025 + $171) is multiplied by the effective interest rate (.11) for the interest period (1/2 year) to compute interest revenue of $5,181 ($94,196 x .11 x 1/2). The interest revenue for the period from January 1, 2010 to July 1, 2010 of $5,171 is added to the interest revenue for the period from July 1, 2010 to December 31, 2010 of $5,181 to equal the total interest revenue for the year of $10,352.

9.   (D)   Investments in debt securities that are in the available-for-sale category are reported at fair value. To apply the fair value method to the Ekberg, Inc. securities, the carrying amount of the bonds at December 31, 2010 must be computed. The bonds were bought at an original cost of $104,158 and the carrying amount was subsequently decreased by $354 and $366 for an end of the year carrying amount of $103,438. Kennedy Co. therefore recognizes an unrealized holding gain by subtracting the carrying value of $103,438 from the fair value of $106,000 to equal $2,562. Because the bonds are available-for-sale securities, the unrealized holding gain will be reported as other comprehensive income and as a separate component of stockholders' equity.

10.   (B)   The realized loss is computed by taking the difference between the carrying value of the bonds ($103,375) and the selling price of the bonds ($103,000) for $375.

11.   (B)   When a premium or discount is amortized under the straight-line method, the interest received is constant from period to period, but the rate of return is not the same year after year. Although the effective interest method results in a varying amount being recorded as interest revenue from period to period, it produces a constant rate of return on the book value of the investment from period to period.

12.   (C)   If a company has acquired a 20% to 50% interest in another corporation, this generally results in a significant level of influence. (A) and (B) If a company has acquired less than a 20% interest in another corporation, this generally results in an insignificant or passive interest. (D) If a company has acquired over a 50% interest in another corporation, this generally results in a controlling interest.

13.   (B)   When a company has acquired a "passive interest" in another corporation, the acquiring company should account for the investment by using the fair value method. (A) If a company has acquired a "significant interest" in another corporation, the acquiring company should account for the investment by using the equity method. (C) The effective interest method would only be required to be used if a company acquired debt securities that were classified as held-to-maturity or available-for-sale debt securities and there was a material difference between using the effective interest method and the straight-line method. (D) If a company has acquired a "controlling interest" in another corporation, the acquiring company should account for the investment by consolidation.

14.   (C)   One of the examples provided by the FASB of an ownership interest in excess of 20% not providing the investor with the ability to exercise significant influence is when the investor attempts to obtain representation on the investee's board of directors and fails. Thus, in this question the investor's inability to exercise significant influence over the investee would result in accounting for the investment in Urban Corporation on the fair value method and the carrying amount of the investment would not change.

15.   (A)   When accounting for available-for-sale equity securities where a company has holdings of less than 20%, unrealized holding gains or losses are recognized but they are included as other comprehensive income and as a separate component of stockholders' equity. (B) When accounting for trading equity securities where a company has holdings of less than 20%, unrealized holding gains or losses are recognized in net income. (C) and (D) when a company has holdings of greater than 20%, unrealized holding gains or losses are not recognized.

16.   (A)   To use the equity method, McCoy Corporation would have to hold an investment of between 20% and 50% of Chudzick's voting stock. The 7,400 shares owned by McCoy represent a little more than 16% of the voting stock (46,000). When an investor cannot exert "significant influence," then the investment should be accounted for under the fair value method.

17.   (A)   The investment account would not be affected if the investment was accounted for under the fair value method. However, under the equity method, the receipt of a dividend out of current earnings will reduce the investment account by the amount of the investment.

18.   (B)   When an investor corporation has holdings of between 20% and 50% in an investee corporation, the investor corporation is considered to exert a "significant influence" over the investee. When an investor exerts a "significant influence" over an investee, the investor should account for the investment under the equity method. Silverman owns 40% (8,000/20,000) of DeFano's outstanding stock; therefore, Silverman should use the equity method to account for the investment in DeFano. Under the equity method, the investment's carrying amount is increased (decreased) by the investor's proportionate share of the earnings (losses) of the investee and decreased by all dividends received by the investor from the investee. Therefore, Silverman's beginning balance in the investment of DeFano would have been increased by Silverman's share of DeFano's earnings ($40,000 = 40% of $100,000) and decreased by Silverman's share of DeFano's dividend distribution ($32,000 = 40% of $80,000). The December 31, 2007 investment in DeFano would therefore have been $208,000 ($200,000 + $40,000 - $32,000).

19.   (D)   Under the equity method, an investor reports as revenue its share of the net income reported by the investee company. Therefore, Silverman should report investment revenue for 2010 of $40,000 (40% of $100,000).

20.   (D)   Transfers of investments between any of the categories are accounted for at fair value.

REVIEW EXERCISES

1.a. Available-for-Sale Securities   88,530
     Cash   88,530

b.

Schmidt Corporation
Schedule of Interest Revenue and Bond Discount Amortization

Date	Cash Received	Interest Revenue	Bond Premium Amortization	Carrying Amount of Bonds
1/1/10				$88,530
7/1/10	$5,000	$5,312	$312	88,842
1/1/11	5,000	5,331	331	89,173
7/1/11	5,000	5,350	350	89,523

c. 7/1/10   Cash   5,000
                Available-for-Sale Securities   312
                    Interest Revenue   5,312

      12/31/10   Interest Receivable   5,000
                Available-for-Sale Securities   331
                    Interest Revenue   5,331

d. 7/l/11   Cash   5,000
                Available-for-Sale Securities   350
                    Interest Revenue   5,350

           Cash   88,000
           Loss on Sale of Securities   1,523
                Available-for-Sale Securities   89,523

2. a.

March 15, 2010

Cash [($2,000 x $10) - $150] 19,850
Loss on Sale of Stock 2,150
     Available-for-Sale Securities 22,000
     (2,000 x $11)

b.

June 1, 2010

Available-for-Sale Securities.. 120,200
     Cash.. 120,200
     [(10,000 x $12) + $200]

c.

Funk Company
Available-for-Sale Equity Security Portfolio
December 31, 2010

Investments	Cost	Fair Value	Unrealized Gain (Loss)
Beem Co.	$ 33,000	$ 24,000	$(9,000)
Lenard Co.	150,000	300,000	150,000
Taylor Co.	120,000	112,000	(8,000)
Chong Co.	120,200	150,000	29,800
Total of portfolio	423,200	586,000	162,800

Previous securities fair value adjustment balance		8,500
Securities fair value adjustment		$171,300

December 31, 2010

Securities Fair Value Adjustment (Available-for-Sale)	171,300	
Unrealized Holding Gain or Loss—Equity		171,300

3.a.

Loss on Impairment..	250,000	
Securities Fair Value Adjustment		
(Available-for-Sale)..	250,000	
Unrealized Holding Gain or Loss—Equity.......................		250,000
Available-for-Sale Securities		250,000

b. $1,150,000. No, amortization of any discount related to debt securities is not permitted after recording the impairment.

c.

Securities Fair Value Adjustment (Available-for-Sale)	125,000	
Unrealized Holding Gain or Loss—Equity.......................		125,000

18

Revenue Recognition

CHAPTER STUDY OBJECTIVES

1. Apply the revenue recognition principle.

2. Describe accounting issues for revenue recognition at point of sale.

3. Apply the percentage-of-completion method for long-term contracts.

4. Apply the completed-contract method for long-term contracts.

5. Identify the proper accounting for losses on long-term contracts.

6. Describe the installment method of accounting.

7. Explain the cost recovery method of accounting.

*8. Explain revenue recognition for franchises and consignment sales.

CHAPTER REVIEW

1. One of the most difficult issues facing accountants concerns the recognition of revenue by a business organization. Although general rules and guidelines exist, the significant variety of marketing methods for products and services make it difficult to apply the rules consistently in all situations. Chapter 18 is devoted to a discussion and illustration of revenue transactions that result from the sale of products and the rendering of services. Throughout the discussion, attention is focused on the theory behind the accounting methods used to recognize revenue. Revenue transactions that result from leasing and the sale of assets other than inventory are discussed in other sections of the text.

Revenue Recognition

2. (S.O. 1) The **revenue recognition principle** provides that revenue is recognized when (1) it is realized or realizable and (2) it is earned. Revenues are **realized** when goods and services are exchanged for cash or claims to cash (receivables). Revenues are **realizable** when assets received in exchange are readily convertible to known amounts of cash or claims to cash. Revenues are **earned** when the entity has substantially accomplished what it must do to be entitled to the benefits represented by the revenues, that is, when the earnings process is complete or virtually complete.

Note: All asterisked (*) items relate to material contained in the Appendix to the chapter.

3.   The conceptual nature of revenue as well as the basis of accounting for revenue transactions are described in the following four statements.

(a)   Revenue from selling products is recognized at the date of sale, usually interpreted to mean the date of delivery to customers.

(b)   Revenue from services rendered is recognized when services have been performed and are billable.

(c)   Revenue from permitting others to use enterprise assets, such as interest, rent, and royalties, is recognized as time passes or as the assets are used.

(d)   Revenue from disposing of assets other than products is recognized at the date of sale.

Point of Sale

4.   (S.O. 2) Sales transactions result in the exchange of products or services of an enterprise for other valuable assets, normally cash or a promise of cash in the future. Although most sales transactions are fundamentally similar, differences in the method or terms of sale lead to real differences in the transactions themselves and thus to differences in the appropriate accounting for them.

5.   The discussion of sales transactions in the chapter is primarily focused on **product sales transactions.** The coverage of product sales transactions is further divided into the following topics: **(a)** revenue recognition at point of sale (delivery), **(b)** revenue recognition before delivery, **(c)** revenue recognition after delivery, and **(d)** revenue recognition for special sales transactions (covered in **Appendix 18-A).** The accounting principles and methods related to product sales transactions are fairly well developed in the accounting literature. Service sales transactions have recently received attention from **AcSEC** and the **FASB.** These efforts are an attempt to develop accounting theory and methodology related to service transactions as distinct from product transactions.

6.   According to the FASB, revenue is recognized when the product is delivered or the service is rendered. This time of recognition is normally at the time of sale when the product or service is delivered to the customer. Some problems in implementing these basic principles arise when **(a)** sales have buyback agreements, **(b)** the right of return exists, and **(c)** trade loading or channel stuffing is present.

7.   In most business enterprises, a far greater proportion of total sales volume is handled on a credit basis than on an ordinary cash sale basis. In situations where the seller gives the buyer the right to return the product, the FASB concluded that the transactions should not be recognized currently as sales unless **all** of the following six conditions are met:

a.   The seller's price to the buyer is substantially fixed or determinable at the date of sale.

b.   The buyer has paid the seller, or the buyer is obligated to pay and the obligation is not contingent on resale of the product

c.   The buyer's obligation to the seller would not be changed in the event of theft or physical destruction or damage of the product.

d.   The buyer has economic substance apart from that provided by the seller.

e.   The seller does not have significant future performance obligations to directly bring about the resale of the product by the buyer.

f.   The amount of future returns can be reasonably estimated.

8.   Even when revenues are recorded at date of delivery, with neither buyback or return provisions, some companies are recognizing revenues and earnings prematurely. This occurs in situations where **trade loading** or **channel stuffing** are present. Trade loading is an attempt to show sales, profits, and market share an entity does not have by inducing wholesale customers to buy more product then they can promptly sell. Channel stuffing is a similar tactic found mostly in the computer software industry. In channel stuffing, the software maker offers deep discounts to its distributors to overbuy and records revenue when the software leaves its loading dock. When this process takes place, the distributors' inventories become bloated and the marketing channel gets stuffed, but the software maker's financial statements are improved.

Long-term Contracts

9.   In most circumstances, revenue is recognized at the point of sale because most of the uncertainties related to the earning process are removed and the exchange price is known. One of the exceptions to the general rule of recognition at point of sale is caused by long-term construction-type projects. The accounting measurements associated with long-term construction projects are difficult because events and amounts must be estimated for a period of years. Two basic methods of accounting for long-term construction contracts are recognized by the accounting profession: (a) **the percentage-of completion method** and (b) **the completed-contract method.**

10.   The AICPA recommends that the percentage-of-completion method and the completed-contract method not be viewed as acceptable, interchangeable alternatives. The percentage-of-completion method should be used when estimates of progress toward completion, revenues, and costs are reasonably dependable and all the following conditions exist:

   a.   The contract clearly specifies the enforceable rights regarding goods or services to be provided and received by the parties, the consideration to be exchanged, and the manner and terms of settlement.
   b.   The buyer can be expected to satisfy all obligations under the contract.
   c.   The contractor can be expected to perform contractual obligations.

The completed-contract method should be used only when **(a)** an entity has primarily short-term contracts, **(b)** the conditions for using the percentage-of-completion method cannot be met, or **(c)** there are inherent hazards in the contract beyond normal, recurring business risks.

Percentage-of-Completion Method

11.   (S.O. 3)   Under the percentage-of-completion method, revenue on long-term construction contracts is recognized as construction progresses. Costs pertaining to the contract plus gross profit earned to date are accumulated in a **Construction in Process account.** The amount of revenue recognized in each accounting period is based on a percentage of the total revenue to be recognized on the contract. This percentage is the **costs incurred on the contract to date divided** by **the most recent estimated total costs (cost-to-cost basis).** Income recognized before completion is recorded by debiting **Construction in Process** and crediting **Revenue from Long-term Contracts.** Use of this method is dependent upon the seller's ability to provide a reliable estimate of both the cost to complete and the percentage of contract performance completed. When such estimates are considered reasonably dependable, the accounting profession has considered the percentage-of-completion method preferable.

Completed-Contract Method

12. (S.O. 4) Under the completed-contract method, revenue and gross profit are recognized when the contract is completed. The principal advantage of the completed-contract method is that reported revenue is based on final results rather than on estimates of unperformed work. Its major disadvantage is the distortion of earnings that may occur. The accounting entries made under the completed-contract method are the same as those made under the percentage-of-completion method, with the notable exception of periodic income recognition.

Contract Losses

13. (S.O. 5) When the current estimates of total contract revenue and contract cost indicate a loss is expected, the entire expected contract loss must be recognized in the period in which it becomes evident under both the percentage-of-completion and the completed-contract-methods.

14. In addition to normal financial statement disclosures, construction contractors should disclose (a) the method of recognizing revenue, **(b)** the basis used to classify assets and liabilities as current, **(c)** the basis for recording inventory, **(d)** the effects of any revisions of estimates, **(e)** the amount of backlog on incomplete contracts, and **(f)** the details about receivables.

Installment Method

15. (S.O. 6) In some cases revenue is recognized after delivery of the product to the buyer. This is due to the fact that, in certain sales situations, the sales price is not reasonably assured and revenue recognition is deferred. The methods generally used to account for the deferral of revenue recognition until cash is received are **(a) the installment method** and **(b) the cost recovery method.**

16. In 1966, the accounting profession concluded that, except in special circumstances, the installment method of recognizing revenue is not acceptable. Use of the installment method is **justified** in situations where receivables are collectible over an extended period of time and there is no reasonable basis for estimating the degree of collectibility. The method is used extensively in tax accounting and has relevance because of the increased emphasis on cash flows.

17. The term **installment sale** describes any type of sale for which payment is required in periodic installments over an extended period of time. The installment method places emphasis on collection, as installment sales lead to income realization in the period of collection rather than the period of sale. This does not mean that revenue is considered unrealized until the entire sale price has been collected but rather that income realization is proportionate to collection. This is due to the fact that the ultimate **profit** is more uncertain in installment sales than in ordinary sales because collection is more doubtful.

18. Under the installment sales method of accounting, the gross profit (sales less cost of goods sold) on installment sales is deferred to those periods in which cash is collected. Operating expenses, such as selling and administrative expenses, are treated as expenses in the period incurred. For installment sales in any one year, the following procedures apply under the installment sales method:

  a.   During the year, record both sales and cost of sales in the regular way using separate installment sales accounts and compute the rate of gross profit on installment sales transactions.
  b.   At the end of the year, apply the rate of gross profit to the cash collections of the current year's installment sales to arrive at the realized gross profit.
  c.   The gross profit not realized should be deferred to future years.

In any year in which collections from prior years' installment sales are received, the gross profit rate of each year's sales must be applied against cash collections of accounts receivable resulting from that year's sales to arrive at the realized gross profit.

19. To illustrate the installment sales method of accounting assume the following facts:

	2010	**2011**	**2012**
Installment sales	$226,000	$248,000	$261,000
Cost of installment sales	164,980	176,080	195,750
Gross profit	$ 61,020	$ 71,920	$ 65,250
Rate of Gross Profit	27%	29%	25%
Cash Receipts			
2010 Sales	$ 85,000	$ 96,000	$ 45,000
2011 Sales		123,000	87,000
2012 Sales			147,000

Only the 2011 journal entries will be shown. The entries for 2010 and 2012 are the same, but the entire set of entries for the installment method are demonstrated by the 2011 entries.

To record 2011 installment sales

Installment Accounts Receivable, 2011	248,000	
Installment Sales		248,000

To record cash collected on
installment receivables

Cash	219,000	
Installment Accounts Receivables, 2010		96,000
Installment Accounts Receivables, 2011		123,000

To record 2011 cost of goods sold
on installment

Cost of Installment Sales	176,080	
Inventory (or Purchases)		176,080

To close installment sales and cost
of installment sales

Installment Sales	248,000	
Cost of Installment Sales		176,080
Deferred Gross Profit, 2011		71,920

To record realized gross profit

Deferred Gross Profit, 2010	25,920 (a)	
Deferred Gross Profit, 2011	35,670 (b)	
Realized Gross Profit		61,590

(a)   ($96,000 X .27)
(b)   ($123,000 X .29)

20.   When interest is involved in installment sales, it should be accounted for separately as interest income in the period received. Uncollectible installment accounts receivable should be accounted for in a manner similar to that used for such losses on other credit sales if repossessions do not normally compensate for uncollectible balances.

Repossessions

21.   The accounting for **repossessions** recognizes that the related installment receivable account is not collectible and that it should be written off. Also, the applicable deferred gross profit must be removed from the ledger.

22.   **Repossessed merchandise** should be recorded in the Repossessed Merchandise Inventory account. The item repossessed should be recorded at its **fair value.** The objective should be to put any asset acquired on the books at its fair value or, when fair value is not ascertainable, at the best possible approximation of fair value. If installment sales transactions represent a significant part of total sales, full disclosure of installment sales, the cost of installment sales, and any expenses allocable to installment sales is desirable. **Deferred gross profit on installment sales** is generally treated as unearned revenue and classified as a current liability.

Cost Recovery Method

23.   (S.O. 7) Under the **cost recovery method,** no profit is recognized until cash payments by the buyer exceed the seller's cost of the merchandise sold. After all the costs have been recovered, any additional cash collections are included in income. The accounting profession allows a seller to use the cost recovery method to account for sales in which "there is no reasonable basis for estimating collectibility." The cost recovery method is required under GAAP where a high degree of uncertainty exists related to the collection of receivables. The cost recovery method is more appropriate than the installment method when there is a greater degree of uncertainty.

Franchises

*24.   (S.O. 8) **Appendix 18A** includes a presentation of franchise sales and consignment sales transactions. In **franchise operations** a franchisor grants business rights under a franchise agreement to a franchisee. Four types of franchise arrangements have evolved in practice: **(a)** manufacturer-retailer, **(b)** manufacturer-wholesaler, **(c)** service sponsor-retailer (McDonald's, Pizza Hut, etc.), and **(d)** wholesaler - retailer. Franchise companies derive their revenue from one or both of two sources: **(a)** the sale of initial franchises and related assets or services and **(b)** continuing fees based on the operations of franchises.

*25. **Initial franchise fees** are to be recorded as revenue only when and as the franchisor makes substantial performance of the services it is obligated to perform and collection of the fee is reasonably assured. **Continuing franchise fees** should be reported as revenue when they are earned and receivable from the franchisee, unless a portion of them has been designated for a particular purpose, such as providing a specified amount for building maintenance or local advertising. When a franchisee is given an option to purchase equipment or supplies by a franchisor at a bargain purchase price (lower than the normal selling price), a portion of the initial franchise fee should be deferred and accounted for as an adjustment to the selling price of equipment or supplies. A franchisor should disclose all significant commitments and obligations resulting from franchise agreements, including a description of services that have not yet been substantially performed.

Consignments

*26. In a **consignment sales arrangement,** merchandise is shipped by the **consignor** to the **consignee,** who acts as an agent for the consignor in selling the merchandise. The merchandise shipped to the consignee remains the **property of the consignor** until a sale is made. When a sale is made, the consignee remits the proceeds, less any related expenses plus a sales commission, to the consignor. When the consignor receives word that a sale has been made, revenue is recognized and inventory is appropriately reduced.

*27. In accounting for consignment sales arrangements, the consignor periodically receives from the consignee an **account sales** that shows the merchandise received, merchandise sold, expenses chargeable to the consignment, and the cash remitted. Revenue is then recognized by the consignor.

GLOSSARY

Account sales.

A document a consignor periodically receives from the consignee that shows the merchandise received, merchandise sold, expenses chargeable to the consignment, and the cash remitted.

Completion of production basis.

The recognition of revenue at the completion of production even though no sale has been made (examples include precious metals or agricultural products with assured prices).

Completed-Contract Method.

The accounting for long-term construction contracts where revenues and gross profit are recognized only when the contract is completed.

*Consignment.**

A contractual arrangement whereby a consignor ships merchandise to a consignee, who is to act as an agent for the consignor in selling the merchandise. The consignor retains title to the goods until the goods are sold.

*Consignor.**

The party (generally a manufacturer) that sends goods to a consignee under consignment.

*Consignee.**

The party (generally a dealer) that receives goods from a consignor under consignment.

*Continuing franchise fees.	The payments made by a franchisee to a franchisor for the continuing rights granted by the franchise agreement and for providing such services as management training, advertising and promotion, legal assistance, and other support.
Cost recovery method.	Income is not recognized until cash payments by the buyer exceed the seller's cost of the merchandise sold.
Cost-to-cost basis.	The method used under the percentage-of-completion method whereby the percentage of completion is measured by comparing costs incurred to date with the most recent estimate of the total costs to complete the contract.
Deposit method.	The seller reports cash received in advance as a deposit on the contract and classifies it as a liability (refundable deposit or customer advance).
Earned.	Revenues are earned when the entity has substantially accomplished what it must do to be entitled to the benefits represented by the revenues, that is, when the earnings process is complete or virtually complete.
*Franchise.	A contractual arrangement whereby a franchisor grants business rights and provides services to a franchisee who in return agrees to pay an initial franchise fee to operate a business and pay continuing fees based on the operations of the business.
*Franchisee.	The party who operates the franchised business.
*Franchisor.	The party who grants business rights under the franchise.
*Initial franchise fee.	Consideration for establishing the franchise relationship and providing some initial services.
Installment sales method.	Income is recognized when it is collected rather than in the period of sale.
Percentage-of-Completion Method.	The accounting for long-term construction contracts where revenues and gross profit are recognized each period based upon the progress of the construction, that is, the percentage of completion.
Realizable.	Revenues are realizable when assets received in exchange are readily convertible to known amounts of cash or claims to cash.
Realized.	Revenues are realized when goods and services are exchanged for cash or claims to cash (receivables).
Revenue recognition principle.	The principle that provides that revenue is recognized when (1) it is realized or realizable and (2) it is earned.

*Substantial performance.   When the franchisor has no remaining obligation to refund any cash received or excuse any nonpayment of a note and has performed all the initial services required under the contract.

CHAPTER OUTLINE

Fill in the outline presented below.

(S.O. 1) The Revenue Recognition Principle

(S.O. 2) Revenue Recognition at Point of Sale (Delivery)

Sales with Buyback Agreements

Sales When Right of Return Exists

Trade Loading and Channel Stuffing

Revenue Recognition Before Delivery

Revenue Recognition During Production

(S.O. 3) Percentage-of-Completion Method

(S.O. 4) Completed-Contract Method

(S.O. 5) Losses on Long-Term Contracts

Chapter Outline *(continued)*

(S.O. 6) Installment Sales Method

Uncollectible Accounts

Defaults and Repossessions

(S.O. 7) Cost Recovery Method

Deposit Method

*(S.O. 8) Franchises

*Initial Franchise Fees

*Continuing Franchise Fees

*Bargain Purchases

*Options to Purchase

*Consignments

REVIEW QUESTIONS AND EXERCISES

TRUE-FALSE

Indicate whether each of the following is true (T) or false (F) in the space provided.

_____ 1. (S.O. 1) FASB Concepts Statement No. 5 provides that revenue is recognized when (a) it is collected and (b) the earning process is complete.

_____ 2. (S.O. 2) Transactions for which sales recognition is postponed because of a high ratio of returned merchandise should **not** be recognized as sales until the return privilege has substantially expired.

_____ 3. (S.O. 2) Trade loading and channel stuffing are management and marketing policy decisions and actions that hype sales, distort operating results, and window dress financial statements.

_____ 4. (S.O. 3) The accounting profession indicates that the percentage-of-completion method is preferred in accounting for long-term construction contracts only when estimates of costs to complete and extent of progress toward completion are verified by an independent certified public accountant.

_____ 5. (S.O. 3) Under the cost-to-cost basis, the percentage of completion is measured by comparing costs incurred to date with the most recent estimate of revenues collected to date.

_____ 6. (S.O. 3) Under the percentage-of-completion method, the difference between the Construction in Process and the Billings on Construction in Process accounts is reported in the balance sheet as a current asset if a debit, and as a contra asset if a credit.

_____ 7. (S.O. 4) The principal advantage of the completed-contract method in accounting for long-term construction contracts is that reported income is based on final results rather than on estimates of unperformed work.

_____ 8. (S.O. 4) The major **disadvantage** of the completed-contract method as compared with the percentage of-completion method is that total net income over the life of the construction contract is normally smaller under the completed-contract method.

_____ 9. (S.O. 4) The annual entries to record costs of construction, progress billings, and collections from customers under the completed-contract method would be identical to those illustrated under the percentage-of-completion method with the significant exclusion of the recognition of revenue and gross profit.

_____ 10. (S.O. 4) When there is a loss in the current period on a profitable contract, under both the percentage-of-completion and the completed-contract methods, the estimated cost increase requires a current period adjustment of excess gross profit recognized on the project in prior periods.

_____ 11. (S.O. 5) The completion of production basis is permitted by GAAP.

_____ 12.   (S.O. 6) Because payment for a product sold on an installment basis is spread over a relatively long period, the risk of loss resulting from uncollectible accounts is greater in installment sales transactions than in ordinary sales.

_____ 13.   (S.O. 6) Under the installment sales method, emphasis is placed on collection rather than on sale, and revenue is considered unrealized until the entire sales price has been collected.

_____ 14.   (S.O. 6) The difference between realized gross profit and deferred gross profit on installment sales is based on the cash collections related to the installment sales.

_____ 15.   (S.O. 6) Repossessed merchandise as a result of a defaulted installment sales contract should be recorded at the best possible estimate of what the item can ultimately be resold for in the second-hand market.

_____ 16.   (S.O. 6) Deferred gross profit on installment sales is generally treated as consisting entirely of unearned revenue and is classified as a current liability.

_____ 17.   (S.O. 6) According to the APB, the installment method of recognizing revenue is restricted to those cases in which receivables are collectible over an extended period of time and there is no reasonable basis for estimating the degree of collectibility.

_____ 18.   (S.O. 6) When interest is involved in installment sales, it should be accounted for as an addition to gross profit recognized on the installment sales collections during the period.

_____ 19.   (S.O. 7) Under the cost recovery method, deferred gross profit is offset against the related receivable--reduced by collections--on the balance sheet.

_____ 20.   (S.O. 7) The deposit method postpones recognizing a sale until a determination can be made as to whether a sale has occurred for accounting purposes.

_____ *21.   (S.O. 8) A franchiser must disclose all significant commitments and obligations resulting from franchise agreements, including a description of services that have not yet been substantially performed.

_____ *22.   (S.O. 8) Franchise companies derive their income almost exclusively from the collection and amortization of initial franchise fees.

_____ *23.   (S.O. 8) In consignment sales accounting, merchandise shipped on consignment remains the property of the consignor until sold.

_____ *24.   (S.O. 8) Expenses paid by the consignor in a consignment arrangement are normally deducted from any commission earned by the consignee.

_____ *25.   (S.O. 8) Consignment accounting represents a method of postponing the recognition of revenue until it is known that a sale to a third party has occurred.

MULTIPLE CHOICE

Select the best answer for each of the following items and enter the corresponding letter in the space.

_____ 1. (S.O. 1) Which of the following is **not** an accurate representation concerning revenue recognition?

A. Revenue from selling products is recognized at the date of sale, usually interpreted to mean the date of delivery to customers.

B. Revenue from services rendered is recognized when cash is received or when services have been performed.

C. Revenue from permitting others to use enterprise assets is recognized as time passes or as the assets are used.

D. Revenue from disposing of assets other than products is recognized at the date of sale.

_____ 2. (S.O. 2) Which of the following is **not** a condition that must be present for a company to recognize revenue at the time of sale when the company gives the buyer the right to return the product?

A. The buyer has paid the seller, or the buyer is obligated to pay the seller and the obligation is not contingent on resale of the product.

B. The present value of the future returns can be reasonably estimated.

C. The seller does not have significant obligations for future performance to directly bring about resale of the product by the buyer.

D. The seller's price to the buyer is substantially fixed or determinable at the date of sale.

_____ 3. (S.O. 3) The profession requires that the percentage-of-completion method be used when estimates of progress toward completion, revenues, and costs are reasonably dependable and three specific conditions exist. Which of the following is **not** one of the three required conditions?

A. The buyer can be expected to satisfy all obligations under the contract.

B. The contract clearly specifies the enforceable rights regarding goods or services to be provided and received by the parties, the consideration to be exchanged, and the manner and terms of settlement.

C. The asset being constructed is a tangible asset to be used in the production of the purchasing entity's product or the rendering of its service.

D. The contractor can be expected to perform the contractual obligation.

_____ 4. (S.O. 3) One of the more popular input measures used to determine the progress toward completion in the percentage-of-completion method is:

A. revenue-percentage basis.

B. cost-percentage basis.

C. progress completion basis.

D. cost-to-cost basis.

The following information relates to questions 5 and 6.

Cushing Corporation recently received a long-term contract to construct a luxury liner. The contract will take 3 years to complete at a cost of $3,500,000. The price of the liner is set at $5,000,000. The cost estimates at the end of the first year are in line with original estimates, and $1,050,000 of costs were incurred during the first year.

_____ 5. (S.O. 3) The amount of income recognized during the first year using the percentage-of-completion method is:

     A. $1,500,000.
     B. $1,050,000.
     C. $ 735,000.
     D. $ 450,000.

_____ 6. (S.O. 3) At the end of the first year which of the following entries would be made to recognize revenue on the contract?

     A.   Accounts Receivable - Construction Contract
              Revenue on Long-Term Contract
     B.   Billings on Construction Contract
              Revenue on Long-Term Contract
     C.   Construction in Process
              Revenue on Long-Term Contract
     D.   Billings on Construction Contract
              Construction in Process

The following information relates to questions 7 and 8.

Bretts Construction Company had a contract starting April 2009, to construct a $6,000,000 building that is expected to be completed in September 2011, at an estimated cost of $5,500,000. At the end of 2009, the costs to date were $2,530,000 and the estimated total costs to complete had not changed. The progress billings during 2009 were $1,200,000 and the cash collected during 2009 was $800,000.

_____ 7. (S.O. 3) For the year ended December 31, 2009, Bretts would recognize gross profit on the building of:
     A. $210,833
     B. $230,000
     C. $270,000
     D. $ 0

_____ 8. (S.O. 3) At December 31, 2009, Bretts would report Construction in Process in the amount of:

     A. $ 230,000
     B. $2,530,000
     C. $2,760,000
     D. $2,360,000

_____ 9.   (S.O. 4) In accounting for long-term construction-type contracts construction costs are accumulated in an inventory account called Construction in Process under the:

	Percentage-of-Completion Method	Completed-Contract Method
A.	Yes	Yes
B.	Yes	No
C.	No	Yes
D.	No	No

_____ 10. (S.O. 4) Under the completed-contract method of accounting for long-term construction contracts, interim charges and/or credits to the income statement are made for:

	Revenues	Costs	Gross Profit
A.	Yes	No	No
B.	No	No	No
C.	No	Yes	No
D.	Yes	Yes	Yes

_____ 11. (S.O. 4) The principal advantage of the completed-contract method is that:

A.   reported revenue is based on final results rather than estimates of unperformed work.
B.   it reflects current performance when the period of a contract extends into more than one accounting period.
C.   it is not necessary to recognize revenue at the point of sale.
D.   a greater amount of gross profit and net income is reported then is the case when the percentage-of-completion method is used.

_____ 12. (S.O. 4) The Nathan Company is involved in the construction of an asset under a long-term construction contract. At the end of the third year of the five year contract, the cost estimates indicate that a loss will result on the completion of the entire contract. In accounting for this contract, the entire expected loss must be recognized in the current period under the:

	Percentage-of-Completion Method	Completed-Contract Method
A.	Yes	No
B.	Yes	Yes
C.	No	Yes
D.	No	No

_____ 13. (S.O. 4) For which of the following products is it appropriate to recognize revenue at the completion of production even though no sale has been made?

A.   Automobiles.
B.   Large appliances.
C.   Single family residential units.
D.   Precious metals.

_____ 14. (S.O. 5) When there is a significant increase in the estimated total contract costs but the increase does **not** eliminate all profit on the contract, which of the following is correct?

A.   Under both the percentage-of-completion and the completed contract methods, the estimated cost increase requires a current period adjustment of excess gross profit recognized on the project in prior periods.

B. Under the percentage-of-completion method only, the estimated cost increase requires a current period adjustment of excess gross profit recognized on the project in prior periods.
C. Under the completed contract method only, the estimated cost increase requires a current period adjustment of excess gross profit recognized on the project in prior periods.
D. No current period adjustment is required.

_____ 15. (S.O. 7) Which of the following methods or bases is used when the collectibility of the receivable is so uncertain that gross profit (or income) is **not** recognized until cash is received?

A. Percentage-of-completion method.
B. Completed-contract method.
C. Installment sales method.
D. Deposit method.

_____ 16. (S.O. 6) Under the installment sales accounting method certain items related to the sale are recognized in the period of the sale and certain items are recognized in the period in which cash is collected. Of the following items, which are recognized in the period of **sale** and which are recognized in the period in which the **cash** is collected?

	Revenues	Cost of Sales	Gross Profit	Other Expenses
A.	Sale	Sale	Cash	Cash
B.	Sale	Cash	Sale	Cash
C.	Sale	Sale	Cash	Sale
D.	Cash	Cash	Sale	Cash

_____ 17. (S.O. 6) The realization of income on installment sales transactions involves:

A. recognition of the difference between the cash collected on installment sales and the cash expenses incurred.
B. deferring the net income related to installment sales and recognizing the income as cash is collected.
C. deferring gross profit while recognizing operating or financial expenses in the period incurred.
D. deferring gross profit and all additional expenses related to installment sales until cash is ultimately collected.

The following information relates to questions 18-20.

During 2010, Trang Corporation sold merchandise costing $500,000 on an installment basis for $800,000. The cash receipts related to these sales were collected as follows: 2010, $250,000; 2011, $450,000; 2012, $100,000.

_____ 18. (S.O. 6) What is the rate of gross profit on the installment sales made by Trang Corporation during 2010?

A. 37.5%.
B. 50%.
C. 60%.
D. 62.5%.

_____ 19. (S.O. 6) If expenses, other than the cost of the merchandise sold, related to the 2010 installment sales amounted to $60,000, by what amount would Trang's net income for 2010 increase as a result of installment sales?

        A. $240,000.
        B. $190,000.
        C. $ 71,250.
        D. $ 33,750.

_____ 20. (S.O. 6) What amounts would be shown in the December 31, 2011 financial statements for realized gross profit on 2010 installment sales, and deferred gross profit on 2010 installment sales, respectively?

        A. $168,750 and $37,500.
        B. $262,500 and $37,500.
        C. $131,250 and $50,000.
        D. $0 and $0.

_____ 21. (S.O. 6) Deferred gross profit on installment sales is generally treated as:

        A. an owners' equity account until collection.
        B. unearned revenue and is classified as a current liability.
        C. unearned revenue and is classified as a deferred charge on the balance sheet.
        D. unearned revenue and is allocated between income tax liability, allowance for bad debts, and net income.

_____ 22. (S.O. 7) Some companies defer the recognition of revenue because the collection of the sales price is **not** reasonably assured. One method employed to defer revenue recognition is the cost recovery method. Under the cost recovery method profit is **not** recognized until:

        A. the entire sales price is collected.
        B. the seller is convinced that collection is assured beyond a reasonable doubt.
        C. the buyer formally accepts delivery of the merchandise involved in the sale.
        D. cash payments by the buyer exceed the seller's cost of the merchandise sold.

_____ *23. (S.O. 8) Initial franchise fees, are recorded as revenue only when and as the franchisor makes substantial performance of the services it is obligated to perform and:

        A. the franchise agreement will last for 5 years or more.
        B. the franchisee has the financial support of a local bank.
        C. collection of the fee is reasonably assured.
        D. the franchisee maintains a specified minimum profit level.

_____ *24. (S.O. 8) Which of the following is **not** an accurate statement regarding consignment arrangements?

        A. The merchandise shipped on consignment remains the property of the consignor until sold.
        B. Since the merchandise shipped remains the property of the consignor, the consignee has no legal obligation regarding any damage to the merchandise.
        C. The consignee is entitled to reimbursement from the consignor for expenses paid in connection with selling the goods and is generally entitled to a commission at an agreed rate on sale actually made.
        D. The consignor accepts the risk that the goods on consignment might not sell and thus relieves the consignee of the need to commit working capital to inventory.

_____*25. (S.O. 8) Theoretically, freight costs incurred in the transfer of consigned goods from the consignor to the consignee should be considered:

     A.   an expense by the consignee.
     B.   an expense by the consignor.
     C.   inventoriable by the consignee.
     D.   inventoriable by the consignor.

REVIEW EXERCISES

1.   (S.O. 1, 2, 3, 4, 6 and *8) Match the revenue transaction listed on the left with the point of revenue realization generally considered appropriate listed on the right.

	Revenue Transaction		**Point of Realization**
____ 1.	Cash sales of merchandise	A.	When accounts receivable are collected
____ 2.	Sales of merchandise on account	B.	When the designated agent collects the
____ 3.	Percentage-of-completion method		purchase price
	on long-term construction project	C.	Date of delivery to customer
____ 4.	Completed-contract method on	D.	When the designated agent submits an
	long-term construction project		"account sales"
____ 5.	Installment sales	E.	As completion of the agreement by the
____ 6.	Consignment sales		seller progresses

2.   (S.0.3) Melanie Construction Company entered into a contract to construct a building for Steve Elbert. The contract called for a flat fee of $900,000, and specified that a progress report be given periodically as to percentage of completion. Construction activities for the first two years are summarized below:

2010:   Construction costs incurred during the year amounted to $172,800; estimated cost to complete, $547,200.

2011:   Construction costs incurred during the year amounted to $385,450; estimated cost to complete, $166,750.

Instructions:
Using the percentage-of-completion method, compute the amount of gross profit Melanie Construction Company should recognize in 2010 and 2011 as a result of this contract.

_____
_____
_____
_____
_____
_____
_____
_____
_____
_____
_____
_____
_____

3.   (S. O. 3 and 4) Meyer Corporation uses the percentage-of-completion method to account for work performed under long-term construction contracts. Meyer began work under contract #7031-21, which provided for a contract price of $3,645,000. Additional data is as follows:

	2010	**2011**
Costs incurred during the year....................................	$563,000	$1,764,000
Estimated costs to complete, as of December 31	1,500,000	-0-
Billings during the year..	580,000	2,875,000
Collections during the year..	525,000	2,670,000

Instructions:

a.   What portion of the total contract price would be recognized as revenue in 2010 and in 2011?

b.   Prepare a complete set of journal entries for 2010 under the (1) percentage-of completion method, and (2) the completed-contract method.

a.

b.

	General Journal		J1
Date	**Account Title**	**Debit**	**Credit**

4.   (S.O. 7) The following information was taken from the records of Locken Corporation for the years indicated. The company's year end is December 31.

	2010	**2011**	**2012**
Sales (on installment)	$450,000	$500,000	$620,000
Cost of sales	342,000	360,000	434,000
Gross Profit	$108,000	$140,000	$186,000
Cash receipts:			
2010 sales	$125,000	$280,000	$ 45,000
2011 sales		210,000	230,000
2012 sales			250,000

Instructions:

Calculate the amount of realized gross profit on installment sales and deferred gross profit to be reported in the year-end financial statements of Locken Corporation for the three years noted.

_____

_____

_____

_____

_____

_____

_____

_____

_____

_____

_____

_____

5.   (S.O.7) Gardin Company uses the installment sales method to account for its installment sales. On January 1, 2010, Gardin Company had an installment account receivable from Silverman Company in the amount of $2,300. Silverman paid a total of $500 on the account during 2010. However, late in 2010 Silverman discontinued payments and the merchandise was repossessed. When the merchandise was repossessed it had a fair market value of $720. Gardin Company spent an additional $75 to recondition the merchandise. When the repossessed merchandise was originally sold, it was to yield a 45% gross profit rate.

Instructions:
Prepare the journal entries on the books of Gardin Company to record all transactions with Silverman Company during 2010.

	General Journal		J1
Date	**Account Title**	**Debit**	**Credit**

SOLUTIONS TO REVIEW QUESTIONS AND EXERCISES

TRUE-FALSE

1. (F) The revenue recognition principle adopted by the FASB has revenue recognized when (1) it is realized or realizable and (2) it is earned. Revenues are realized when goods and services are exchanged for cash or claims to cash (receivables). Revenues are realizable when assets received in exchange are readily convertible to known amounts of cash or claims to cash. Revenues are earned when the entity has substantially accomplished what it must do to be entitled to the benefits represented by the revenues.

2. (T)

3. (T)

4. (F) The accounting profession considers the percentage-of-completion method preferable when estimates of cost to complete and extent of progress toward completion of long-term contracts are reasonably dependable. There is no necessity to have these estimates verified by an independent third party. In 1981, the AICPA recommended that the completed-contract method and the percentage-of-completion method be used in specified circumstances and that these two methods not be viewed as acceptable alternatives in the same circumstances.

5. (F) Under the cost-to-cost basis, the percentage-of-completion is measured by comparing costs incurred to date with the most recent estimate of the total costs to complete the contract.

6. (F) Under the percentage-of-completion method, the difference between the Construction in Process and the Billings on Construction in Process accounts is reported in the balance sheet as a current asset if a debit, and as a current liability if a credit.

7. (T)

8. (F) The total net income or gross profit over the life of a construction contract is the same under both the percentage-of-completion method and the completed-contract method. The major difference between the methods is the timing of the recognition of gross profit during the life of the contract.

9. (T)

10. (F) When there is a loss in the current period on a profitable contract, under the percentage-of-completion method **only,** the estimated cost increase requires a current period adjustment of excess gross profit recognized on the project in prior periods.

11. (T)

12. (T)

13. (F) This statement is false because each time a portion of the revenue from an installment sale is collected, it is recognized as revenue. The statement in this question reads "...until the entire sales price is collected" which makes it false.

14. (T)

15. (F) The objective with respect to repossessed merchandise is to put it on the books at its fair value or, when fair value is not ascertainable, at the best possible approximation of fair value.

16. (T)

17. (T)

18. (F) When interest is involved in installment sales, it should be accounted for separately as interest revenue distinct from the gross profit recognized on the installment sales collections during the period.

19. (T)

20. (T)

*21. (T)

*22. (F) Franchise companies derive their revenue from one or both of two sources: (1) from the sale of initial franchise and related assets or services and (2) from continuing fees based on the operations of franchises.

*23. (T)

*24. (F) The consignee acts as an agent for the consignor in selling merchandise. The consignee earns a commission upon the sale of the consigned merchandise. However, expenses incurred by the consignor are not deducted from the commissions earned by the consignee.

*25. (T)

MULTIPLE CHOICE

1. (B) Revenues from services rendered is recognized when services have been performed and are billable. The receipt of cash does not necessarily signal the recognition of revenue.

2. (B) The FASB has concluded that if a company sells its product but gives the buyer the right to return it, then revenue from the sales transaction shall be recognized at the time of sale only if **all** of the following six conditions have been met:

    1. The seller's price to the buyer is substantially fixed or determinable at the date of sale.
    2. The buyer has paid the seller, or the buyer is obligated to pay the seller and the obligation is not contingent on resale of the product.
    3. The buyer's obligation to the seller would not be changed in the event of theft or physical destruction or damage of the product.
    4. The buyer acquiring the product for resale has economic substance apart from that provided by the seller.
    5. The seller does not have significant obligations for future performance to directly bring about resale of the product by the buyer.
    6. The amount of future returns can be reasonably estimated.

3. (C)   The specific conditions make no mention of the asset which is the subject of the contract. The other three alternatives include conditions which must be met for mandatory use of the percentage-of-completion method.

4. (D)   The cost-to-cost basis is a popular input method and is often used to determine the progress toward completion when the percentage-of-completion method is used. Under the cost-to-cost basis, the percentage of completion is measured by dividing the costs incurred to date by the most recent estimate of the total costs to complete the contract.

5. (D)   Total cost.. $3,500,000
          Cost incurred.. $1,050,000

          % of total cost incurred $1,050,000 ÷ $3,500,000 =.30

          Estimated income: $5,000,000 - $3,500,000 = $1,500,000
              Income recognized in the first year
              $1,500,000 x .30 = $450,000

6. (C)   Under the percentage-of-completion method, the Construction in Process account is used to record revenue throughout the contract period.

7. (B)   Bretts would calculate the estimated total gross profit and the percentage completed on the building as follows:

Contract price		$6,000,000
Less estimated cost:		
Costs to date	$2,530,000	
Estimated costs to complete	2,970,000	
Estimated total costs		5,500,000
Estimated total gross profit		$ 500,000
Percent complete ($2,530,000/$5,500,000):		46%

          Therefore the gross profit recognized in 2009 would be $230,000 (46 % of $500,000).

8. (C) $2,530,000 of costs are accumulated in the Construction in Process account to maintain a record of the total costs incurred. In addition, the gross profit of $230,000 computed in 7. above would also be debited to Construction in Process. Therefore at December 31, 2009, the account Construction in Process would have an ending balance of $2,760,000 ($2,530,000 + $230,000).

9. (A)   Both the percentage-of-completion method and the completed-contract method use the Construction in Process account to accumulate construction costs during the period of the contract. In addition to construction costs, gross profit earned to date is included in the Construction in Process account under the percentage-of-completion method.

10. (B)   Under the completed-contract method, costs of long-term contracts in process and current billings are accumulated, but there are no interim changes or credits to income statement accounts for revenues, costs, and gross profit.

11.   (A)   The completed-contract method recognizes revenue and gross profit only at the point of sale, that is, when the contract is completed. Thus, reported revenue is based on final results rather than estimates of unperformed work as is the case with the percentage-of-completion method. The final amount of gross profit is the same under the completed-contract method as it is under the percentage-of-completion method. The major difference is the pattern of recognition.

12.   (B)   Cost estimates at the end of the current period may indicate that a loss will result on completion of the entire contract. Under both the percentage-of-completion method and the completed-contract method, the entire expected contract loss must be recognized in the current period.

13.   (D)   In the case of precious metals with assured prices, revenue is recognized at the completion of production even though no sale has been made. Revenue is recognized when these metals are mined because the sales price is reasonably assured, the units are interchangeable, and no significant costs are involved in distributing the product. The other three products noted in alternatives A, B, and C do not meet all these characteristics.

14.   (B)   When there is a significant increase in the estimated total contract costs but the increase does not eliminate all profit on the contract, under the percentage-of-completion method only, the estimated cost increase requires a current period adjustment of excess gross profit recognized on the project in the prior periods.

15.   (C)   The installment sales method is used when the collectibility of the receivable is so uncertain that gross profit (or income) is not recognized until cash is received. (A) The percentage-of-completion method is used for long-term contracts when estimates of progress toward completion, revenues, and costs are reasonably dependable and (1) the contract clearly specifies certain enforceable rights, (2) the buyer can be expected to satisfy all obligations under the contract, and (3) the contractor can be expected to perform the contractual obligation. (B) The completed-contract method is used when (1) an entity has primarily short-term contracts, or (2) when the conditions for using the percentage-of-completion method cannot be met, or (3) when there are inherent hazards in the contract beyond the normal, recurring business risks. (D) The deposit method is used when there is not sufficient transfer of the risks and rewards of ownership.

16.   (C)   Both revenues and cost of sales are recognized in the period of sale but the related gross profit is deferred to those periods in which cash is collected. Thus, instead of the sale being deferred to the future periods of anticipated collection and then related costs and expenses being deferred, only proportional gross profit is deferred. Other expenses, that is, selling expense, administrative expense, and so on, are not deferred.

17.   (C)   Under the installment method of accounting, gross profit recognition is deferred until the period of cash collection. Both revenues and cost of sales are recognized in the period of sale, but the related gross profit is deferred to those periods in which cash is collected. Thus, instead of the sale being deferred to the future periods of anticipated collection and then related costs and expenses being deferred, only the proportional gross profit is deferred, which is equivalent to deferring both sales and cost of sales. Other expenses such as selling expense and administrative expense are not deferred.

18.   (A)   Rate of gross profit is computed by dividing the gross profit by the sales price.

G.P. ($800,000 - $500,000)......................	$300,000
Sales Price..	800,000
Rate of G.P. ($300,000 ÷ $800,000)........	37.5%

19.   (D)

Realized gross profit ($250,000 x 37.5%)	$ 93,750
Less expenses	60,000
Increase in net income	$33,750

20.   (A)

Total gross profit ($800,000 - $500,000)	$300,000
Gross profit realized in:	
2010 ($250,000 x 37.5%)	$ 93,750
2011 ($450,000 x 37.5%)	168,750
2012 ($100,000 x 37.5%)	37,500

The December 31, 2011, financial statements will show realized gross profit of $168,750 and deferred gross profit of $37,500 resulting from 2010 installment sales.

21.   (B)   Deferred gross profit on installment sales is generally treated as unearned revenue and is classified as a current liability. Theoretically, deferred gross profit consists of three elements: (1) income tax liability to be paid when the sales are reported as realized revenue; (2) allowance for collection expense, bad debts, and repossession losses; and (3) net income. Because of the difficulty in allocating deferred gross profit among these three elements, however, the whole amount is frequently reported as unearned revenue.

22.   (D)   Under the cost recovery method, after all costs have been recovered, any additional cash collections are included in income. Thus, profit is not recognized until cash payments by the buyer exceed the seller's cost of merchandise sold. This method is used where a high degree of uncertainty exists related to collection of receivables.

*23.   (C)   The initial franchise fee is considered for establishing the franchise relationship and providing some initial services. Such fees are recorded as revenue only upon substantial performance by the franchiser and when collection of the initial franchise fee is reasonably assured.

*24.   (B)   When a consignee accepts merchandise on a consignment arrangement, he or she agrees to exercise due diligence in caring for and selling the merchandise. If the consignee does not exercise due diligence in caring for the merchandise, he or she will be liable for damages sustained.

*25.   (D)   Freight costs are necessary costs incurred in bringing consigned goods to the condition and location required for sale. This is the responsibility of the consignor and should be recognized as an inventoriable cost.

REVIEW EXERCISES

1. 1. C   4. C
    2. C   5. A
    3. E   6. D

2.   2010:

Contract price		$900,000
Less:		
Cost to date..	$172,800	
Estimated cost to complete............................	547,200	
Estimated total cost		720,000
Estimated total income..		$180,000

Income recognized in 2010:
($172,800 ÷ 720,000) X $180,000 $43,200

2011:

Contract price...		$900,000
Less:		
Cost to date ($172,800 + $385,450)	$558,250	
Estimated cost to complete...	166,750	
Estimated total cost..		725,000
Estimated total income		$175,000

Income recognized in 2011:
($558,250 ÷725,000) X $175,000 $134,750
Less 2010 recognized income   43,200
$ 91,550

3. a. 2010: $\dfrac{\$563,000}{\$2,063,000}$ X $3,645,000 = $994,733

2011:	Contract Price	$3,645,000
	Revenue Recognized in 2010	994,733
	Revenue Recognized in 2011	$2,650,266

    b. (1) **Percentage-of-Completion Method - 2010**

Construction in Process	563,000	
Materials, Cash, Payable, etc.		563,000
Accounts Receivable	580,000	
Billings on Construction in Process		580,000
Cash	525,000	
Accounts Receivable		525,000
Construction in Process	431,733*	
Construction Expense	563,000	
Revenue-Long-Term Contracts (see a)		994,733

*[$3,645,000 - ($563,000 + $1,500,000) x ($563,000/($563,000 + $1,500,000)]

        (2) **Completed-Contract Method - 2010**
        Under the completed-contract method, all the above entries are made except for the last
        entry. No income is recognized until the contract is completed.

4.

	2010	**2011**	**2012**
Rate of Gross Profit on sales..........................	24%	28%	30%
Realized Gross Profit			
2010 sales..	$30,000	$67,200	$10,800
2011 sales..		58,800	64,400
2012 sales..			75,000
Realized Gross Profit 12-31	$30,000	$126,000	$150,200
Deferred Gross Profit:			
2010 sales..	$78,000	$ 10,800	
2011 sales..		81,200	$ 16,800
2012 sales..			111,000
Deferred Gross Profit 12-31	$78,000	$ 92,000	$127,800

5.

Cash	500	
Accounts Receivable		500
(To record collection of cash on installment receivables)		
Deferred Gross Profit ($500 X 45%)	225	
Realized Gross Profit		225
(To recognize gross profit on installment sale)		
Repossessed Merchandise	720	
Deferred Gross Profit (45% X $1,800)	810	
Loss on Repossession	270	
Installment Accounts Receivable		1,800
(To record default and repossessed merchandise)		
Repossessed Merchandise	75	
Cash		75
(To record cash spent on reconditioning)		

19

Accounting for Income Taxes

CHAPTER STUDY OBJECTIVES

1. Identify differences between pretax financial income and taxable income.

2. Describe a temporary difference that results in future taxable amounts.

3. Describe a temporary difference that results in future deductible amounts.

4. Explain the purpose of a deferred tax asset valuation allowance.

5. Describe the presentation of income tax expense in the income statement.

6. Describe various temporary and permanent differences.

7. Explain the effect of various tax rates and tax rate changes on deferred income taxes.

8. Apply accounting procedures for a loss carryback and a loss carryforward.

9. Describe the presentation of deferred income taxes in financial statements.

10. Indicate the basic principles of the asset-liability method.

*11. Understand and apply the concepts and procedures of interperiod tax allocation.

CHAPTER REVIEW

Introduction

1. Chapter 19 addresses the issues related to accounting for income taxes. Taxable income is computed in accordance with prescribed tax regulations and rules, whereas accounting income is measured in accordance with generally accepted accounting principles. Unfortunately for accountants, tax regulations and accounting principles are not always in agreement.

2. (S.O. 1) Due to the fact that tax regulations and generally accepted accounting principles differ in many ways, taxable income and financial income frequently differ. The following represent examples of events that can result in such differences: **(a)** depreciation computed on a straight-line basis for financial reporting purposes and on an accelerated basis for tax purposes, **(b)** income recognized on the accrual basis for financial reporting purposes and on the installment basis for tax purposes, and **(c)** warranty costs recognized in the period incurred for financial reporting purposes and when they are paid for tax purposes.

Note: All asterisked (*) items relate to material contained in the Appendix to the chapter.

3.   The items discussed in paragraph 2 above can result in temporary differences between the amounts reported for book purposes and those reported for tax purposes. A **temporary difference** is the difference between the tax basis of an asset or liability and its reported amount in the financial statements that will result in taxable amounts (increase in taxable income) or deductible amounts (decrease in taxable income) in future years when the reported amount of the asset is recovered or when the reported amount of the liability is settled. When the book amount of an asset or liability differs from the tax basis as a result of a temporary difference, the future tax effects on taxable income must be reported in the current financial statements.

Deferred Tax Liability

4.   (S.O. 2) A **deferred tax liability** is the amount of deferred tax consequence attributable to the temporary differences that will result in net taxable amounts (taxable amounts less deductible amounts) in future years. The liability is the amount of taxes payable on these net taxable amounts in future years based on existing provisions of the tax law.

5.   The following example is presented to demonstrate the deferred tax liability concept. Assume that Bobbie Company earns $50,000 of net operating income before depreciation for each of five consecutive years. The company depreciates its fixed assets using the straight-line method for accounting purposes and an acceptable accelerated method for tax purposes over this five-year period. The following schedule shows taxable income, income tax payable, accounting income, and income tax expense for the five-year period assuming a 40% tax rate.

Year	Taxable Income	Income Tax Payable	Accounting Income	Income Tax Expense
1	$ 40,000	$16,000	$ 44,000	$17,600
2	42,000	16,800	44,000	17,600
3	44,000	17,600	44,000	17,600
4	46,000	18,400	44,000	17,600
5	48,000	19,200	44,000	17,600
Totals	$220,000	$88,000	$220,000	$88,000

6.   At the end of year one the entry to recognize the tax expense and the tax liability is:

Income Tax Expense	17,600	
Income Tax Payable		**16,000**
Deferred Tax Liability		**1,600**

Each year (two through five) the entry is made debiting the tax expense account and crediting the tax liability for the amounts indicated. Note that the **Deferred Tax Liability** account will increase in years one and two, remain unchanged in year three, and then decrease in years four and five so that a zero balance results at the end of the five-year period which represents the assets' useful life.

Deferred Tax Asset

7.   (S.O. 3) Due to the fact that deductible amounts can arise in the future as a result of temporary differences at the end of the current year, the deferred tax consequences of these deductible amounts should be recognized as a **deferred tax asset.** A deferred tax asset is the amount of taxes (computed in accordance with provisions of the tax law) that will be refundable in future years as a result of these deductible amounts. A key issue in accounting for income taxes is whether a deferred tax asset should be recognized in the financial records. Previously, the FASB took a strong position against recording

deferred tax assets. In their most recent pronouncement, the FASB reversed their position noting that deferred tax assets meet the definition of an asset and should be reported in the financial statements. The three main conditions for an item to be reported as an asset are: **(a)** it results from past transactions; **(b)** it gives rise to a probable benefit in the future; and **(c)** the company controls access to the benefits. These conditions are met by the deferred tax asset.

8. (S.O. 4) A deferred tax asset is recognized for all deductible temporary differences. However, deferred tax assets should be reduced by a valuation allowance if, based on available evidence, it is more likely than not that some portion or all of the deferred tax asset will not be realized. For example, assume Angie Company has a deductible temporary difference of $2,500,000 at the end of its initial year of operations. Its tax rate is 45%, which means a deferred tax asset of $1,125,000 or ($2,500,000 X .45) is recorded. Assuming taxes payable are $2,000,000, the required journal entry is:

Income Tax Expense	875,000	
Deferred Tax Asset	1,125,000	
Income Tax Payable		2,000,000

If, after further consideration, it is considered more likely than not that $300,000 of this deferred tax asset will not be realized then the following entry is appropriate.

Income Tax Expense	300,000	
Allowance to Reduce Deferred Tax Asset		
to Expected Realizable Value		300,000

The Allowance account is a contra account and is deducted from the Deferred Tax Asset account in the financial statements.

9. (S.O. 5) The formula to compute income tax expense (benefit) is as follows:

Income Tax Payable or Refundable	±	Change in Deferred Income Taxes	=	Total Income Tax Expense or Benefits

In the income statement or in the notes to the financial statements, the significant components of income tax expense attributable to continuing operations should be disclosed.

Temporary and Permanent Differences

10. (S.O. 6) Differences between taxable income and accounting income can be categorized as either **(a) temporary differences** or **(b) permanent differences.** Temporary differences arise when the tax basis of an asset or liability and its reported amount in the financial statements differ. This difference will reverse and result in taxable or deductible amounts in future years as the asset is recovered or the liability is settled at its reported amount.

11. Temporary differences originate in one period and reverse or "turn around" in one or more subsequent periods. For example, when a company records a product warranty liability, an expense is recognized for accounting purposes but not for tax purposes. In future years when the product warranty liability is settled, tax deductible amounts result which reverse the effect of the original timing differences.

12. Two concepts related to temporary differences are **originating differences** and **reversing differences.** An originating difference is the initial temporary difference between the book basis and the

tax basis of an asset or liability regardless of whether the tax basis of the asset of liability exceeds or is exceeded by the book basis of the asset or liability. A reversing difference, on the other hand, occurs when a temporary difference that originated in a prior period is eliminated and the tax effect is removed from the deferred tax account. In the depreciation example presented in paragraph 5 above, the originating difference was $1,600 and $800 in the first two years, and the reversing difference was $800 and $1,600 in the final two years.

13.   Permanent differences are items that **(a)** enter into financial income but *never* into taxable income or **(b)** enter into taxable income but *never* into financial income. Examples of permanent differences include interest received on state and municipal obligations, proceeds from life insurance on key executives, and compensation expense associated with certain employee stock options. These items are not included in the computation of taxable income, and the profession has concluded that the tax consequences of these differences should not be recognized.

Future Tax Rates

14.   (S.O. 7) When recording deferred income taxes consideration must be given to the tax rate in effect when the timing differences reverse. Normally, the current tax rate is used to compute deferred income taxes. However, future tax rates, other than the current rate **should be used** when such rates **have been enacted into law.** When an unexpected change in the tax rate has been enacted into law, its effect on deferred income tax and related tax expense should be recorded immediately. The effects are reported as an adjustment to tax expense in the period of the change.

Accounting for Tax Losses

15.   (S.O. 8) A **net operating loss** occurs for tax purposes in a year when tax-deductible expenses exceed taxable revenues. Under certain circumstances the federal tax laws permit taxpayers to use the losses of one year to offset the profits of other years. This income-averaging provision is accomplished through the **carryback** and **carryforward** of net operating losses. Under these rules, a company pays no income taxes for a year in which it incurs a net operating loss.

16.   A company may carry a net operating loss back two years and receive refunds for income taxes paid in those years. The loss must be applied to the earliest year first and then to the second year. Any loss remaining after the two year carryback may be carried forward up to 20 years to offset future taxable income. A company may elect the loss carryforward only, offsetting future taxable income for up to 20 years.

17.   When a company carries a tax loss back, the tax loss gives rise to a refund that is both measurable and currently realizable; therefore, the associated tax benefit should be recognized in the current loss period. When a company carries a tax loss forward, a deferred tax asset should be established for the benefits of future tax savings. If it is more likely than not that the entire future tax loss will not be realized in future years, a valuation allowance is required.

Balance Sheet Presentation

18.   (S.O. 9) Deferred income taxes are reported on the balance sheet as assets and liabilities. An individual deferred tax liability or asset is classified as current or noncurrent based on the classification of the related asset or liability for financial reporting purposes. A deferred tax asset or liability is considered to be related to an asset or liability if reduction of the asset or liability will cause the temporary difference to reverse or turn around. A deferred tax liability or asset that is not related to an asset or liability for financial reporting shall be classified according to the expected reversal date of the temporary difference. The balance in the deferred income tax account should be analyzed into its

components and classified on the balance sheet into two categories: **one for net current amount** and **one for net noncurrent (or long-term) amount.**

19.   The following is a summarization of the considerations related to balance sheet presentation of deferred tax accounts.

     a.   Classify the amounts as current or noncurrent. If they are related to a specific asset or liability, they should be classified in the same manner as the related asset or liability. If not so related, they should be classified on the basis of the expected reversal date.

     b.   Determine the net current amount by summing the various deferred tax assets and liabilities classified as current. If the net result is an asset, report on the balance sheet as a current asset; if a liability, report as a current liability.

     c.   Determine the net noncurrent amount by summing the various deferred tax assets and liabilities classified as noncurrent. If the net result is an asset, report on the balance sheet as a noncurrent asset; if a liability, report as a long-term liability.

Income Statement Presentation

20.   Income tax expense (or benefit) should be allocated to continuing operations, discontinued operations, extraordinary items, the cumulative effect of accounting changes, and prior period adjustments. This approach is referred to as **intraperiod tax allocation.** In addition, the significant components of income tax expense attributable to continuing operations should be disclosed. Companies are also required to reconcile income tax expense on continuing operations with the amount that results from applying domestic federal statutory tax rates to pretax income from continuing operations. The amounts of any operating loss carryforwards not recognized in the loss period, along with the expiration of these loss carryforwards, should be disclosed. When companies have uncertain tax positions, if the probability is more than 50 percent, companies may reduce their liability or increase their assets. If the probability is less than 50 percent, companies may not record the tax benefit.

Asset-Liability Method

21.   (S.O. 10) The FASB believes that the asset-liability viewpoint (balance sheet approach) is the most consistent method for accounting for income taxes. One objective of this approach is to recognize the amount of taxes payable or refundable for the current year. A second objective is to recognize deferred tax liabilities and assets for the future tax consequences of events that have been recognized in the financial statements or tax returns. To implement the objectives, the following basic principles are applied in accounting for income taxes at the date of the financial statements:

     a.   A current tax liability or asset is recognized for the estimated taxes payable or refundable on tax returns for the current year.

     b.   A deferred tax liability or asset is recognized for the estimated future tax effects attributed to temporary differences and carryforwards.

     c.   The measurement of current and deferred tax liabilities and assets is based on provisions of the enacted tax law; the effects of future changes in tax laws or rates are not anticipated.

     d.   The measurement of deferred tax assets is reduced, if necessary, by the amount of any tax benefits that, based on available evidence, are not expected to be realized.

Interperiod Tax Allocation

*22.   (S.O. 11) A comprehensive illustration of a deferred income tax problem is included in **Appendix 19-A.** This illustration is one that should be analyzed and studied as it will provide a sound basis for an understanding of the many aspects of accounting for income taxes.

GLOSSARY

Alternative minimum tax.	An alternative tax system used to ensure that corporations do not avoid paying a fair share of income taxes through various tax avoidance approaches.
Asset-liability method.	A method used to account for income taxes that recognizes the amount of taxes payable or refundable for the current year and records deferred tax liabilities and assets for the future tax consequences of events that have been recognized in the financial statements or tax returns.
Average tax rate.	The amount of income taxes payable for the period divided by taxable income.
Carrybacks.	Deductions or credits that cannot be utilized on the tax return during a year and that may be carried back to reduce taxable income or taxes paid in a prior year.
Carryforwards.	Deductions or credits that cannot be utilized on the tax return during a year and that may be carried forward to reduce taxable income or taxes payable in a future year.
Current tax expense (benefit).	The amount of income taxes paid or payable (or refundable) for a year as determined by applying the provisions of the enacted tax law to the taxable income or excess of deductions over revenues for that year.
Deductible temporary difference.	Temporary differences that result in deductible amounts in future years when the related asset or liability is recovered or settled, respectively.
Deferred tax asset.	The deferred tax consequences attributable to deductible temporary differences and carryforwards.
Deferred tax consequences.	The future effects of income taxes as measured by the enacted tax rate and provisions of the enacted tax law resulting from temporary differences and carryforwards at the end of the current year.

Deferred tax expense (benefit). The change during the year in an enterprise's deferred tax liabilities and assets.

Deferred tax liability. The deferred tax consequences attributable to taxable temporary differences.

Effective tax rate. Total income tax expense for the period divided by pretax financial income.

Income taxes. Domestic and foreign (national), state, and local (including franchise) taxes based on income.

Income taxes currently payable (refundable). Refer to current tax expense (benefit).

Income tax expense (benefit). The sum of current tax expense (benefit) and deferred tax expense (benefit).

*Interperiod tax allocation. The allocation of income tax between periods whereby there is a recognition of deferred income taxes.

Intraperiod tax allocation. The allocation of income tax expense (or benefit) to continuing operations, discontinued operations, extraordinary items, cumulative effect of accounting changes and prior period adjustments.

Net operating loss (NOL). When tax-deductible expenses exceed taxable revenues for the tax year.

Originating temporary difference. The initial difference between the book basis and the tax basis of an asset or liability, regardless of whether the tax basis of the asset or liability exceeds or is exceeded by the book basis of the asset or liability.

Permanent differences. Differences between taxable income and pretax financial income that are caused by items that (1) enter into pretax financial income but never into taxable income or (2) enter into taxable income but never into pretax financial income.

Pretax financial income. Financial accounting term often referred to as income before income taxes, income for financial reporting purposes, or income for book purposes.

Reversing difference. A temporary difference that originated in prior periods is eliminated and the related tax effect is removed from the deferred tax account.

Taxable income. The excess of taxable revenues over tax deductible expenses and exemptions for the year as defined by the governmental taxing authority.

Taxable temporary difference.

Temporary differences that result in taxable amounts in future years when the related asset or liability is recovered or settled, respectively.

Tax-planning strategy.

An action that meets certain criteria and that would be implemented to realize a tax benefit for an operating loss or tax credit carryforward before it expires.

Temporary difference.

A difference between the tax basis of an asset or liability and its reported amount in the financial statements that will result in taxable or deductible amounts in future years when the reported amount of the asset or liability is recovered or settled, respectively.

Valuation allowance.

The portion of a deferred tax asset for which it is more likely than not that a tax benefit will not be realized.

CHAPTER OUTLINE

Fill in the outline presented below.

(S.O. 1) Pretax Financial Income and Taxable Income

(S.O. 2) Future Taxable Amounts and Deferred Taxes

Deferred Tax Liability

(S.O. 3) Future Deductible Amounts and Deferred Taxes

Deferred Tax Asset

(S.O. 4) Deferred Tax Asset-Valuation Allowance

(S.O. 5) Income Statement Presentation

(S.O. 6) Temporary Differences

Revenues or gains that are taxable after they are recognized in financial income
1.

2.

3.

4.

Chapter Outline *(continued)*

Expenses or losses that are deductible after they are recognized in financial income.
1.

2.

3.

4.

Revenues or gains that are taxable before they are recognized in financial income.
1.

2.

3.

4.

Expenses or losses that are deductible before they are recognized in financial income
1.

2.

3.

Permanent Differences

   Items that are recognized for financial reporting purposes but not for tax purposes.

      1.

      2.

      3.

      4.

      5.

      6.

Chapter Outline *(continued)*

Items that are recognized for tax purposes but not for financial reporting purposes

1.

2.

(S.O. 7) Future Tax Rates

(S.O. 8) Accounting for Net Operating Losses

Loss Carryback

Loss Carryforward

(S.O. 9) Financial Statement Presentation

Balance Sheet Presentation

Income Statement Presentation

(S.O. 10) Principles of the Asset-Liability Approach

*(S.O. 11) Interperiod Tax Allocation

REVIEW QUESTIONS AND EXERCISES

TRUE-FALSE

Indicate whether each of the following is true (T) or false (F) in the space provided.

_____ 1. (S.O. 2) A temporary difference is the difference between the tax basis of an asset or liability and its reported amount in the financial statements that will result in taxable amounts or deductible amounts in future years.

_____ 2. (S.O. 2) When the book amount of an asset or liability differs from the tax basis as a result of a temporary difference, the future tax effects on taxable income must be reported solely in the future financial statement that the difference affects.

_____ 3. (S.O. 2) A deferred tax liability is the amount of deferred tax consequences attributable to existing temporary differences that will result in net taxable amounts in future years.

_____ 4. (S.O. 2) Deferred tax expense is the decrease in the deferred tax liability balance from the beginning to the end of the accounting period.

_____ 5. (S.O. 2) The concept of a deferred tax liability meets the definition of a liability established according to GAAP because it (a) results from past transactions, (b) is a present obligation, and (c) represents a future sacrifice.

_____ 6. (S.O. 3) An objective of accounting for income taxes is to recognize deferred tax liabilities and assets for the future tax consequences of events that have already been recognized in the financial statements.

_____ 7. (S.O. 3) A deferred tax asset represents the increase in taxes payable in future years as a result of taxable temporary differences existing at the end of the current year.

_____ 8. (S.O. 3) Deferred tax assets should **not** be recognized in the accounts because they fail to meet the definition of an asset.

_____ 9. (S.O. 4) A deferred tax asset should be reduced by a valuation allowance if, based on available evidence, it is more likely than not that some portion or all of the deferred tax asset will **not** be realized.

_____ 10. (S.O. 4) All positive and negative information should be considered in determining whether a valuation allowance is needed.

_____ 11. (S.O. 6) Depreciable property relates to expenses or losses that are deductible from taxable income after they are recognized in financial income.

_____ 12. (S.O. 6) An originating temporary difference is the initial difference that occurs when the book basis of an asset exceeds, but is **not** exceeded by, the tax basis of a liability.

_____ 13. (S.O. 6) A reversing difference occurs when a temporary difference that originated in prior periods is eliminated and the related tax effect is removed from the deferred tax account.

_____ 14. (S.O. 6) A permanent difference results when the tax laws cause an item reported on the income statement to be different from that same item reported on the balance sheet.

_____ 15. (S.O. 7) A corporation that has tax-free income has an effective tax rate that is less than the statutory (regular) tax rate.

_____ 16. (S.O. 7) In computing deferred income taxes a new tax rate should be used if (a) it is probable that a future tax rate change will occur, and (b) the rate is reasonably estimatable.

_____ 17. (S.O. 8) Under the carryback and carryforward provisions of the federal tax laws a company pays no tax in a year in which it incurs a net operating loss and can carry that loss back two years and forward 20 years in offsetting past and future taxable income.

_____ 18. (S.O. 8) In general, the tax benefits of loss carryforwards, should **not** be recognized in the loss year when the benefits arise, but rather in the year they are realized.

_____ 19. (S.O. 8) The only way a tax loss carryforward can be recognized in the current year is when an entity has incurred net losses during the past two calendar years and has no ability to carry any of the loss back.

_____ 20. (S.O. 9) In classifying deferred taxes on the balance sheet, an entity should net the current deferred tax asset and liability amount and net the noncurrent deferred tax asset and liability amount thus reporting only one current and one noncurrent deferred tax amount.

_____ 21. (S.O. 10) The asset-liability approach to accounting for income taxes requires a journal entry at the end of each year which either increases an asset or decreases a liability.

MULTIPLE CHOICE

Select the best answer for each of the following items and enter the corresponding letter in the space provided.

_____ 1. (S.O. 1) In 2010, Delaney Company had revenues of $180,000 for book purposes and $150,000 for tax purposes. Delaney also had expenses of $100,000 for both book and tax purposes. If Delaney has a 35% tax rate, what is Delaney's income tax payable for 2010?

    A. $10,500
    B. $17,500
    C. $28,000
    D. $35,000

_____ 2. (S.O. 1) Maureen Corporation reports income before taxes of $500,000 in its income statement, but because of timing differences taxable income is only $200,000. If the tax rate is 45%, what amount of net income should the corporation report?

    A. $337,500.
    B. $275,000.
    C. $225,000.
    D. $ 90,000.

_____ 3.   (S.O. 2) According to GAAP, a deferred tax liability:

	Results from a Past Transaction	Is a Present Obligation	Represents Future Sacrifice
A.	Yes	No	Yes
B.	Yes	Yes	No
C.	Yes	Yes	Yes
D.	No	No	No

_____ 4.   (S.O. 4) Gleim Inc. has a deductible temporary difference of $100,000 at the end of its first year of operations. Its tax rate is 40%. Income taxes payable are $90,000. Gleim properly recorded a deferred tax asset. Later, after careful review of all available evidence, it is determined that it is more likely than not that $15,000 of the deferred tax asset will **not** be realized. What entry should Gleim make to record the reduction in asset value?

A.	Income Tax Expense	15,000	
	Deferred Tax Asset		15,000
B.	Income Tax Payable	15,000	
	Income Tax Expense		15,000
C.	Allowance to Reduce Deferred		
	Tax Asset to Expected Realizable Value	15,000	
	Income Tax Expense		15,000
D.	Income Tax Expense	15,000	
	Allowance to Reduce Deferred		
	Tax Asset to Expected Realizable Value		15,000

_____ 5.   (S.O. 6) A major distinction between temporary and permanent differences is:

A.   permanent differences are not representative of acceptable accounting practice.

B.   temporary differences occur frequently, whereas permanent differences occur only once.

C.   once an item is determined to be a temporary difference, it maintains that status; however, a permanent difference can change in status with the passage of time.

D.   temporary differences reverse themselves in subsequent accounting periods, whereas permanent differences do not reverse.

_____ 6.   (S.O. 6) The use of accelerated depreciation for tax purposes and straight-line depreciation for accounting purposes results in:

A.   a larger amount of depreciation expense shown on the tax return than on the income statement, over the asset's useful life.

B.   the asset being fully depreciated for tax purposes in half the time it takes to become fully depreciated for accounting purposes.

C.   a larger amount of depreciation expense shown on the income statement than on the tax return in the last year of the asset's useful life.

D.   a loss on the sale of the asset in question if it is sold for its book value before its useful life expires.

_____ 7.   (S.O. 6) Which of the following are temporary differences that are normally classified as expenses or losses that are deductible after they are recognized in financial income?

   A.   Advance rental receipts.
   B.   Product warranty liabilities.
   C.   Depreciable property.
   D.   Fines and expenses resulting from a violation of law.

_____ 8.   (S.O. 6)   Which of the following is a permanent difference that is recognized for tax purposes but **not** for financial reporting purposes?

   A.   The deduction for dividends received from U.S. corporations.
   B.   Interest received on state and municipal bonds.
   C.   Compensation expense associated with certain employee stock options.
   D.   A litigation accrual.

_____ 9.   (S.O. 6) Which of the following is a temporary difference classified as a revenue or gain that is taxable after it is recognized in financial income?

   A.   Subscriptions received in advance.
   B.   Prepaid royalty received in advance.
   C.   An installment sale accounted for on the accrual basis for financial reporting purposes and on the installment (cash) basis for tax purposes.
   D.   Interest received on a municipal obligation.

_____ 10.   (S.O. 6) Kubitz Company reported the following items on its income statement for the year ended December 31, 2010.

   Interest received on municipal bonds $16,000
   Fines from a violation of law   11,000

   For Kubitz Company the amount of temporary differences used to measure deferred income taxes amount to:

   A. $0
   B. $11,000
   C. $16,000
   D. $27,000

The following information should be used to answer questions 11, 12 and 13.

Sandy Company deducts insurance expense of $21,000 for tax purposes in 2010, but the expense is not yet recognized for accounting purposes. In 2011, 2012 and 2013 taxable income will be higher than financial income because no insurance expense will be deducted for tax purposes, but $7,000 of insurance expense will be reported for accounting purposes in each of these years. Sandy Company has a tax rate of 45% and income taxes payable of $18,000 at the end of 2010. There were no deferred taxes at the beginning of 2010.

_____ 11.   (S.O. 6) What is the amount of the deferred tax liability at the end of 2010?
   A. $0
   B. $3,000
   C. $8,100
   D. $9,450

_____ 12.   (S.O. 6) What journal entry should be made for the income tax expense at the end of 2010?

A.	Income Tax Expense	18,000	
	Income Tax Liability		18,000
B.	Income Tax Expense	27,450	
	Income Tax Liability		18,000
	Deferred Tax Liability		9,450
C.	Income Tax Expense	26,100	
	Income Tax Liability		18,000
	Deferred Tax Liability		8,100
D.	Income Tax Expense	30,450	
	Income Tax Liability		21,000
	Deferred Tax Liability		9,450

_____ 13.   (S.O. 6) Assuming that income tax payable for 2011 is $24,000, the income tax expense for 2011 would be what amount?

   A. $20,850
   B. $24,000
   C. $27,150
   D. $33,450

_____ 14.   (S.O. 6) Which of the following differences would result in future taxable amounts?

   A.   Expenses or losses that are tax deductible after they are recognized in financial income.
   B.   Revenues or gains that are taxable before they are recognized in financial income.
   C.   Revenues or gains that are recognized in financial income but are never included in taxable income.
   D.   Expenses or losses that are tax deductible before they are recognized in financial income.

The following information should be used to answer questions 15 and 16.

Annette Company made the following journal entry in late 2010 for rent on property it leases to Hrubec Corporation.

Cash	80,000	
Unearned Rent		80,000

The payment represents rent for the years 2011 and 2012, the period covered by the lease. Annette Company is a cash basis taxpayer. Annette has income tax payable of $123,000 at the end of 2010, and its tax rate is 38%.

_____ 15.   (S.O. 6) What amount of income tax expense should Annette Company report at the end of 2010?

   A. $153,400
   B. $107,800
   C. $ 92,600
   D. $ 73,400

_____ 16.   (S.O. 6) Assuming the taxes payable at the end of 2011 is $136,000, which journal entry
would Annette Company use to record its tax expense for 2011?

A.	Income Tax Expense	166,400	
	Deferred Tax Asset		30,400
	Income Tax Payable		136,000
B.	Income Tax Expense	151,200	
	Deferred Tax Asset		15,200
	Income Tax Payable		136,000
C.	Income Tax Expense	105,600	
	Deferred Tax Asset	30,400	
	Income Tax Payable		136,000
D.	Income Tax Expense	120,800	
	Deferred Tax Asset	15,200	
	Income Tax Payable		136,000

_____ 17.   (S.O. 6) The following information is taken from the accounts of Milar Company after its
first year of operations:

Income before taxes		$100,000
Federal income tax payable	$41,600	
Deferred income tax	(1,600)	
Income tax expense		40,000
Net income		$ 60,000

Milar estimates its annual warranty expense as a percentage of sales. The amount charged
to warranty expense on its books was $38,000. No other differences existed between
accounting and taxable income. Assuming a 40% income tax rate, what amount was
actually paid this year on the Company's warranty?

    A. $34,000.
    B. $38,000.
    C. $40,000.
    D. $42,000.

_____ 18.   (S.O. 6) Nolan Company sells its product on an installment basis, earning a $450 pretax
gross profit on each installment sale. For accounting purposes the entire $450 is recognized
in the year of sale, but for income tax purposes the installment method of accounting is
used. Assume Nolan makes one sale in 2009, another sale in 2010, and a third sale in 2011.
In each case, one-third of the gross sales price is collected in the year of sale, one-third in
the next year, and the final installment in the third year. If the tax rate is 50%, what amount
of deferred tax liability should Nolan Company show on its December 31, 2011 balance
sheet:

    A. $150.
    B. $225.
    C. $300.
    D. $450.

_____ 19.   (S.O. 7) When a change in the tax rate is enacted into law, its effect on existing deferred income tax accounts should be:

   A.   handled retroactively in accordance with the guidance related to changes in accounting principles.
   B.   considered, but it should only be recorded in the accounts if it reduces a deferred tax liability or increases a deferred tax asset.
   C.   reported as an adjustment to tax expense in the period of change.
   D.   applied to all temporary or permanent differences that arise prior to the date of the enactment of the tax rate change, but not subsequent to the date of the change.

_____ 20.   (S.O. 7) Fesmire Co. had a deferred tax liability balance due to a temporary difference at the beginning of 2009 related to $200,000 of excess depreciation. In December of 2009, a new income tax act is signed into law that raises the corporate rate from 35% to 40%, effective January 1, 2011. If taxable amounts related to the temporary difference are scheduled to be reversed by $100,000 for both 2010 and 2011, Fesmire should increase or decrease deferred tax liability by what amount?

   A.   Decrease by $10,000.
   B.   Decrease by $5,000.
   C.   Increase by $5,000.
   D.   Increase by $10,000.

_____ 21.   (S.O. 8) A net operating loss occurs for tax purposes in a year when tax-deductible expenses exceed taxable revenues. Under certain circumstances the federal tax laws permit taxpayers to use the losses of one year to offset the profits of other years. For what period of time can net operating losses be offset against prior or future years' profits?

	Loss Carryback	Loss Carryforward
A.	10 years	10 years
B.	2 years	20 years
C.	3 years	15 years
D.	15 years	3 years

_____ 22.   (S.O. 9) A deferred tax liability is classified on the balance sheet as either a current or a noncurrent liability. The current amount of a deferred tax liability should generally be:

   A.   the net deferred tax consequences of temporary differences that will result in net taxable amounts during the next year.
   B.   totally eliminated from the financial statements if the amount is related to a noncurrent asset.
   C.   based on the classification of the related asset or liability for financial reporting purposes.
   D.   the total of all deferred tax consequences that are not expected to reverse in the operating period or one year, whichever is greater.

REVIEW EXERCISES

1.   (S.0. 6) Numerous items create differences between taxable income and pretax financial income. For purposes of accounting recognition, these differences are of two types: (1) temporary differences and (2) permanent differences. These two classifications are further divided into other categories. Six of those categories are:

Temporary Differences:
   A.   Expenses or losses that are tax deductible after they are recognized in financial income.
   B.   Expenses or losses that are tax deductible before they are recognized in financial income.
   C.   Revenues or gains that are taxable before they are recognized in financial income.
   D.   Revenues or gains that are taxable after they are recognized in financial income.

Permanent Differences:
   E.   Items recognized for accounting purposes but not for tax purposes.
   F.   Items recognized for tax purposes but not for accounting purposes.

Instructions:
For each of the items listed below, indicate by letter which of the four categories it represents.

_____   1.   Litigation accruals.
_____   2.   Fines and expenses resulting from a violation of law.
_____   3.   Percentage depletion.
_____   4.   Proceeds from life insurance carried by the company on a key officer.
_____   5.   Advance rental receipts.
_____   6.   Depreciable property.
_____   7.   Installment sale accounted for on accrual basis for accounting and cash basis for tax purposes.
_____   8.   Royalties received in advance.
_____   9.   Product warranty liability.
_____ 10.   Deduction for dividends received from U.S. corporations.
_____ 11.   Interest received on state and municipal obligations.

2.   (S.0.2) Heiden Company reported the following net income before taxes and depreciation for the years indicated.

| | **2009:** $80,000 | **2010:** $100,000 | **2011:** $75,000 |

The Company purchased assets costing $90,000 on January 1, 2009. The assets have a three-year useful life and no salvage value. For tax purposes the Company used an acceptable accelerated depreciation method that resulted in depreciation expense of $45,000; $30,000; and $15,000 for the three years respectively. For financial reporting purposes the straight-line method was used. A 30% tax rate was in effect for the three years.

Instructions:
Prepare the necessary calculations and make the end of year entries for the Heiden Company for the years 2009, 2010, 2011.

	2009		2010		2011	
	Acct.	**Tax**	**Acct.**	**Tax**	**Acct.**	**Tax**
Income before tax and depreciation						
Depreciation expense						
Subtotal						
Income tax						
Net						

	General Journal		J1
Date	Account Title	Debit	Credit

3.   (S.0.6) Karma Company reports pretax financial income of $300,000 in each of the years 2009, 2010, and 2011. The company is subject to a 20% tax rate, and has the following differences between pretax financial income and taxable income:

a.   An installment sale of $48,000 in 2009 is reported for tax purposes over a 2-year period at a constant amount per month beginning July 1, 2009. The entire sale is recognized for book purposes in 2011.

b.   Interest received by the company on state and municipal bonds is $3,000 in 2010 and 2011. This is not recognized as revenue for tax purposes, but is recognized for book purposes.

Instructions
Prepare the necessary calculations and make the journal entries to record income taxes for Karma Company for 2009, 2010, and 2011.

	General Journal		J1
Date	Account Title	Debit	Credit

**4.   (S.O.11) Helmkamp Company began business on January 1, 2010. The following information pertains to the Company's 2010 operations.

1.   Pretax financial income for 2010 is $128,000.
2.   The tax rate enacted for 2010 and future years is 42%.
3.   The differences between the 2010 income statement and tax return are as follows:
   a.   The company earned gross profit on construction contracts in the amount of $38,000 using the percentage-of-completion method for accounting purposes. Use of the completed-contract method for tax purposes resulted in gross profit of $10,000.
   b.   Premium for life insurance on company president used in computing pretax financial income amounted to $4,200.
   c.   Depreciation of fixed assets for accounting purposes: $57,000. Depreciation of fixed assets for tax purposes: $77,000.
   d.   Warranty expense:
Tax Return	$2,600
Accounting Records	$4,900
   e.   Received $3,800 in interest revenue on the tax exempt bonds of the city purchased early in the year.

4.   Treat the construction profit and depreciation as noncurrent and the warranty expense as current.

Instructions
a.   Compute taxable income for 2010.
b.   Compute the deferred taxes at December 31, 2011 that relate to the temporary differences described above and indicate whether each is an asset or a liability.
c.   Prepare the journal entry to record income tax expense, deferred taxes, and income taxes payable for 2010.

a.

_____

_____

_____

_____

_____

_____

_____

_____

_____

_____

_____

_____

b.

_____

_____

_____

_____

_____

_____

_____

_____

_____

_____

_____

c.

	General Journal		J1
Date	**Account Title**	**Debit**	**Credit**

SOLUTIONS TO REVIEW QUESTIONS AND EXERCISES

TRUE-FALSE

1.   (T)

2.   (F)   When the book amount of an asset or liability differs from the tax basis as a result of a temporary difference, the future tax effects on taxable income must be reported in the current financial statements.

3.   (T)

4.   (F)   Deferred tax expense is the **increase** in the deferred tax liability balance from the beginning to the end of the accounting period.

5.   (T)

6.   (T)

7.   (F)   A deferred tax asset represents the increase in taxes refundable (or saved) in future years as a result of deductible temporary differences existing at the end of the current year. A deferred tax liability represents the increase in taxes payable in future years as a result of taxable temporary differences existing at the end of the current year.

8.   (F)   This statement is false because a deferred tax asset meets the three main conditions for an item to be reported as an asset:

   (a)   It results from past transactions.
   (b)   It gives rise to a probable benefit in the future.
   (c)   The company controls access to the benefits.

9.   (T)

10.   (T)

11.   (F)   Depreciable property relates to expenses or losses that are deductible from taxable income before they are recognized in financial income.

12.   (F)   An originating temporary difference is the initial difference between the book basis and the tax basis of an asset or liability regardless of whether the tax basis of the asset or liability exceeds or is exceeded by the book basis of the asset or liability.

13.   (T)

14.   (F)   Permanent differences are items that (1) enter into pretax financial income but never into taxable income, or (2) enter into taxable income but never into pretax financial income.

15.   (T)

16.   (F)   Even if it is probable that future tax rate change will occur, if it is not yet enacted into law, the current rate should be used.

17.   (T)

18.   (F)   The tax benefits of loss carryforwards are always recognized in the current year since they represent future deductible amounts. However, if it is more likely than not that some or all of the NOL carryforward will not be realized, the deferred tax asset is reduced by a valuation account.

19.   (F)   Tax loss carryforwards are always recognized in the current year since they represent future deductible amounts. However, if it is more likely than not that some or all of the NOL carryforward will not be realized, the deferred tax asset is reduced by a valuation account.

20.   (T)

21.   (F)   Under the asset-liability approach, the one objective of accounting for income taxes is to recognize the amount of taxes payable or refundable for the current year. A second objective is to recognize deferred tax liabilities and assets for the future tax consequences of events that have been recognized in the financial statements or tax returns.

MULTIPLE CHOICE

1.   (B)   The computation of income tax payable is calculated as follows:

Revenues	$150,000
Expenses..	100,000
Taxable income for 2010.................................	50,000
Tax rate..	X 35%
Income tax payable...	$ 17,500

2.   (B)

Income...	$500,000
Tax expense..	225,000
Net income	$275,000

The tax expense is $225,000, which is reported on the income statement. Due to the temporary difference the company's tax liability is only $90,000 ($200,000 x .45). Thus, Deferred Income Taxes would be credited for $135,000 ($225,000 - $90,000) due to the temporary difference.

3.   (C)   According to GAAP a deferred tax liability meets the definition of a liability. Thus, **(a)** it results from a past transaction, **(b)** it is a present obligation, and **(c)** it represents a future sacrifice.

4.   (D)   In the journal entry, income tax expense is increased in the current period because a favorable tax benefit is not expected to be realized for a portion of the deductible temporary difference. A valuation account is simultaneously established to recognize the reduction in the carrying amount of the deferred tax asset.

5.   (D)   The only correct alternative regarding temporary differences and permanent differences is alternative D. Temporary and permanent differences occur with the same general frequency. Also, permanent differences do not change in status with the passage of time.

6.   (C)   Depreciation expense under an accelerated depreciation method will be larger in the early years of an asset's life and smaller in the later years. When compared to depreciation expense calculated under the straight-line method, the expense calculated under the accelerated method will be greater in the early years and less in the later years of an asset's useful life.

7.   (B)   Product warranty liabilities are temporary differences normally classified as expenses or losses that are deductible after they are recognized in financial income. (A) Advance rental receipts are temporary differences that are normally classified as revenues or gains that are taxable before they are recognized in financial income. (C) Depreciable property is a temporary difference that is normally classified as expenses or losses that are deductible **before** they are recognized in financial income. (D) Fines and expenses resulting from a violation of law are permanent differences that are normally recognized for financial reporting purposes but not for tax purposes.

8.   (A)   The deduction for dividends received from U.S. corporations is a permanent difference that is recognized for tax purposes but not for financial reporting purposes. (B) Interest received on state and municipal bonds and (C) compensation expense associated with certain employee stock options are permanent differences that are recognized for financial reporting purposes but not for tax purposes. (D) A litigation accrual is a temporary difference that is classified as an expense or loss that is deductible after it is recognized in financial income.

9.   (C)   An installment sale accounted for on the accrual basis for financial reporting purposes and on the installment (cash) basis for tax purposes is a temporary difference classified as a revenue or gain that is taxable after it is recognized in financial income. (A) Subscriptions received in advance and (B) a prepaid royalty received in advance are temporary differences classified as revenues or gains that are taxable **before** they are recognized in financial income. (D) Interest received on a municipal obligation is a permanent difference that is recognized for financial reporting purposes but not for tax purposes.

10.   (A)   Temporary differences are differences which exist between taxable income and accounting income. These differences originate in one period and reverse in one or more subsequent periods. Temporary differences are used to measure deferred income taxes. However, the items noted in this question are permanent differences. Permanent differences affect either accounting income or tax income, but not both, so they do not result in deferred income taxes.

11.   (D)

Books basis of unexpired insurance	$21,000
Tax basis of unexpired insurance	-0-
Cumulative temporary differences	21,000
Tax rate	45%
Deferred tax liability at end of 2010	$ 9,450

12.   (B)   Taxes due and payable are credited to Income Tax Payable; the increase in deferred taxes is credited to Deferred Tax Liability; and the sum of those two items is debited to Income Tax Expense.

13.   (A)   At the end of 2011 (the second year) the difference between the book value and the tax basis of the unexpired insurance is $14,000 ($21,000 - $7,000). This difference is multiplied by the tax rate to arrive at the deferred tax liability to be reported at the end of 2011.

Deferred tax liability at end of 2011	$ 6,300
Deferred tax liability at end of 2010	9,450
Deferred tax expense (benefit)	(3,150)
Current tax expense (income tax payable)	24,000
Income tax expense (total) for 2011	$20,850

14.   (D)   Expenses or losses that are tax deductible before they are recognized in financial income would result in future taxable amounts. Alternatives A and B are temporary differences which result in future deductible amounts. Alternative C is a permanent difference that does not result in either future taxable or deductible amounts.

15.   (C)

Books basis of unearned revenue	$80,000
Tax basis of unearned revenue	-0-
Cumulative temporary difference end of 2010	80,000
Tax rate	38%
Deferred tax asset at end of 2010	$30,400

2010 Income Tax Payable	$123,000
Deferred Tax Asset	(30,400)
Income Tax Expense - 2010	$ 92,600

16.   (B)   At the end of 2009 the difference between the book value and the tax basis of the unearned revenue is $40,000. The difference is multiplied by the tax rate to arrive at the deferred tax asset to be reported at the end of 2011.

Deferred tax asset at end of 2011	$ 15,200
Deferred tax asset at beginning of 2011	30,400
Deferred tax expense benefit	15,200
Current tax expense (liability)	136,000
Income tax expense 2011	$151,200

17.   (A)   The $1,600 difference between tax expense and tax liability is caused by the warranty expense. Because the tax liability is greater by $1,600, the amount of warranty expense charged on the tax return was smaller than the $38,000 charged against accounting income. We also know that 40% of the difference between warranty expense and the warranty payments actually made is $1,600. Thus, the total difference is $4,000 ($1,600 ÷ .40). The amount actually paid this year on the Company's warranty was $34,000 ($38,000 - $4,000).

18.   (B)

	2009	2010	2011
Tax Expense	$225	$225	$225
Tax Liability	75	150	225
Deferred Tax [(decrease)/increase]	150	75	-0-
Deferred Tax Liability	$150	$225	$225

19.   (C)   When a change in the tax rate is enacted into law, its effect on deferred income tax should be recorded immediately. The effects are reported as an adjustment to tax expense in the period of the change.

20.   (C)   At the beginning of 2009 the Deferred Tax Liability account would have had a balance of $70,000 ($200,000 X 35%). Because of the change in future tax rates, the deferred tax liability at the end of 2009 should be $75,000 computed as follows:

	2010	2011	Total
Future taxable amounts	$100,000	$100,000	$200,000
Tax rates	35%	40%	
Deferred tax liability	$ 35,000	$ 40,000	$ 75,000

Therefore in order to change the deferred tax liability balance from $70,000 to $75,000, it will have to be increased by $5,000.

21.   (B)   A company may carry the net operating loss back two years and receive refunds for income taxes paid in those years. The loss may be applied to the earliest year first and then subsequently to the second year. Any loss remaining after the two-year carryback may be carried forward up to 20 years to offset future taxable income. A company may elect the loss carryforward only, offsetting future taxable income up to 20 years.

22.   (C)   Deferred tax assets and liabilities are generally classified as current or noncurrent based on the classification of   the specific asset or liability to which it is related.

REVIEW EXERCISES

1.
1.	A	7.	D
2.	E	8.	C
3.	F	9.	A
4.	E	10.	F
5.	C	11.	E
6.	B		

2.

	2009		2010		2011	
	Acct.	**Tax**	**Acct.**	**Tax**	**Acct.**	**Tax**
Income before tax and depreciation	$80,000	$80,000	$100,000	$100,000	$75,000	$75,000
Depreciation expense	(30,000)	(45,000)	(30,000)	(30,000)	(30,000)	(15,000)
	$50,000	$35,000	$70,000	$70,000	$45,000	$60,000
Income tax	(15,000)	(10,500)	(21,000)	(21,000)	(13,500)	(18,000)
	$35,000	$24,500	$49,000	$49,000	$31,500	$42,000

2009:

Income Tax Expense	15,000	
Deferred Tax Liability		4,500
Income Taxes Payable		10,500

2010:

Income Tax Expense	21,000	
Income Taxes Payable		21,000

2011:

Income Tax Expense	13,500	
Deferred Tax Liability..	4,500	
Income Taxes Payable...		18,000

3.   Karma Company

	2009	**2010**	**2011**
Pretax financial income	$300,000	$300,000	$300,000
Permanent difference			
Unrecognized revenue		(3,000)	(3,000)
Temporary difference			
Installment sale	(36,000)	24,000	12,000
Taxable income	264,000	321,000	309,000
Tax rate	20%	20%	20%
Income tax payable	$52,800	$64,200	$61,800

December 31, 2009

Income Tax Expense ($52,800 + $7,200).............................	60,000	
Income Tax Payable ($264,000 x 20%)............................		52,800
Deferred Tax Liability ($36,000 x 20%)		7,200

December 31, 2010

Income Tax Expense ($64,200 - $4,800)	59,400	
Deferred Tax Liability ($24,000 x 20%)................................	4,800	
Income Tax Payable ($321,000 x 20%)............................		64,200

December 31, 2011

Income Tax Expense ($61,800 - 2,400)	59,400	
Deferred Tax Liability ($12,000 x 20%)................................	2,400	
Income Tax Payable ($309,000 x 20%)............................		61,800

4. a. Pretax financial income $128,000

Permanent differences:

Life insurance premium	$4,200	
Tax-exempt interest	(3,800)	400

Temporary differences:

Excess construction profits per books ($38,000 - $10,000)	(28,000)
Excess depreciation per tax ($77,000 - $57,000)	(20,000)
Excess warranty expense per books ($4,900 - $2,600)	2,300
Taxable income	$82,700

b.

Temporary Difference	Deferred Tax Asset		Deferred Tax Liability	
Construction Profit			$28,000 x 42%	= $11,760
Depreciation			20,000 x 42%	= 8,400
Warranty Expense	$2,300 x 42 % =	$966		
		$966		$20,160

c.

Income Tax Expense..	53,928	
Deferred Tax Asset (Current).................................	966	
Income Tax Payable..		34,734(a)
Deferred Tax Liability (Noncurrent)........................		20,160

(a)$82,700 x 42% = $34,734

Accounting for Pensions and Postretirement Benefits

CHAPTER STUDY OBJECTIVES

1. Distinguish between accounting for the employer's pension plan and accounting for the pension fund.

2. Identify types of pension plans and their characteristics.

3. Explain alternative measures for valuing the pension obligation.

4. List the components of pension expense.

5. Use a work sheet for employer's pension plan entries.

6. Describe the amortization of prior service costs.

7. Explain the accounting for unexpected gains and losses.

8. Explain the corridor approach to amortizing gains and losses.

9. Describe the requirements for reporting pension plans in financial statements.

*10. Identify the differences between pensions and postretirement healthcare benefits.

*11. Contrast accounting for pensions to accounting for other postretirement benefits.

CHAPTER REVIEW

1. Chapter 20 discusses the various aspects of accounting for the cost of pension plans. Accounting for pension costs is somewhat complicated because of the variety of social concepts, legal considerations, actuarial techniques, income tax regulations, and varying business philosophies that affect the development and maintenance of pension plans. This chapter relates these issues to the recommended accounting treatment for the costs associated with a pension plan.

Nature of Pension Plans

2. (S.O. 1) A **pension plan** is an arrangement whereby an employer provides benefits (payments) to employees after they retire for services they provided while they were working. In the accounting for a pension plan, consideration must be given to accounting for the employer and accounting for the pension plan itself. A pension plan is said to be **funded** when the employer sets funds aside for future pension benefits by making payments to a funding agency that is responsible for accumulating the assets of the pension fund and for making payment to the recipients as the benefits come due. In an insured plan, the funding agency is an insurance company; in a trust fund plan, the funding agency is a trustee.

Note: All asterisked (*) items relate to material contained in the Appendix to the chapter.

3.   Pension plans can be **contributory** or **noncontributory.** In a contributory plan, the employees bear part of the cost of the stated benefits or voluntarily make payments to increase their benefits. If the plan is noncontributory, the employer bears the entire cost. Because the problems associated with pension plans involve complicated actuarial considerations, actuaries are engaged to ensure that the plan is appropriate for all employee groups covered. Actuaries make predictions (actuarial assumptions) of mortality rates, employee turnover, interest and earnings rates, early retirement frequency, future salaries, and other factors necessary to operate a pension plan. Thus, accounting for defined benefit pension plans is highly reliant upon information and measurements provided by actuaries.

Types of Pension Plans

4.   (S.O. 2) The most common types of pension arrangements are **defined contribution plans** and **defined benefit plans.** In a defined contribution plan, the employer agrees to contribute a certain sum each period based on a formula. The formula might consider such factors as age, length of service, employer's profits, and compensation level. The accounting for a defined contribution plan is straightforward. The employer's responsibility is simply to make a contribution each year based on the formula established in the plan. Thus, the employer's annual cost is the amount it is obligated to contribute to the pension trust. If the contribution is made in full each year no pension asset or liability is reported on the balance sheet.

5.   A defined benefit plan defines the benefits that the employee will receive at the time of retirement. The formula that is typically used provides for the benefits to be a function of the level of compensation near retirement and of the number of years of service. The accounting for a defined benefit plan is complex. Because the benefits are defined in terms of uncertain future variables, an appropriate funding pattern must be established to insure that enough monies will be available at retirement to meet the benefits promised.

Measures of Liability

6.   (S.O. 3) Most accountants agree that an employer's **pension obligation** is the deferred compensation obligation it has to its employees for their services under the terms of the pension plan. However, there are three ways to measure this liability. One approach is to base the obligation on the **vested benefits** current employees are entitled to. The vested benefits pension obligation is computed using current salary levels and includes only vested benefits. A second approach to the measurement of the pension obligation is to base the computation on all years of service performed by employees under the plan-both vested and nonvested—using **current** salary levels. This measurement of the pension obligation is called the **accumulated benefit obligation.** A third measurement technique bases the computation on both vested and nonvested service using **future** salaries. Because future salaries are expected to be higher than current salaries, this approach, known as the **projected benefit obligation,** results in the largest measurement of the pension obligation.

7.   Regardless of the approach used, the estimated future benefits to be paid are discounted to present value. While the accumulated benefit obligation is used in certain situations, the profession generally has adopted the projected benefit obligation to measure the liability for the pension obligation.

8.   Under older accounting rules, accounting for pension plans followed a **noncapitalization approach.** Noncapitalization, often referred to as off-balance-sheet financing, was achieved because the balance sheet reported an asset or liability for the pension plan arrangement only if the amount actually funded during the year by the employer was different from the amount reported by the employer as pension expense for the year. The current rule leans toward a **capitalization approach.** Under a capitalization approach, the employer has a liability for pension benefits that it has promised to pay for employee services already performed. As pension expense is incurred--as the employees work--the employer's liability increases. The pension liability is reduced through the payment of benefits to retired

employees. The current rule represents a compromise that combines some of the features of capitalization with some of the features of noncapitalization.

Components of Pension Expense

9. (S.O. 4) There is now broad agreement that pension cost should be accounted for on the accrual basis. Accounting for pension plans requires measurement of the cost and its identification with the appropriate time periods. The determination of pension cost is very complicated because it is a function of a number of factors. These factors are identified and described below.

Service Cost. The expense caused by the increase in pension benefits payable (the projected benefit obligation) to employees because of their services rendered during the current year. Actuaries compute service cost as the present value of the new benefits earned by employees during the year.

Interest. Because a pension is a deferred compensation arrangement, it is recorded on a discounted basis. Interest expense accrues each year on the projected benefit obligation based on a selected interest rate called the **settlement rate.**

Actual Return on Plan Assets. Annual expense is adjusted for interest and dividends that accumulate within the fund as well as increases and decreases in the market value of the fund assets. Computation of the actual return on plan assets is illustrated by the following schedule:

Fair value of plan assets at end of the period		$2,500,000
Deduct: Fair value of plan assets at beginning of period		1,800,000
Increase/decrease in fair value of plan assets		700,000
Deduct: Contributions to plan during period	$275,000	
Less benefits paid during the period	120,000	155,000
Actual return on plan assets		$ 545,000

If the actual return on the plan assets is positive (gain) during the period, it is subtracted in the computation of pension expense. If the actual return is negative (loss) during the period, it is added in the computation of pension expense.

Amortization of Prior Service Cost. Because plan amendments are granted with the expectation that the employer will realize economic benefits in future periods, the cost (prior service cost) of providing these retroactive benefits is allocated to pension expense in the future, specifically to the remaining service-years of the affected employees.

Gain or Loss. Two items comprise gain or loss: (1) the difference between the actual return and the expected return on plan assets and (2) amortization of the unrecognized net gain or loss from previous periods.

The Pension Work Sheet

10. (S.O. 5) In illustrating the accounting for these factors the text material makes use of a work sheet approach. The work sheet is unique to pension accounting and is utilized to record both the formal entries and memo entries that are necessary to keep track of all the employer's relevant pension plan items and components. The format of the work sheet is as follows:

	Pension Work Sheet				
	General Journal Entries			**Memo Record**	
Items	Annual Pension Expense	Cash	Prepaid/ Accrued Cost	Projected Benefit Obligation	Plan Assets

The left-hand "General Journal Entries" columns of the work sheet record entries in the formal general ledger accounts. The right-hand "Memo Record" columns maintain balances on the unrecognized (noncapitalized) pension items. On the first line of the work sheet, the beginning balances (if any) are recorded. Subsequently, transactions and events related to the pension plan are recorded, using debits and credits and using both sets of records as if they were one for recording the entries. For each transaction or event, the debits must equal the credits. The balance in the Prepaid/Accrued Cost column should equal the net balance in the memo record. The work sheet approach to accumulating balances for pension accounting is a most effective means of keeping track of complicated computations.

2010 Entries and Work Sheet

11. To illustrate the use of a work sheet, the following facts apply to Oehler Company for the year 2010:

Plan assets, 1/1/10	$450,000
Projected benefit obligation, 1/1/10	$450,000
Annual service cost for 2010	27,000
Settlement rate for 2010	7%
Actual return on plan assets for 2010	30,000
Contributions (funding) in 2010	32,000
Benefits paid to retirees in 2010	17,000

The work sheet would be completed as follows:

	General Journal Entries			Memo Record	
Items	Annual Pension Expense	Cash	Prepaid/ Accrued Cost	Projected Benefit Obligation	Plan Assets
Balance, 1/1/10				450,000 Cr.	450,000 Dr.
(a) Service Cost	27,000 Dr.			27,000 Cr.	
(b) Interest Cost	*31,500 Dr.			31,500 Cr.	
(c) Actual Return	30,000 Cr.				30,000 Dr.
(d) Contributions		32,000 Cr.			32,000 Dr.
(e) Benefits				17,000 Dr.	17,000 Cr.
Journal Entry for 2010	28,500 Dr.	32,000 Cr.	3,500 Dr.		
Balance, 12/31/10			3,500 Dr.	491,500 Cr.	495,000 Dr.

Oehler Company (table title)

*$450,000 X .07

2011 Entries and Work Sheet

12. To illustrate the use of a work sheet with amortization of unrecognized prior service costs, the following facts continue to apply to Oehler Company for the year 2011:

Present value of prior service benefits granted 1/1/11	$42,000
Annual service cost for 2011	28,000
Settlement rate for 2011	7%
Actual return on plan assets for 2011	31,000
Contributions (funding) in 2011	29,000
Benefits paid retirees in 2011	24,000
Amortization of prior service costs	17,500

The work sheet would be completed as follows:

	General Journal Entries			Memo Record		
Oehler Company						
Items	Annual Pension Expense	Cash	Prepaid/ Accrued Cost	Projected Benefit Obligation	Plan Assets	Unrecognized Prior Service Cost
Balance, 12/31/10			3,500 Dr.	491,500 Cr.	495,000 Dr.	
(f) Prior Service Cost				42,000 Cr.		42,000 Dr.
Balance, 1/1/11			3,500 Dr.	533,500 Cr.	495,000 Dr.	42,000 Dr.
(g) Service Cost	28,000 Dr.			28,000 Cr.		
(h) Interest Cost	*37,345 Dr.			37,345 Cr.		
(i) Actual Return	31,000 Cr.				31,000 Dr.	
(j) Amortization of PSC	17,500 Dr.					17,500 Cr.
(k) Contributions		29,000 Cr.			29,000 Dr.	
(l) Benefits				24,000 Dr.	24,000 Cr.	
Journal Entry for 2011	51,845 Dr.	29,000 Cr.	22,845 Cr.			
Balance, 12/31/11			19,345 Cr.	574,845 Cr.	531,000 Dr.	24,500 Dr.

*$533,500 X .07

The pension reconciliation schedule is as follows:

Projected benefit obligation (Credit)	$(574,845)
Plan assets at fair value (Debit)	531,000
Funded status	(43,845)
Unrecognized prior service cost (Debit)	24,500
Prepaid/accrued pension cost (Credit)	$ (19,345)

Amortization of Prior Service Cost (PSC)

13. (S.O. 6) Prior Service Costs (PSC) occur when a company provides benefits to employees for years of service before the date of initiation or amendment. These costs should be initially recorded as an adjustment to other comprehensive income and then recognize the prior service cost as a component of pension expense over the remaining service lives of the employees who are expected to benefit from the change in the plan. The cost of the retroactive benefits (including any benefits provided to existing retirees) is the increase in the projected benefit obligation at the date of the amendment.

Gain or Loss

14. (S.O. 7) Because of the concern to companies that pension plans would have uncontrollable and unexpected swings in pension expense, the profession decided to reduce the volatility by using **smoothing techniques.** Asset gains (occurring when actual return is greater than expected return) and asset losses (occurring when actual return is less than expected return) are recorded in an Unrecognized Net Gain or Loss account and combined with unrecognized gains and losses accumulated in prior years. Liability gains (resulting from unexpected decreases in the liability balance) and liability losses (resulting

from unexpected increases) are deferred and combined in the same Unrecognized Net Gain or Loss account used for asset gain or losses.

15. (S.O. 8) The Unrecognized Net Gain or Loss account can continue to grow if asset gains and losses are not offset by liability gains and losses. To limit this potential growth, the FASB invented the **corridor approach** for amortizing the accumulated balance in the Unrecognized Gain or Loss account when it gets too large. The unrecognized net gain or loss account balance gets too large and must be amortized when it exceeds the arbitrarily selected FASB criterion of 10% **of the larger of the beginning balance of the projected benefit obligation or the market-related value of plan assets.** Any systematic method of amortizing the excess may be used but it cannot be less than the amount computed using straight-line amortization over the average remaining service-life of all active employees. Amortization of the excess unrecognized net gain or loss should be included as a component of pension expense only if, as of the **beginning of the year,** the unrecognized net gain or loss exceeded the corridor.

16. To illustrate the amortization of unrecognized gains and losses, assume the following information related to Scott Inc.'s pension plan:

Beginning of the Year

	2010	**2011**	**2012**
Projected Benefit Obligation	$3,600,000	$4,100,000	$4,400,000
Market-Related Asset Value	4,100,000	4,300,000	4,200,000
Unrecognized- Net Loss	-0-	900,000	800,000

If the average remaining service life of all remaining employees is 8 years, the schedule to amortize the unrecognized net loss is as follows:

Corridor Test and Gain/Loss Amortization Schedule

Year	Projected Benefit Obligation	Plan Assets	Corridor	Cumulative Unrecognized Net Loss	Minimum Amortization of Loss (Current Year)
2010	$3,600,000	$4,100,000	$410,000	$ -0-	$ -0-
2011	4,100,000	4,300,000	430,000	900,000	58,750(a)
2012	4,400,000	4,200,000	440,000	1,641,250(b)	150,156(b)

(a) $900,000 - 430,000 = $470,000; $470,000/8 = $58,750
(b) $900,000 - 58,750 + 800,000 = $1,641,250
    $1,641,250 - 440,000 = $1,201,250; $1,201,250/8 = $150,156

The loss recognized in 2010 would increase pension expense by $58,750. This amount is far less than the $900,000 that would be recognized if the corridor method was not applied. The rationale for the corridor is that gains and losses result from refinements in estimates as well as real changes in economic value and that, over time, some of these gains and losses will offset one another.

2010 Entries and Work Sheet

17. Continuing the Oehler Company illustration into 2012, the following facts apply to the pension plan:

Annual service cost for 2012	$29,000
Settlement rate is 7%; expected earnings rate is 7%	
Actual return on plan assets for 2012	28,000
Amortization of PSC in 2012	21,000
Contributions (funding) in 2012	32,000
Benefits paid to retirees in 2012	20,000
Changes in actuarial assumptions establish	
the end-of-year projected benefit obligation	640,000

The work sheet would be completed as follows:

Oehler Company

Items	General Journal Entries			Memo Record			
	Annual Pension Expense	Cash	Prepaid/ Accrued Cost	Projected Benefit Obligation	Plan Assets	Unrecognized Prior Service Cost	Unrecognized Net Gain or Loss
Balance, 12/31/11			19,345 Cr.	574,845 Cr.	531,000 Dr.	24,500 Dr.	
(m) Service Cost	29,000 Dr.			29,000 Cr.			
(n) Interest Cost	40,239 Dr.			40,239 Cr.			
(o) Actual Return	28,000 Cr.				28,000 Dr.		
(p) Unexpected loss	*9,170 Cr.						9,170 Dr.
(q) Amortization of PSC	21,000 Dr.					21,000 Cr.	
(r) Contributions		32,000 Cr.			32,000 Dr.		
(s) Benefits				20,000 Dr.	20,000 Cr.		
(t) Liability increase				**15,916 Cr.			15,916 Dr.
Journal Entry for 2012	53,069 Dr.	32,000 Cr.	21,069 Cr.				
Balance, 12/31/12			40,414 Cr.	640,000 Cr.	571,000 Dr.	3,500 Dr.	25,086 Dr.

*($531,000 X .07) - $28,000 = $9,170
**$574,845 + $29,000 + $40,239 - $20,000 = $624,084
  $640,000 - $624,084 = $15,916

The pension reconciliation schedule is as follows:

Projected benefit obligation (Credit)	$(640,000)
Plan assets at fair value (Debit)	571,000
Funded status	(69,000)
Unrecognized prior service cost (Debit)	3,500
Unrecognized net loss (Debit)	25,086
Prepaid/accrued pension cost (Credit)	$ (40,414)

Financial Statement Disclosure

18. (S.O. 9) If the amount paid (credit to Cash) by the employer to the pension trust is less than the annual provision (debit to Pension Expense), a credit balance accrual in the amount of the difference arises. This accrued pension cost usually appears in the long-term liability section and should be titled Accrued Pension Cost, Liability for Pension Expense Not Funded, or Due to Pension Fund. Classification as a current liability occurs when the liability requires the disbursement of cash within the next year. When the cash paid to the pension trust during the period is greater than the amount charged to expense, a deferred charge equal to the difference arises. This deferral should be reported as Prepaid Pension Cost, Deferred Pension Expense, or Prepaid Pension Expense in the current assets section if it is current in nature and in the other assets section if it is long-term in nature.

19. The current financial statement disclosure requirements for pension plans are as follows:

   a. A schedule showing all the major components of pension expense.
   b. A reconciliation showing how the projected benefit obligation and the fair value of the plan assets changed from the beginning to the end of the period.
   c. The funded status of the plan (difference between the projected benefit obligation and fair value of the plan assets) and the amounts recognized and not recognized in the financial statements.
   d. A disclosure of the rates used in measuring the benefit amounts (discount rate, expected return on plant assets, rate of compensation).

   In addition, disclosure of the reconciling schedule of the off-balance sheet assets, liabilities and unrecognized gains and losses with the on-balance sheet asset or liability should be provided.

Pension Reform Act

20. The **Pension Reform Act of 1974** (ERISA) set out specific requirements for companies providing a pension plan for their employees. These requirements are designed to safeguard employees' pension rights, specifically in the areas of funding, participation, and vesting. The Act also created the **Pension Benefit Guaranty Corporation** (PBGC) to administer terminated plans and to impose liens on the corporate assets for certain unfunded pension liabilities.

Pension Terminations

21. **ERISA** prevents companies from recapturing excess assets (pension plan assets in excess of projected benefit obligations) unless they pay participants what is owed to them and then terminate the plan. The accounting issue that arises from these terminations is whether a gain should be recognized by the corporation when these assets revert back to the company. Up to this point the profession has required that these gains be reported if the companies switched from a defined benefit plan to a defined contribution plan. Otherwise, the gain is deferred and amortized over at least 10 years in the future.

Post-Retirement Benefits

*22. (S.O. 10) Health care and other **postretirement benefits** (other than pensions) for current and future retirees and their dependents are forms of deferred compensation earned through employee service and subject to accrual during the years an employee is working. The period of time over which the postretirement benefit is accrued, called the **attribution period,** is the period of service during which the employee earns the benefits under the terms of the plan. The attribution period generally begins when an employee is hired and ends on the date the employee is eligible to receive the benefits and ceases to earn additional benefits by performing service, called the vesting date.

*23. Employers are required to account for post retirement benefits other than pensions on an accrual basis. Like pension accounting, the accrual basis necessitates measurement of the employer's obligation to provide future benefits and accrual of the cost during the years that the employee provides service.

*24. (S.O. 11) **Appendix 20-A** provides an example using a worksheet in accounting for a postretirement benefits plan.

GLOSSARY

Accumulated benefit obligation.	The employer's pension obligation that is computed using the deferred compensation amount on all years of service performed by employees under the plan--both vested and nonvested--using current salary levels.
*Accumulated Postretirement Benefit Obligation (APBO).	The actuarial present value of future benefits attributed to employees' services rendered to a particular date.
Actual return on plan assets.	The return earned by the accumulated pension fund assets in a particular year. The return can be from interest, dividends, and realized and unrealized changes in the fair market value of the plan assets.
Actuaries.	Individuals who are trained through a long and rigorous certification program to assign probabilities to future events and their financial effects.
Amortization of unrecognized prior service cost.	Recognition of the cost of pension plan amendments that provide for an increase in benefits for employee service provided in prior years.
Attribution period.	The period of service during which the employee earns postretirement benefits under the terms of the plan.
Capitalization approach.	The approach for recording pension plans that represents the economic substance of the pension plan arrangement over its legal form.
Contributory pension plan.	A pension plan where the employees bear part of the cost of the stated benefits or voluntarily make payments to increase their benefits.
Corridor approach.	An approach used to limit the growth in the Unrecognized Net Gain or Loss account by amortizing the accumulated balance in the account when it gets too large.
Defined benefit plan.	A pension plan which defines the benefits that the employee will receive at the time of retirement.

Defined contribution plan.
A pension plan where the employer agrees to contribute to a pension trust a certain sum each period based on a formula.

Employer's pension obligation.
The deferred compensation obligation the employer has to its employees for their service under the terms of the pension plan.

*Expected Postretirement Benefit Obligation (EPBO).
The actuarial present value as of a particular date of all benefits expected to be paid after retirement to employees and their dependents.

Funded pension plan.
A pension plan where the employer (company) sets funds aside for future pension benefits by making payments to a funding agency that is responsible for accumulating the assets of the pension fund and for making payments to the recipients as the benefits become due.

Interest on the liability.
The interest expense which accrues each year on the projected benefit obligation.

Multiemployer pension plans.
Pension plans sponsored by two or more different employers.

Noncapitalization approach.
The approach for recording pension plans off the balance sheet.

Noncontributory pension plan.
A pension plan where the employer bears the entire cost.

Pension Benefit Guaranty Corporation.
A corporation created by ERISA who's purpose is to administer terminated pension plans and impose liens on the employer's assets for certain unfunded pension liabilities.

Pension plan.
An arrangement whereby an employer provides benefits (payments) to employees after they retire for services they provided while employed.

Pension plan gain or loss.
The difference between the actual return and the expected return on plan assets and amortization of the unrecognized net gain or loss from previous periods.

Projected benefit obligation.
The employer's pension obligation that is computed using the deferred compensation amount on all years of service performed by employees under the plan—both vested and nonvested—using future salaries.

Qualified pension plan.
A pension plan in accordance with federal income tax requirements that permits deductibility of the employer's contributions to the pension fund and tax-free status of earnings from pension fund assets.

Service cost.
The expense caused by the increase in pension benefits payable (the projected benefit obligation) to employees because of their services rendered during the current year.

Vested benefits.   Benefits that the employee is entitled to receive even if the employee renders no additional services under the plan.

Vested benefit obligation.   The employer's pension obligation that is computed using current salary levels and includes only vested benefits.

CHAPTER OUTLINE

Fill in the outline presented below.

(S.O. 1) Nature of Pension Plans

Contributory Plan

Noncontributory Plan

Qualified Pension Plan

(S.O. 2) Types of Pension Plans

Defined Contribution Plan

Defined Benefit Plan

(S.O. 3) Measures of Pension Obligation (Liability)

Vested Benefit Obligation

Chapter Outline *(continued)*

      Accumulated Benefit Obligation

      Projected Benefit Obligation

      Capitalization vs. Noncapitalization

(S.O. 4) Components of Pension Expense

      Service Cost

      Interest on the Liability

      Actual Return on Plan Assets

(S.O. 6) Amortization of Unrecognized Prior Service Cost

(S.O. 7) Gain or Loss

(S.O. 8) Corridor Amortization

(S.O. 9) Reporting Pension Plans in Financial Statements

      The Pension Reform Act of 1974

Chapter Outline *(continued)*

Multiemployer Plans

Pension Terminations

*(S.O. 10) Accounting for Postretirement Benefits

REVIEW QUESTIONS AND EXERCISES

TRUE-FALSE

Indicate whether each of the following is true (T) or false (F) in the space provided.

_____ 1. (S.O. 1) When a pension plan is funded, the company sets aside funds for future pension benefits by making payments to a funding agency that is responsible for accumulating the assets of the pension fund.

_____ 2. (S.O. 1) A noncontributory pension plan and defined contribution plan refer to the same type of plan.

_____ 3. (S.O. 2) Measuring the amount of pension obligation resulting from a pension plan is a problem involving actuarial consideration.

_____ 4. (S.O. 2) The accounting for defined benefit pension plans is highly reliant upon information and measurements provided by actuaries.

_____ 5. (S.O. 3) Vested benefits are those that the employee is entitled to receive even if the employee renders no additional services under the plan.

_____ 6. (S.O. 3) Once the actuary has computed the amount of money it will take to pay for all retirement benefits for both active and retired employees, a company is best advised to fund this obligation immediately.

_____ 7. (S.O. 3) The difference between the vested benefit obligation and the accumulated benefit obligation concerns the use of current salaries versus future salaries in the measurement process.

_____ 8. (S.O. 3) Assuming salary increases for employees covered by a pension plan, the accumulated benefit obligation will be greater than the projected benefit obligation.

_____ 9. (S.O. 3) In accounting for pension plans, the accounting profession has taken the noncapitalization approach, often referred to as "off-balance-sheet" financing.

_____ 10. (S.O. 4) The projected benefit obligation provides a more realistic measure on a going concern basis of the employer's obligation under the plan and, therefore, should be used as the basis for determining service cost.

_____ 11. (S.O. 4) The service cost component of a pension plan recognized in a period should be determined as the actuarial present value of benefits attributed by the pension benefit formula to employee services during that period.

_____ 12. (S.O. 4) When considering the interest rate component used in the determination of pension cost the FASB concluded that the rate selected should reflect conservatism.

_____ 13. (S.O. 4) The interest rate used to compute the projected benefit obligation should also be used as the rate of return on plan assets.

_____ 14. (S.O. 4) Interest on the liability (or interest expense) is the interest for the period on the projected benefit obligation outstanding during the period.

_____ 15. (S.O. 4) Actual return on plan assets increases pension expense (assuming the actual return is positive).

_____ 16. (S.O. 4) The employer is required to disclose in notes to the financial statements the projected benefit obligation, pension plan assets, unrecognized prior service costs and unrecognized net gain or loss.

_____ 17. (S.O. 6) When a defined benefit pension plan is amended, the expense and related liability for the prior service costs should be fully reported in the year in which the amendment was adopted.

_____ 18. (S.O. 7) The market-related asset value of pension plan assets is a calculated value that recognizes changes in fair value in a systematic and rational manner over not more than 5 years.

_____ 19. (S.O. 8) Under the corridor approach, the unrecognized net gain or loss balance is considered too large and must be amortized when it exceeds 20% of the larger of the ending balances of the accumulated benefit obligation or the market-related value of the plan assets.

_____ 20. (S.O. 9) In pension accounting, an entity is required to recognize a liability when the accumulated benefit obligation exceeds the fair value of plan assets and recognize an asset if the fair value of pension plan assets exceeds the accumulated benefit obligation.

_____ 21. (S.O. 9) If the cash paid to the pension trust fund during a period is greater than the amount charged to expense, a loss on pension plan funding is shown on the statement of income.

_____ 22. (S.O. 9) An employer is required to present a reconciliation showing how the projected benefit obligation and the fair value of the plan assets changed from the beginning to the end of the period.

_____ 23. (S.O. 9) The Pension Benefit Guaranty Corporation's purpose is to administer terminated plans and to impose liens on the employer's assets for certain unfunded pension liabilities.

_____ *24. (S.O. 10) Health care and other postretirement benefits for current and future retirees and their dependents are forms of deferred compensation earned through employee service and subject to accrual during the years an employee is working.

_____ *25. (S.O. 10) The Expected Postretirement Benefit Obligation (EPBO) is the actuarial present value of the future benefits attributed to employees' services rendered to a particular date.

MULTIPLE CHOICE

Select the best answer for each of the following items and place the corresponding letter in the space provided.

_____ 1. (S.O. 1) The difference between a contributory pension plan and a noncontributory pension plan is:

    A. contributory plans tend to be fully funded, whereas noncontributory plans are based on "pay-as-you-go" funding.

    B. in contributory plans employees bear part of the cost of stated benefits or voluntarily make payments to the plan, whereas the costs of noncontributory plans are borne by the employer.

    C. noncontributory plans are dependent upon a company's ability to consistently earn a net income for pension payments, whereas contributory plans are not dependent upon operating results.

    D. in a contributory plan contributions are made, but in a noncontributory plan no contributions are made.

_____ 2. (S.O. 1) When an employer sets funds aside for future pension benefits by making payments to a funding agency that is responsible for accumulating the assets of the pension fund and for making payments to the recipients as the benefits become due, the pension plan is said to be:

    A. insured.
    B. qualified.
    C. risk free.
    D. funded.

_____ 3. (S.O. 2) Which of the following is **not** a characteristic of a defined contribution pension plan?

    A. The employer's contribution each period is based on a formula.
    B. The benefits to be received by employees are defined by the terms of the plan.
    C. The accounting for a defined contribution plan is straightforward and uncomplicated.
    D. The benefit of gain or the risk of loss from the assets contributed to the pension fund are borne by the employee.

_____ 4. (S.O. 2) In accounting for a defined benefit pension plan:

     A.   an appropriate funding pattern must be established to insure that enough monies will be available at retirement to meet the benefits promised.

     B.   the employer's responsibility is simply to make a contribution each year based on the formula established in the plan.

     C.   the expense recognized each period is equal to the cash contribution.

     D.   the liability is determined based upon known variables that reflect future salary levels promised to employees.

_____ 5. (S.O. 2) The use of a formula in developing the parameters of a pension fund is used when the plan is a

	Defined Benefit Plan	Defined Contribution Plan
A.	Yes	No
B.	No	Yes
C.	Yes	Yes
D.	No	No

_____ 6. (S.O. 3) The present value of the pension plan benefits that will have to be paid to both active and retired employees covered by a pension plan is dependent on all of the following factors **except**:

     A.   the benefit provisions of the plan.

     B.   characteristics of the employee group.

     C.   actuarial assumptions.

     D.   the income level of the entity setting up the plan.

_____ 7. (S.O. 3) Alternative methods exist for the measurement of the pension obligation (liability). Which measure requires the use of future salaries in its computation?

     A.   Vested benefit obligation.

     B.   Accumulated benefit obligation.

     C.   Projected benefit obligation.

     D.   Restructured benefit obligation.

_____ 8. (S.O. 3) Pension cost should be accounted for on the:

     A.   cash basis of accounting, recognizing the amount paid as the pension expense for the period.

     B.   accrual basis, in a manner similar to other costs and expenses.

     C.   current value basis, because employees need to be aware of the value of the retirement benefits they will receive.

     D.   prospective basis, because even though the expense is a current period item, the benefits and the related liability belong to future periods.

_____ 9. (S.O. 4) Which of the following is **not** a factor considered in the determination of pension cost?

     A.   Service cost.

     B.   Interest.

     C.   Prior service cost.

     D.   Inflation.

_____ 10. (S.O. 4) Of the following components of pension expense, which is most likely to result in a decrease in pension expense?

   A.   Actual return on plan assets.
   B.   Amortization of unrecognized prior service cost.
   C.   Interest on the liability.
   D.   Service cost.

_____ 11. (S.O. 4) Malikowski Company had the fair value of its plan assets increase by $620,000 during 2010. During 2010 Malikowski Company contributed $280,000 to the pension plan and had benefits of $167,000 paid to retired employees. Based on these facts, the actual return on plan assets for Malikowski Company during 2010 is:
   A. $620,000
   B. $507,000
   C. $340,000
   D. $173,000

_____ 12. (S.O. 5) If the pension expense for a pension plan for a particular year amounts to $14,000 and the amount funded amounts to $11,000 for the same year, Prepaid/Accrued Pension Cost account would be:

   A.   unaffected.
   B.   debited for $3,000.
   C.   credited for $3,000.
   D.   either debited or credited, but the amount cannot be determined from the data given.

Use the following information for questions 13 and 14.

On January 1, 2010, Sanders Co. has the following balances:

Projected benefit obligation	$1,400,000
Fair value of plan assets	1,200,000

The settlement rate is 10%. Other data related to the pension plan for 2010 are:

Service cost	$120,000
Amortization of unrecognized prior service costs	40,000
Contributions	200,000
Benefits paid	70,000
Actual return on plan assets	158,000
Amortization of unrecognized net gain	12,000

_____ 13. (S.O. 5) The balance of the projected benefit obligation at December 31, 2010 is:

   A. $1,558,000
   B. $1,570,000
   C. $1,590,000
   D. $1,790,000

_____   14.   (S.O. 5) The fair value of plan assets at December 31, 2010 is:

     A. $1,476,000
     B. $1,488,000
     C. $1,500,000
     D. $1,620,000

_____   15.   (S.O. 6) Presented below is pension information related to Durkin, Inc. for the year 2010:

Actual return on plan assets	$ 8,000
Interest on vested benefits	5,000
Service cost	10,000
Interest on projected benefit obligation	7,000
Amortization of prior service cost due to increase in benefits	6,000

The amount of pension expense to be reported for 2010 is

     A. $15,000
     B. $20,000
     C. $23,000
     D. $31,000

_____   16.   (S.O. 6) When a defined benefit plan is amended and credit is given to employees for years of service provided before the date of amendment:

     A.   both the accumulated benefit obligation and the projected benefit obligation are usually greater than before.
     B.   both the accumulated benefit obligation and the projected benefit obligation are usually less than before.
     C.   the expense and the liability should be recognized at the time of the plan change.
     D.   the expense should be recognized immediately, but the liability may be deferred until a reasonable basis for its determination has been identified.

_____   17.   (S.O. 7) The unexpected gains or losses that result from changes in the projected benefit obligation are called:

	Asset Gains & Losses	Liability Gains & Losses
A.	Yes	Yes
B.	No	No
C.	Yes	No
D.	No	Yes

_____ 18. (S.O. 8) McDonough, Inc. received the following information from its pension plan trustee concerning the operation of the company's defined benefit pension plan for the year ended December 31, 2010.

	1/1/10	12/31/10
Market-related asset value	$5,000,000	$5,750,000
Projected benefit obligation	9,500,000	9,800,000
Accumulated benefit obligation	2,000,000	2,300,000
Unrecognized net (gains) and losses	-0-	200,000

The service cost component of pension expense for 2010 is $700,000 and the amortization unrecognized prior service cost is $150,000. The settlement rate is 10% and the expected rate of return is 8%. What is the amount of pension expense for 2010?

A. $1,200,000
B. $1,340,000
C. $1,400,000
D. $1,430,000

_____ 19. (S.O. 8) The following information relates to the De Maet Company's pension plan:

Projected benefit obligation	$870,000
Plan assets	920,000
Cumulative unrecognized net loss	320,000
Average remaining service life of all active employees	5 years

Based on the above information, and use of the corridor test, what is the minimum amortization of the loss for the current period?

A. $ 45,600
B. $ 46,600
C. $228,000
D. $233,000

_____ 20. (S.O. 9) The financial statement disclosures related to a pension plan should include:

	Fair Value of the Plan Assets	Rates used in Measuring Benefit Amounts	Projected Benefit Obligation
A.	Yes	Yes	No
B.	Yes	Yes	Yes
C.	No	No	No
D.	No	Yes	Yes

_____ 21. (S.O. 9) Which of the following is **not** one of the provisions of The Employee Retirement Income Security Act of 1974 (ERISA)?

A. Plan administrators are required to publish a comprehensive description and summary of their plans and detailed annual reports accompanied by supplementary schedules and statements.

B. An employer must fund the pension plan in accordance with an actuarial funding method that over time will be sufficient to pay for all pension obligations.

C. The Pension Benefit Guarantee Corporation, established by ERISA, can impose a lien against an employer's assets for up to 80% of corporate net worth when the present value of guaranteed vested benefits exceeds the pension fund assets.

D. Required reports, statements, and supplementary schedules pertaining to the pension plan must be subjected to audit by independent public accountants.

_____ *22. (S.O. 11) The following facts relate to the Muno Co. postretirement benefits plan for 2010:

Service cost	$ 45,000
Discount rate	10%
APBO, 1/1/10	350,000
EPBO, 1/1/10	500,000
Benefit payments to employees	34,000

The amount of postretirement expense for 2010 is:
A. $74,000
B. $80,000
C. $84,000
D. $90,000

REVIEW EXERCISES

1. Listed below on the left are a number of terms related to pension accounting. Match the terms on the left with the appropriate definitions on the right.

A. Defined benefit plan.
B. Funded pension plan.
C. Corridor approach.
D. Projected benefit obligation.
E. Defined contribution plan.
F. Prior service cost.
G. Qualified pension plan.
H. Liability gains and losses.
I. Service cost.
J. Accumulated benefit obligation.

_____ 1. Unexpected changes in the projected benefit obligation.

_____ 2. Computation of the deferred compensation amount based on both vested and nonvested service using future salaries.

_____ 3. This arises when a defined benefit plan is amended and credit is given to employees for services provided before the amendment.

_____ 4. The employer sets funds aside for future pension benefits by making payments to an agency such as a financial institution.

_____ 5. Present value of benefits accrued to date based on current salary levels.

_____ 6. In this plan it is necessary to determine what the contribution should be today to meet the pension benefit commitments that will arise at retirement.

_____ 7. Portion of the cost of a pension plan based on the work an employee provides to the employer.

_____ 8. Determines the amount in the Unrecognized Gain or Loss account that should be amortized.

_____ 9. The employer agrees to contribute a certain sum to the plan each period based on a formula.

_____ 10. A pension plan designed in accord with federal income tax requirements that permits deductibility of the employer's contributions to the pension fund and tax-free status of the earnings of the pension fund assets.

2.   (S.O. 5) On January 1, 2010, Leo Company started a defined benefit pension plan. Data related to the pension plan is presented below.

Plan assets, 1/1/10	$150,000
Projected benefit obligation, 1/1/10	150,000
Annual service cost, 2010	17,000
Settlement rate, 2010	12%
Actual return on plan assets, 2010	15,000
Employer's contribution, 2010	16,000
Benefits paid to retirees, 2010	10,000

Instructions:
Based upon the information presented above prepare a pension work sheet for Leo Company for 2010, and record the journal entry to formally recognize pension expense for 2010.

Leo Company
Pension Worksheet --2010

	General Journal Entries			Memo Record	
Items	Annual Pension Expense	Cash	Prepaid/ Accrued Cost	Projected Benefit Obligation	Plan Assets

General Journal			J1
Date	Account Title	Debit	Credit

3.   (S.0.6) Larsen Company has a defined benefit pension plan which covers 220 employees. Based upon negotiations with the employees, Larsen Company amends its pension plan as of 1/l/10 and grants $111,600 of prior service cost to its employees. The following schedule reflects employee groups based on expected years of retirement.

Group	Number of Employees	Expected Retirement on 12/31
A	30	2010
B	40	2011
C	35	2012
D	70	2013
E	45	2014
	220	

Instructions:

Compute the annual amortization of the prior service cost using the
a.   years-of-service method, and
b.   straight-line amortization over the average remaining service life of employees.

a.   Computation of Service Years

Year	A	B	C	D	E	TOTAL
2010						
2011						
2012						
2013						
2014						

Computation of Annual Prior Service Cost Amortization

Year	Total Service-Years	Cost Per Service Year	Annual Amortization
2010			
2011			
2012			
2013			
2014			

b.

4.   (S.O. 5 and 6) On January 1, 2010 Bengston Company amended its pension plan to provide greater benefits to its employees. The amendment to the plan resulted in prior service costs with a present value of $90,000. Also, the following facts relate to the pension plan for 2010

Projected benefit obligation, 12/31/09	$175,000
Plan assets, 12/31/09	171,000
Prior service cost, 1/1/10	90,000
Annual service cost, 2010	18,000
Settlement rate, 2010	12%
Actual return on plan assets	18,500
Employer's contribution, 2010	42,000
Benefits paid to retirees, 2010	12,000
Balance in prepaid/accrued pension cost, 12/31/09	4,000Cr
Amortization of prior service cost using	
the years-of-service method	23,800

Instructions:

a.   Based upon the information presented above prepare a pension worksheet for Bengston Company for 2010.

b.   Record the journal entry to formally recognize the pension expense for 2010.

c.   Prepare the reconciliation schedule to reconcile the 2010 ending balance of prepaid/accrued pension cost.

Bengston Company
Pension Work Sheet - 2010

	General Journal Entries			Memo Record		
Items	Annual Pension Expense	Cash	Prepaid/ Accrued Cost	Projected Benefit Obligation	Plan Assets	Unrecognized Prior Service Cost

b.

General Journal			J1
Date	Account Title	Debit	Credit

c.

_____
_____
_____
_____
_____
_____
_____

5.   (S.O. 4 and 6) Solkey Company sponsors a defined benefit pension plan. The following information related to the pension plan is provided by the firm's actuary.

	1/1/10	**12/31/10**
Vested Benefit Obligation	$3,600	$4,200
Accumulated Benefit Obligation	4,300	5,650
Projected Benefit Obligation	5,800	6,860
Plan Assets (Fair Value)	3,500	4,600
Settlement Rate and Expected Rate of Return		10%
Prepaid/(Accrued) Pension Cost	600Cr	?
Unrecognized Prior Service Cost	1,700	1,530
Service Cost - 2010		1,200
Contributions - 2010		1,500
Benefits Paid - 2010		800

Average remaining service life per employee is 10 years.

Instructions:

a.   Compute the actual return on plan assets in 2010.
b.   Compute the unrecognized net gain or loss as of December 31, 2010 (assuming the January 1, 2010 balance was zero).
c.   Compute the amount of unrecognized net gain or loss amortization for 2011 (corridor approach).
d.   Compute the amount of prior service cost amortization for 2010.
e.   Compute pension expense for 2010.
f.   Compute the minimum liability to be reported at December 31, 2010.
g.   Prepare a schedule reconciling the plan's funded status with the amounts reported in the December 31, 2010 balance sheet.

a.

_____

_____

_____

_____

_____

_____

b.

_____

_____

_____

_____

_____

_____

_____

_____

_____

c.

d.

e.

f.

g.

SOLUTIONS TO REVIEW QUESTIONS AND EXERCISES

TRUE-FALSE

1.   (T)

2.   (F)   A noncontributory pension plan is a plan wherein the employer bears the entire cost. This is different from contributory plans where the employees bear part of the cost of the stated benefits or voluntarily make payments to increase their benefits. Under a defined contribution plan, the employer agrees to contribute to a pension trust a certain sum each period based on a formula; however, often times employees are also allowed to contribute.

3.   (T)

4.   (T)

5.   (T)

6.   (F)   Funding the pension plan obligation immediately is not a wise decision. First, most companies would not find immediate funding an efficient use of their liquid resources. Secondly, the IRS has established certain minimum and maximum amounts that can be taken as tax deductions in any given year. If a company were to fund the plan immediately, a substantial portion of this deduction would usually be lost.

7.   (F)   The major difference between the vested benefit obligation and the accumulated benefit obligation is that the accumulated benefit obligation includes benefits for vested and nonvested employees at current salaries, whereas, the vested benefit obligation includes benefits for only vested employees at current salaries.

8.   (F)   The accumulated benefit obligation does not consider future compensation levels as does the projected benefit obligation. Thus, if salaries are assumed to increase as a result of raises, the projected benefit obligation will yield the greater liability as it is based on the larger amount.

9.   (F)   Under the old rules, accounting for pension plans followed a noncapitalization approach. Under the current rules, however, the profession has adopted an approach that leans toward capitalization.

10.   (T)

11.   (T)

12.   (F)   The Board requires companies to select their assumptions regarding the interest rate in an explicit fashion. That is, the interest rate assumption used should represent the best estimate of the plan's expert experience solely with respect to interest rates. The rates should reflect current market conditions.

13.   (F)   The interest rate used to compute the projected benefit obligation need not be used as the rate of return on plan assets.

14. (T)

15. (F) Actual return on plan assets reduces pension expense (assuming the actual return is positive).

16. (T)

17. (F) The FASB has taken the position that no expense and, in some cases, no liability should be recognized at the time of the plan change. Its rationale is that the employer would not provide credit for past years of service unless it expected to receive benefits in the future. The retroactive benefits should not be recognized as pension expense entirely in the year of amendment but should be recognized during the service periods of those employees who are expected to receive benefits under the plan.

18. (T)

19. (F) Under the corridor approach, the unrecognized net gain or loss balance is considered too large and must be amortized when it exceeds **10%** of the larger of the **beginning** balances of the **projected** benefit obligation or the market-related value of the plan assets.

20. (F) Recognition of the liability is required. However, based solely on conservatism, the FASB does not permit the recognition of an asset when the fair value of the pension plan assets exceed the accumulated benefit obligation.

21. (F) When the cash paid exceeds the amount charged to expense, a deferred charge equal to the difference is recorded. This deferral should be reported in the current asset section of the balance sheet if it is current in nature and in the other assets section if it is long-term in nature.

22. (T)

23. (T)

*24. (T)

*25. (F) The Expected Postretirement Benefit Obligation (EPBO) is the actuarial present value as of a particular date of all benefits expected to be paid after retirements to employees and their dependents.

MULTIPLE CHOICE

1. (B) In a contributory pension plan, the employees bear part of the cost of the benefits or make voluntary contributions. In a noncontributory plan, the employer bears the entire cost.

2. (D) When funds are set aside by an employer to accomplish the objectives of a pension plan, the plan is said to be funded. An insured plan is one that has an insurance company as the funding agency. A qualified pension plan is one that is designed in accordance with federal income tax requirements. There is no formal concept known as a risk free pension plan.

3. (B) If the benefits that the employee will receive are defined by the plan, then it is a defined benefit plan rather than a defined contribution plan. The characteristics described in alternatives A, C, and D are representative of a defined contribution plan.

4. (A) The accounting for a defined benefit plan is complex. Because the benefits are defined in terms of uncertain future variables, an appropriate funding pattern must be established to insure that enough monies will be available at retirement to meet the benefits promised.

5. (C) In a defined contribution plan, the employer agrees to contribute to a pension trust a certain sum each period based on a formula. This formula considers such things as age, length of employee service, employer's profits, and compensation level. A defined benefit plan defines the benefits that the employee will receive at the time of retirement. A formula is typically used to provide for the benefits which basically are a function of the employee's years of service and an employee's compensation level when he or she nears retirement.

6. (D) The present value of pension plan benefits is not affected by the income of the entity setting up the plan. These benefits are, however, dependent upon the benefit provisions, the employee group covered, and the actuarial assumptions employed.

7. (C) As its name implies, the projected benefit obligation bases the computation of the deferred compensation amount on both vested and nonvested services using future salaries. Vested benefit obligation and accumulated benefit obligation use current salary levels in computing the deferred compensation amount. There is no such concept as the restructured benefit obligation.

8. (B) Pension cost should be accounted for on the accrual basis. Most accountants recognize that accounting for pension plans requires measurement of the cost and its identification with the appropriate time periods, which involves application of accrual, deferral, and estimation concepts in the same manner that they are applied in the measurement and the time-period identification of other costs and expenses.

9. (D) Inflation is not a component used in determining pension cost. One could argue that inflation does in fact have an impact on the other factors that go into the determination of pension cost, but it is not in and of itself a primary factor. The determination of pension cost is a function of (1) service cost, (2) interest, (3) return on plan assets, (4) prior service cost, and (5) gains and losses.

10. (A)   The actual return on plan assets (assuming the return is positive) serves to decrease pension expense as the return represents an amount earned on the investment of plan assets. This return is the increase in pension funds from interest, dividends, and realized and unrealized changes in the fair market value of the plan assets. It generally follows that such return should decrease the pension expense.

11. (B)   The actual return on plan assets for Malikowski Company would be computed as follows:

Increase in fair value of plan assets		$620,000
Deduct: Contributions to plan	$280,000	
Less benefits paid	167,000	113,000
Actual return on plan assets		$507,000

12. (C)   The $3,000 difference between the pension expense and the funded amount (cash credit) represents a liability because of the underfunding. The journal entry would be:

Pension Expense	14,000	
Cash		11,000
Prepaid/Accrued Pension Cost		3,000

13. (C)   The balance of the projected benefit obligation at December 31, 2010 is calculated as follows:

Projected benefit obligation, 1/1/10	$1,400,000
Service cost	120,000
Interest cost ($1,400,000 x 10%)	140,000
Benefits	(70,000)
Projected benefit obligation, 12/31/10	$1,590,000

14. (B)   The fair value of plan assets at December 31, 2010 is calculated as follows:

Fair value of plan assets, 1/1/10	$1,200,000
Actual return on plan assets	158,000
Contributions	200,000
Benefits	(70,000)
Fair value of plan assets, 12/31/10	$1,488,000

15. (A)   The amount of pension expense to be reported for 2010 should be calculated as follows:

Service cost	$10,000
Interest on projected benefit obligation	7,000
Amortization of prior service cost due to increase in benefits	6,000
Actual return on plan assets	(8,000)
Pension expense	$15,000

16. (A)   When a plan is amended both the accumulated benefit obligation and the projected benefit obligation are usually greater because employees have been given more benefits. With respect to the expense and liability, the FASB has taken the position that no expense and in some cases no liability should be recognized at the time of the plan change. Its rationale is that the employer would not provide credit for past years of service unless it expected to receive benefits in the future.

17. (D)   Asset gains and losses occur when the expected return on plan assets differs from the actual return on plan assets. Asset gains occur when the actual return exceeds the expected return. Asset losses occur when the expected return exceeds the actual return. The unexpected gains and losses resulting from changes in the projected benefit obligation are called liability gains and losses. Liability gains result from unexpected decreases in the liability balance, and liability losses result from unexpected increases.

18. (C)   The pension expense for 2010 would be computed as follows:

Service cost	$ 700,000
Interest cost ($9,500,000 x 10%)	950,000
*Expected return ($5,000,000 x 8%)	(400,000)
Amortization of unrecognized prior service cost	150,000
Pension expense	$1,400,000

*The actual entries the company would have to make would include a debit or credit to the account Actual Return and then an adjusting entry of an Unexpected Gain or Loss to result in the net of expected return.

Also, the company needs to be concerned with amortizing any of the balance in Unrecognized Net Gain or Loss. If the balance in Unrecognized Net Gain or Loss exceeds 10% of the larger of the beginning-of-the-year projected benefit obligation or the plan asset's market-related asset value, then the excess should be amortized in some systematic manner. In this case, however, 10% of the larger of the beginning-of-the-year projected benefit or the plan asset's market-related asset value is $950,000 ($9,500,000 x 10%), which is greater than the 0 beginning balance in Unrecognized Net Gain or Loss.

19. (A)   The computation requires the calculation of the corridor amount which is 10% of the greater of the projected benefit obligation or the plan assets. This amount is subtracted from the cumulative unrecognized net loss and the resulting amount is divided by the average remaining service life of all active employees. The computation is as follows:

$320,000 - $92,000 = $228,000; $228,000/5 = $45,600

20.   (B)   The current financial statement disclosure requirements for pension plans are as follows:

    a.   A schedule showing all the major components of pension expense.

    b.   A reconciliation showing how the projected benefit obligation and the fair value of the plan assets changed from the beginning to the end of the period.

    c.   The funded status of the plan (difference between the projected benefit obligation and fair value of the plan assets) and the amounts recognized and not recognized in the financial statements.

    d.   A disclosure of the rates used in measuring the benefit amounts (discount rate, expected return on plant assets, rate of compensation).

21.   (C)   While the Pension Benefit Guarantee Corporation is empowered by ERISA to administer terminated pension plans and impose liens on assets, the maximum lien amount that can be imposed is 30% of net worth.

*22.   (B)   The amount of postretirement expense for 2010 is calculated by adding the service cost ($45,000) to the interest cost ($350,000 x 10%).

REVIEW EXERCISES

1.
1.	H	6.	A
2.	D	7.	I
3.	F	8.	C
4.	B	9.	E
5.	J	10.	G

2.

Leo Company
Pension Work Sheet - 2010

	General Journal Entries			Memo Report	
	Annual Pension		**Prepaid/ Accrued**	**Projected Benefit**	**Plan**
Items	**Expense**	**Cash**	**Cost**	**Obligation**	**Assets**
Balance 1/1/10				$150,000Cr	$150,000Dr
Service cost	$17,000Dr			17,000Cr	
Interest cost	*18,000Dr			18,000Cr	
Actual return	15,000Cr				15,000Dr
Contributions		$16,000Cr			16,000Dr
Benefits				10,000Dr	10,000Cr
Entry 12/31	20,000Dr	16,000Cr	4,000Cr		
Balance 12/31/10			4,000Cr	$175,000Cr	$171,000Dr

*$150,000 x .12 = $18,000

Journal Entry:	Pension Expense	20,000	
	Cash		16,000
	Prepaid/Accrued Pension Cost		4,000

3. a.

Computation of Service Years

Year	A	B	C	D	E	Total
2010	30	40	35	70	45	220
2011		40	35	70	45	190
2012			35	70	45	150
2013				70	45	115
2014	—	—	—	—	45	45
	30	80	105	280	225	720

Computation of Annual Prior Service Cost Amortization

Year	Total Service Years	X	Cost Per Service Year	=	Annual Amortization
2010	220		155*		$ 34,100
2011	190		155		29,450
2012	150		155		23,250
2013	115		155		17,825
2014	45		155		6,975
					$111,600

*$111,600/720 $155

b. $720 \div 220 = 3.27$

$111,600 \div 3.27 = \$34,128$

Straight-line amortization:	2010	-	$ 34,128
	2011	-	34,128
	2012	-	34,128
	2013	-	9,214 *
			$11,600

*($34,128.44 x .27)

4.

Bengston Company
Pension Work Sheet - 2010

| | General Journal Entries | | | Memo Report | | |
	Annual Pension Expense	Cash	Prepaid/ Accrued Cost	Projected Benefit Obligation	Plan Assets	Unrecognized Prior Service Cost
Balance 12/31/09			$ 4,000Cr	$175,000Cr	$171,000Dr	
Prior service cost				90,000Cr		$90,000Dr
Balance 1/1/10			4,000Cr	265,000Cr	171,000Dr	90,000Dr
Service cost	$18,000Dr			18,000Cr		
Interest cost	*31,800Dr			31,800Cr		
Actual return	18,500Cr				18,500Dr	
Amortization PSC	23,800Dr					23,800Cr
Contributions		$42,000Cr			42,000Dr	
Benefits				12,000Dr	12,000Cr	
Entry 12/31	55,100Dr	42,000Cr	13,100Cr			
Balance 12/31/10			$17,100Cr	$302,800Cr	$219,500Dr	$66,200Dr

*$265,000 x .12 = $31,800

b.

Journal Entry:	Pension Expense	55,100	
	Cash		42,000
	Prepaid/Accrued Pension Cost		13,100

c.

Projected benefit obligation (Credit)	$(302,800)
Plan assets at fair value (Debit)	219,500
Funded status	(83,300)
Unrecognized prior service cost (Debit)	66,200
Prepaid/accrued pension cost (Credit)	$ (17,100)

5. a.   Actual Return on Plan Assets:

Fair value of plan assets, 12/31/10		$4,600
Less fair value of plan assets 1/1/10		3,500
Change in fair value		1,100
Deduct: Contributions	$1,500	
Less benefits paid	(800)	(700)
Actual return on plan assets		$ 400

b.   Unrecognized net gain or loss:

1.   Liability gain or loss:

12/31/10 actuarially computed PBO		$6,860
1/1/10 PBO	$5,800	
Add interest (10%)	580	
Add service cost	1,200	
Less benefit payment	(800)	6,780
Liability loss		

80

2.   Asset gain or loss:

Actual return on plan assets	$ 400
Less expected return $3,500 X 10%	(350)
Asset gain	(50)
Unrecognized net (gain) or loss	$ 30

c.   Corridor test:

Year	Beg PBO	Plan Assets (FV)	10% Corridor	Unrecognized Net Loss	Loss Amortization
2011	$6,860	$4,600	$686	$30	-0-

d.   Prior Service Cost Amortization:

$1,700 X 1/10 = $170 per year

e.   Pension Expense - 2010:

Service cost	$ 1,200
Interest cost ($5,800 X 10%)	580
Actual return on plan assets (see a)	(400)
Unexpected gain (see b2)	50
Amortization of prior service cost (d)	170
Pension expense for 2010	$1,600

f.   Minimum Liability Computation:

Accumulated benefit obligation 12/31/10	$(5,650)
Plan assets at fair value	4,600
Minimum liability	(1,050)
Accrued pension cost, 12/31/10 [($1,600 - $1,500) + $600]	700
Additional liability	$ (350)

g.   Reconciliation schedule:

Projected benefit obligation	$(6,860)
Fair value of plan assets	4,600
Unfunded PBO	(2,260)
Unrecognized prior service cost ($1,700 - $170)	1,530
Unrecognized net gain or (loss)	30
Accrued pension cost	(700)
Additional liability	(350)
Accrued pension cost liability recognized in the balance sheet	$(1,050)

21

Accounting for Leases

CHAPTER STUDY OBJECTIVES

1. Explain the nature, economic substance, and advantages of lease transactions.
2. Describe the accounting criteria and procedures for capitalizing leases by the lessee.
3. Contrast the operating and capitalization methods of recording leases.
4. Identify the classifications of leases for the lessor.
5. Describe the lessor's accounting for direct-financing leases.
6. Identify special features of lease arrangements that cause unique accounting problems.
7. Describe the effect of residual values, guaranteed and unguaranteed, on lease accounting.
8. Describe the lessor's accounting for sales-type leases.
9. List the disclosure requirements for leases.
*10. Understand and apply lease accounting concepts to various lease arrangements.
*11. Describe the lessee's accounting for sale-leaseback transactions.

CHAPTER REVIEW

1.   Many businesses lease substantial portions of the property and equipment they use in their business organization as an alternative to ownership. Because leasing provides some financial, operating, and risk advantages over ownership, it has become the fastest growing form of capital investment. This increased significance of lease arrangements in recent years has intensified the need for uniform accounting and complete informative reporting of leasing transactions. Chapter 21 presents a discussion of the accounting issues related to leasing arrangements from the point of view of **both the lessee and the lessor.** Among the issues discussed are: (1) the classification of leasing arrangements, (2) the various methods used in accounting for leases, and (3) the financial statement disclosure requirements when leases are present.

The Leasing Environment

2.   (S.O. 1) A **lease** is a contractual agreement between a lessor and a lessee that gives the lessee the right to use specific property, owned by the lessor, for a specified period of time. In return for this right, the lessee agrees to make rental payments over the lease term to the lessor.

Note: All asterisked (*) items relate to material contained in the Appendix to the chapter.

Advantages of Leasing

3.   In discussing the advantages of leasing arrangements, advocates point out that leasing allows for: (a) **100% financing,** (b) **protection against obsolescence,** (c) **flexibility,** (d) **less costly financing,** (e) **tax advantages,** and (f) **off-balance sheet financing.**

4.   A variety of opinions exist regarding the manner in which certain long-term lease arrangements should be accounted for. These opinions range from total capitalization of all long-term leases to the belief that leases represent executory contracts that should not be capitalized. The FASB *Statements* dealing with lease accounting can be characterized as advocating capitalization of lease arrangements that are similar to installment purchases. In short, lease arrangements that transfer substantially all of the risks and rewards of ownership of property should be capitalized by the lessee.

Transfer of Ownership Criteria

5.   (S.O. 2) For accounting purposes of the **lessee,** all leases may be classified as **operating leases** or **capital leases.** For a lease to be recorded as a capital lease, the lease must be noncancelable and meet one of the following four criteria:

      a.   The lease transfers ownership of the property to the lessee.

      b.   The lease contains a bargain purchase option.

      c.   The lease term is equal to 75% or more of the estimated economic life of the leased property.

      d.   The present value of the minimum lease payments (excluding executory costs) equals or exceeds 90% of the fair value of the leased property.

If the lease meets none of the four criteria, the lease should be classified and accounted for as an operating lease.

6.   The **transfer of ownership** criteria is straightforward and easy to apply in practice. A **bargain purchase option** is a provision allowing the lessee to purchase the leased property for a price that is significantly lower than the property's expected fair value at the date the option becomes exercisable. The **75% of economic life test** is based on the belief that when a lease period equals or exceeds 75% of the asset's economic life, the risks and rewards of ownership are transferred to the lessee and capitalization is appropriate. The reason for the **90% of fair market value** test is that if the present value of the minimum lease payments are reasonably close to the market price of the asset, the asset is effectively being purchased. A major exception to the 75% and 90% rules is when the inception of the lease occurs during the last 25% of the asset's life. When this occurs the 75% and 90% tests should not be used.

Capital Leases for Lessees

7.   Under the capital lease method the lessee treats the lease transaction as if an asset were being purchased on time (installment basis). For a capital lease, the lessee records an asset and a liability at the lower of **(a)** the present value of the minimum lease payments during the term of the lease or **(b)** the fair market value of the leased asset at the inception of the lease. In determining the present value of the minimum lease payments, three important concepts are involved: **(a)** minimum lease payments, **(b)** executory costs, and **(c)** the discount rate.

8.   **Minimum lease payments** include **(a)** minimum rental payments, **(b)** any guaranteed residual value, **(c)** penalty for failure to renew or extend the lease, and **(d)** any bargain purchase option. Minimum rental payments are the minimum payments the lessee is obligated to make to the lessor under the lease agreement. A guaranteed residual value is the estimated fair (market) value of the leased property at the end of the lease term. This allows the lessor to transfer the risk of loss in the fair value of the asset to the lessee. The guaranteed residual value is **(a)** the certain or determinable amount at which the lessor has the right to require the lessee to purchase the asset or **(b)** the amount the lessee or the third-party guarantor guarantees the lessor will realize.

9.   **Executory costs** include the cost of insurance, maintenance, and tax expense related to the leased asset. If the lessor makes these payments, such amounts should reduce the present value of the minimum lease payments. When the lease agreement specifies that executory costs are assumed by the lessee, the rental payments can be used without adjustment in the present value computation. The lessee uses its **incremental borrowing rate (discount rate)** to compute the present value of the minimum lease payments. This rate, often determined by the exercise of professional judgment, is defined as the rate that, at the inception of the lease, the lessee would have incurred to borrow the funds necessary to buy the leased asset. There is one exception to use of the incremental borrowing rate by the lessee in computing the present value of the minimum lease payments. If the lessee knows the **implicit rate computed by the lessor,** and that rate is less than the lessee's incremental borrowing rate, then the lessee must use the implicit rate.

10.   When the lessee uses the capital lease method, each lease payment is allocated between a reduction of the lease obligation and interest expense applying the **effective interest method.** The lessee should amortize the leased asset by applying one of the conventional depreciation methods. During the term of the lease, assets recorded under capital leases are separately identified in the lessee's balance sheet. Likewise, the related obligations are separately identified with the portion due within one year or the operating cycle, whichever is longer, classified with current liabilities and the balance with noncurrent liabilities.

11.   A complete illustration of the accounting for a capital lease by the lessee is found in the text. It is important to understand the preparation of the Lease Amortization Schedule. This schedule provides the basis for the entire range of journal entries for the lease transaction. The basic entries include: **(a)** initial capitalization which requires a debit to the asset and a credit to the liability, **(b)** annual lease payments which include a debit to the liability and a credit to cash, and **(c)** the annual depreciation entry. Of course, any interest accrual or executory costs would be included in the entries made for the lease obligation.

Operating Leases for Lessees

12.   In accounting for an operating lease, the lessee would use the accounting method known as the **operating method.** When the lessee uses the operating method, the periodic rent associated with the lease is recognized in the period benefited by the leased asset. Under this method, the commitment to make future rental payments is not recognized in the accounts. Only footnote recognition is given to the commitment to pay future rentals. The journal entry the lessee would make to record operating lease payments includes a debit to Rent Expense and a credit to Cash.

13.   If the lessee **guarantees the residual value,** the present value of this residual value should be reported as part of the lease liability. If a bargain purchase option exists instead of a guaranteed residual value, the lessee should increase the present value of the minimum lease payments by the present value of the option price. In both the guaranteed residual value and the bargain purchase option cases, the lessee is

committed to making these payments, and therefore the payments should be reported as an increase to the lease liability.

Comparison of Capital Lease with Operating Lease

14.   (S.O. 3)   While the total charges to operations are the same over the lease term whether the lease is accounted for as a capital lease or as an operating lease, under the capital lease treatment the charges are higher in the earlier years and lower in the later years.   If an accelerated method of depreciation is used, the differences between the amounts charged to operations under the two methods would be even larger in the earlier and later years.   The following differences occur if a capital lease instead of an operating lease is employed:

   a.   an increase in the amount of reported debt (both short-term and long-term),
   b.   an increase in the amount of total assets (specifically long-lived assets), and
   c.   a lower income early in the life of the lease and, therefore, lower retained earnings.

Accounting by Lessors

15.   (S.O. 4)   Three benefits available to the lessor are **(a)** competitive interest margins, **(b)** tax incentives, and **(c)** high residual values.   For **lessor** accounting purposes, all leases may be classified as: (a) **operating leases,** (b) **direct financing leases,** or (c) **sales-type leases.**   The lessor should classify and account for an arrangement as a direct financing lease or a sales-type lease if at the date of the lease agreement **one or more** of the following **Group I** criteria are met and **both of** the following **Group II** criteria are met.

Group I

   a.   The lease transfers ownership of the property to the lessee.
   b.   The lease contains a bargain purchase option.
   c.   The lease term is equal to 75% or more of the estimated economic life of the leased property.
   d.   The present value of the minimum lease payments (excluding executory costs) equals or exceeds 90% of the fair value of the leased property.

Group II

   a.   Collectibility of the payments required from the lessee is reasonably predictable.
   b.   No important uncertainties surround the amount of unreimbursable costs yet to be incurred by the lessor under the lease.

16.   The distinction between a direct financing lease and a sales-type lease is that **a sales-type lease involves manufacturer's or dealer's profit (or loss) and a direct financing lease does not.**   The primary difference between applying the financing method to a direct financing lease and applying it to a sales-type lease is the recognition of the manufacturer's or dealer's profit at the inception of the lease.   The profit or loss to the lessor is evidenced by the difference between the fair value of the leased property at the inception of the lease and the lessor's cost or carrying amount (book value).   All leases that do not qualify as direct financing or sales-type leases are classified and accounted for by the lessors as operating leases.

17. A lessor should account for an operating lease using the operating method. Under the **operating method,** each rental receipt of the lessor is recorded as rent revenue on the use of an item carried as a fixed asset. The fixed asset is depreciated in the normal manner, with the depreciation expense of the period
being matched against the rental revenue.

Direct Financing Method (Lessor)

18. (S.O. 5) Leases that are in substance the financing of an asset purchase by the lessee are called direct financing leases. In this type of lease, the lessee records a lease receivable instead of a leased asset. The lease receivable is the present value of the minimum lease payments. Remember that "minimum lease payments" includes:
   1. rental payments (excluding executory costs),
   2. bargain purchase option (if any),
   3. guaranteed residual value (if any), and
   4. penalty for failure to renew (if any).

Special Accounting Problems

19. (S.O. 6) Leases have certain characteristics that create unique accounting problems. The next paragraphs review these characteristics.

Residual Value

20. (S.O. 7) The **residual value** of a leased asset is the **estimated fair value** of the asset at the end of the lease term. The residual value may be **guaranteed** or **unguaranteed** by the lessee. A guaranteed residual value is said to exist when the lessee agrees to make up any deficiency below a stated amount in the value of the asset at the end of the lease term. A guaranteed residual value affects the lessee's computation of the minimum lease payments and, therefore, the amounts capitalized as a leased asset and a lease obligation. The lessor assumes the residual value will be realized at the end of the lease term whether guaranteed or unguaranteed.

21. To understand the accounting implications of a guaranteed residual value, assume a lessee guarantees the residual value of an asset will be $8,000. If, at the end of the lease, the fair market value of the residual value is less than $8,000, the lessee will have to record a loss for the difference. For example, if the lessee depreciated the asset down to its residual value of $8,000 but the fair market value of the residual value was $4,000, the lessee would have to record a loss of $4,000. If the fair market value of the asset exceeds the $8,000, a gain may be recognized. Gains on guaranteed residual values may be apportioned to the lessor and lessee in whatever ratio the parties initially agree.

Sales-Type Leases

22. (S.O. 8) Under sales-type leases, the profit recorded by the lessor at the point of sale is the same whether the residual value is guaranteed or unguaranteed, but the sales revenue and cost of goods sold amounts are different. The present value of the unguaranteed residual value is deducted from sales revenue and cost of goods sold.

Bargain Purchase Options

23. A **bargain purchase option** is a provision allowing the lessee, at his or her option, to purchase the leased property at a price that is sufficiently lower than the expected fair value of the property at the date the option becomes exercisable. When a bargain purchase option exists, the lessee must increase the present value of the minimum lease payments by the present value of the option price. The only difference between accounting for a bargain purchase option and a guaranteed residual value of identical amounts is in the computation of the annual depreciation. In the case of a guaranteed residual value, the lessee depreciates the asset over the **lease life.** When a bargain purchase option is present, the lessee uses the economic life of the asset in computing depreciation.

Initial Direct Costs

24. **Initial direct costs** are the costs incurred by the lessor that are directly associated with negotiating and consummating a **completed** leasing transaction. There are two types of initial direct costs, **incremental direct costs** and **internal direct costs.** Incremental direct costs are costs incurred in originating a lease arrangement that are paid to third parties. Internal direct costs are costs directly related to specified activities performed by the lessor on a given lease. When an operating lease is present, the initial direct costs are deferred and amortized over the life of the lease in proportion to rental income. In a sales-type lease, these costs are expensed in the period that profit on the sale is recognized. For direct financing leases, initial direct costs are added to the net investment in the lease and amortized over the life of the lease as a yield adjustment.

Disclosure

25. (S.O. 9) The FASB requires that specific information with respect to operating leases and capital leases be disclosed in the lessee's financial statements or in the footnotes as of the date of the latest balance sheet presented. This section includes both a listing of lessee and lessor disclosure requirements and actual disclosure illustrations. The general information required to be disclosed by the lessee **for all leases** includes, but is not necessarily limited to, the following:

   a.   The basis on which contingent rental payments are determined.
   b.   The existence and terms of renewal or purchase options and escalation clauses.
   c.   Restrictions imposed by lease agreements, such as those concerning dividends, additional debt, and future leasing.

*Lease Accounting Concepts

26. (S.O. 10) Lease accounting is based on criteria that assess whether substantially all of the risks and benefits of ownership of the asset have been transferred from the lessor to the lessee.

*Sale-Leaseback

27. (S.O. 11) A **"sale-leaseback"** transaction is one in which the owner of property sells it to another and simultaneously leases it back from the new owner. The seller-lessee, in a sale-leaseback transaction, should apply the same criteria mentioned earlier in deciding whether to account for the lease as a capital lease or an operating lease. Likewise, the purchaser-lessor should apply the criteria mentioned earlier in deciding whether the sale-leaseback transaction should be accounted for using the operating method or the financing method.

GLOSSARY

Bargain purchase option.

A provision allowing the lessee to purchase the leased property for a price that is significantly lower than the property's expected fair value at the date the option becomes exercisable.

Bargain renewal option.

A provision allowing the lessee to renew the lease for a rental that is lower than the expected fair rental at the date the option becomes exercisable.

Capital lease.

A lease that is treated as if the lessor has transferred ownership of the property to the lessee and the rental payments made by the lessee to the lessor constitute a financing arrangement.

Cost of goods sold (sales-type lease).

The cost of the asset to the lessor, less the present value of any unguaranteed residual value.

Direct financing lease.

Leases that are in substance the financing of an asset purchase by the lessee.

Discount rate.

The interest rate used by the lessee to compute the present value of the minimum lease payments: which is the lesser of (1) lessee's incremental borrowing rate or (2) the known implicit rate computed by the lessor.

Executory costs.

The costs incurred during the economic life of leased tangible assets, such as insurance, maintenance and tax expenses.

Guaranteed residual value.

The certain or determinable amount at which the lessor has the right to require the lessee to purchase the asset or the amount the lessee or a third-party guarantor guarantees the lessor will realize.

Implicit interest rate.

The interest rate implicit in the lease that when applied to the minimum lease payments and any unguaranteed residual value accruing to the lessor, which causes the aggregate present value to be equal to the fair value of the leased property to the lessor.

Incremental borrowing rate.

The rate that, at the inception of the lease, the lessee would have incurred to borrow the funds necessary to buy the leased asset on a secured loan with repayment terms similar to the payment schedule called for in the lease.

Incremental direct costs.

The costs paid to independent third parties incurred in originating a lease arrangement, such as the cost of independent appraisal of collateral used to secure a lease, the cost of an outside credit check of the lessee, or a broker's fee for finding the lessee.

Initial direct costs.

Incremental direct costs and internal direct costs.

Internal direct costs.

The costs directly related to specified activities performed by the lessor on a given lease, such as evaluating the prospective lessee's financial condition and evaluating and recording guarantees, collateral, and other security arrangements.

Internal indirect costs.

The costs indirectly related to specified activities performed by the lessor on a given lease, such as advertising, servicing existing leases, and establishing and monitoring credit policies.

Lease.

A contractual agreement between a lessor and a lessee that gives the lessee the right to use specific property, owned by the lessor, for a specific period of time in return for stipulated, and generally periodic, cash payments (rents).

Lessee.

The party that receives the right to use property owned by the lessor, in return for cash payments (rents) under the terms of a lease.

Lessor.

The party that gives the lessee the right to use specific property, owned by the lessor, for a specific period of time under the terms of a lease.

Minimum lease payments.

Minimum rental payments adjusted for any guaranteed residual value, any penalty for failure to renew, and a bargain purchase option.

Minimum rental payments.

Minimum payments the lessee is obligated to make to the lessor under the lease agreement.

*Minor leaseback.

A leaseback in which the present value of the rental payments are 10% or less of the fair value of the asset.

Noncancelable.

The lease contract is cancelable only upon the outcome of some remote contingency or that the cancellation provisions and penalties of the contract are so costly to the lessee that cancellation probably will not occur.

Off-balance-sheet financing.

The result when a lease does not add debt on a balance sheet or affect financial ratios.

Operating lease.

Leases that are not classified as capitalized leases.

Operating method.

The method of accounting for an operating lease whereby rent expense (and a compensating liability) accrues day by day to the lessee as the property is used.

Residual value.

The estimated fair (market) value of the leased property at the end of the lease term.

*Sale-leaseback.

A transaction in which the owner of property (seller-lessee) sells the property to another and simultaneously leases it back from the new owner.

Sales price of the asset (sales-type lease).

Under a sales-type lease, it is the present value of the minimum lease payments.

Sales-type lease.

A direct financing lease which also accounts for the manufacturer's or dealer's gross profit (or loss).

Third-party guarantor.

A separate party which acts like an insurer by guaranteeing the residual value of leased assets.

Unguaranteed residual value.

The amount of residual value which is not guaranteed.

CHAPTER OUTLINE

Fill in the outline presented below.

(S.O. 1) Lease Provisions

Advantages of Leasing

Accounting by Lessees for Capitalized Leases

(S.O. 2) The Four Criteria for Determining a Capital Lease

1.

2.

Chapter Outline *(continued)*

        3.

        4.

        Determination of Minimum Lease Payments

        Accounting for the Asset

        Accounting for the Liability

(S.O. 3) Accounting by Lessees for Operating Leases

        Accounting by Lessors for Capitalized Leases

(S.O. 5) Direct Financing Leases

        Sales-Type Leases

        Accounting by Lessor for Operating Leases

(S.O. 6) Special Accounting Problems

(S.O. 7) Residual Values

Chapter Outline *(continued)*

        Lessee accounting for residual value

        Lessor accounting for residual value

(S.O. 8) Sales-Type Leases

        Bargain Purchase Option

        Initial Direct Costs

(S.O. 9) Presentation and Disclosures of Lease Data

*(S.O. 10) Lease Accounting Concepts

*(S.O. 11) Sales Leasebacks

REVIEW QUESTIONS AND EXERCISES

TRUE-FALSE

Indicate whether each of the following is true (T) or false (F) in the space provided.

_____ 1.   (S.O. 1) A lease is a contractual agreement conveying ownership of certain property from one party to another party.

_____ 2.   (S.O. 1) Under a leasing arrangement, it is possible to write off the full cost of a leased asset including land and residual values.

_____ 3.   (S.O. 3) An operating lease refers to a lease agreement for property used in the operations of the lessee's business.

_____ 4.   (S.O. 3) One of the major distinctions between an operating lease and a capital lease is the fact that annual rental payments under a capital lease are higher than rental payments under an operating lease.

_____ 5.   (S.O. 2) If a lease contains a bargain purchase option, the lessee shall classify and account for the arrangement as a capital lease.

_____ 6.   (S.O. 2) Under the operating method, the lessee assigns rent to the periods benefiting from the use of the asset and does **not** record the commitment to make future payments.

_____ 7.   (S.O. 2) Under the capital lease method, the lessee treats the lease transaction as if an asset were being purchased on an installment payment basis.

_____ 8.   (S.O. 2) The lessee records a capital lease as an asset, using the fair market value of the leased asset on the date of the lease as the asset's cost.

_____ 9.   (S.O. 2) The rental payments paid to a lessor in a capital lease transaction constitute a payment of principal plus interest because of the financing-type nature of the transaction.

_____ 10.   (S.O. 2) When the lessee accounts for a capital lease, the amortization (depreciation) of the asset and the discharge of the lease obligation should be handled in a consistent manner over the same number of accounting periods.

_____ 11.   (S.O. 2) If the lessee has knowledge of the lessor's implicit interest rate and it is lower than the lessee's incremental borrowing rate, the implicit interest rate should be used in computing the present value of minimum rental payments.

_____ 12.   (S.O. 4) A lessor must be a manufacturer or dealer to realize a profit (or loss) at the inception of a lease that requires application of sales-type lease accounting.

_____ 13.   (S.O. 4) All leases that do **not** qualify as direct financing or sales-type leases are classified and accounted for by the lessors as capital leases.

_____ 14.   (S.O. 5) Leases that are in substance the financing of an asset purchase by the lessee are called direct financing leases.

_____ 15.   (S.O. 5) The lease receivable is the present value of the minimum lease payments.

_____ 16.   (S.O. 6) The residual value is the actual fair value of the leased asset at the end of the lease term.

_____ 17.   (S.O. 7) When the lessor accounts for minimum lease payments, the basis for capitalization includes the guaranteed residual value but excludes the unguaranteed residual value.

_____ 18.   (S.O. 7) A lessee would treat guaranteed residual value as an additional lease payment that will be paid in property or cash, or both, at the end of the lease term.

_____ 19.   (S.O. 8) Initial direct costs are those costs associated with negotiating and consummating completed lease transactions.

_____ 20.   (S.O. 8) In a sales-type lease, the gross profit amount on the sale of the asset is the same whether a guaranteed or unguaranteed residual value is involved.

_____ 21.   (S.O. 9) During the term of the lease, assets recorded under capital leases are separately identified in the lessee's balance sheet.

_____ 22.   (S.O. 9) Lease disclosure requirements on the part of the lessor apply only to lessors whose predominant business activity is leasing.

_____ *23.   (S.O. 11) The criteria a lessee uses to determine whether a lease is a capital lease or an operating lease apply in the case of a sale-leaseback transaction.

_____ *24.   (S.O. 11) Any profit or loss experienced by the seller-lessee in a sale-leaseback transaction must be included in income at the date of the lease agreement.

_____ *25.   (S.O. 11) Leasebacks in which the present value of the rental payments are 20% or less of the fair market value of the asset are defined as minor leasebacks and the transaction is considered a sale.

MULTIPLE CHOICE

Select the best answer for each of the following items and enter the corresponding letter in the space provided.

_____   1. (S.O. 1) An essential element of a lease conveyance is that the:

    A.   lessor conveys less than his or her total interest in the property.
    B.   lessee provides a sinking fund equal to one year's lease payments.
    C.   property that is the subject of the lease agreement must be held for sale by the lessor prior to the drafting of the lease agreement.
    D.   term of the lease is substantially equal to the economic life of the leased property.

_____   2. (S.O. 1) Which of the following is **not** one of the commonly discussed advantages of leasing?

    A.   Leasing permits 100% financing versus 60 to 80% when purchasing an asset.
    B.   Leasing permits rapid changes in equipment, thus reducing the risk of obsolescence.
    C.   Leasing improves financial ratios by increasing assets without a corresponding increase in debt.
    D.   Leasing permits write-off of the full cost of the asset.

_____   3. (S.O. 1) The accounting principles used in lease accounting attempt to provide symmetry between the lessee and lessor. With respect to lease rental payments in a capital lease, they are considered to consist of both interest and principal by the:

	Lessee	Lessor
A.	Yes	No
B.	No	Yes
C.	Yes	Yes
D.	No	No

_____   4. (S.O. 2) Which of the following lease arrangements would most likely be accounted for as an operating lease by the lessee?

    A.   The lease agreement runs for 15 years and the economic life of the leased property is 20 years.
    B.   The present value of the minimum lease payments is $55,600 and the fair value of the leased property is $60,000.
    C.   The lease agreement allows the lessee the right to purchase the leased asset for $1.00 when half of the asset's economic useful life has expired.
    D.   The lessee may renew the two-year lease for an additional two years at the same rental.

_____   5.   (S.O. 2) If the lease term is equal to 75% or more of the estimated economic life of the leased property, the asset should be capitalized by the lessee. The one exception to this rule is when:

   A.   the lease term is for 5 years or less.
   B.   the lessee does not intend to exercise its option to purchase the asset at the conclusion of the lease term.
   C.   the lessor refuses to offer a bargain purchase option and the leased property will revert to the lessor at the end of the lease term.
   D.   the inception of the lease occurs during the last 25% of the life of the asset.

_____   6.   (S.O. 2) Minimum lease payments are payments the lessee is obligated to make or can be expected to make in connection with the leased property. In computing minimum lease payments all of the following would be included, **except** the:

   A.   present value of the cost of the leased asset.
   B.   penalty for failure to renew or extend the lease.
   C.   bargain purchase option.
   D.   minimum rental payments.

_____   7.   (S.O. 2) In computing the present value of the minimum lease payments the lessee must use a discount rate. Normally, use of the lessee's incremental borrowing rate is appropriate unless:

   A.   the lessee's incremental borrowing rate exceeds the prime interest rate on the date of the lease agreement, in which case the prime interest rate should be used.
   B.   the incremental borrowing rate is less than two-thirds of the prime interest rate, in which case the prime interest rate should be used.
   C.   the lessee knows the implicit rate computed by the lessor and it is greater than the lessee's incremental borrowing rate, then the lessee must use the lessor's implicit rate.
   D.   the lessee knows the implicit rate computed by the lessor and it is less than the lessee's incremental borrowing rate, then the lessee must use the lessor's implicit rate.

_____   8.   (S.O. 2) What impact does a bargain purchase option have on the present value of the minimum lease payments computed by the lessee?

   A.   No impact as the option does not enter into the transaction until the end of the lease term.
   B.   The lessee must increase the present value of the minimum lease payments by the present value of the option price.
   C.   The lessee must decrease the present value of the minimum lease payments by the present value of the option price.
   D.   The minimum lease payments would be increased by the present value of the option price if, at the time of the lease agreement, it appeared certain that the lessee would exercise the option at the end of the lease and purchase the asset at the option price.

Use the following information for questions 9 and 10.

On January 1, 2010, Kinney Corporation signed a five-year noncancelable lease for certain machinery. The terms of the lease called for Kinney to make annual payments of $20,000 at the end of each year for five years with title to pass to Kinney at the end of this period. The machinery has an estimated useful life of 7 years and no salvage value. Kinney uses the straight-line method of depreciation for all of its fixed assets. Kinney accordingly accounts for this lease transaction as a capital lease. The minimum lease payments were determined to have a present value of $75,816 at an effective interest rate of 10%.

_____ 9. (S.O. 2) With respect to this capitalized lease, for 2010 Kinney should record:

    A.   lease expense of $20,000.
    B.   interest expense of $7,582 and depreciation expense of $10,831.
    C.   interest expense of $7,582 and depreciation expense of $15,163.
    D.   interest expense of $10,000 and depreciation expense of $15,163.

_____ 10. (S.O. 2) With respect to this capitalized lease, for 2011 Kinney should record:

    A.   interest expense of $4,823 and depreciation expense of $10,831.
    B.   interest expense of $6,340 and depreciation expense of $10,831.
    C.   interest expense of $6,823 and depreciation expense of $10,831.
    D.   interest expense of $7,582 and depreciation expense of $10,831.

_____ 11. (S.O. 2) Under the operating method, a rent expense accrues day by day to the lessee as the property is made available for use. This amount of rent expense is:
    A.   capitalized in an asset account and charged against income as the asset depreciates.
    B.   capitalized in an asset account and netted against the corresponding lease liability each time a balance sheet is prepared.
    C.   charged against income in the periods benefiting from the use of the asset.
    D.   charged against income at the same rate as the reduction in the corresponding lease liability.

_____ 12. (S.O. 3) If a lease transaction is accorded capital lease treatment rather than operating lease treatment, it would have what impact on the following financial items of the lessee?

	Reported Debt	Total Assets	Return on Total Assets
A.	Increase	Increase	Increase
B.	Increase	Increase	Decrease
C.	Decrease	Increase	Increase
D.	Increase	Increase	No Effect

_____ 13. (S.O. 3) Wilson Company has a machine with a cost of $250,000 which also is its fair market value on the date the machine is leased to Berger Company. The lease is for 6 years and the machine is estimated to have a residual value of zero. If the lessor's interest rate implicit in the lease is 12%, the six beginning-of-the-year lease payments would be:

    A. $30,806
    B. $41,667
    C. $54,291
    D. $60,807

14.   (S.O. 4) In addition to the four criteria that a lessee must assess in deciding whether to classify a lease transaction as a capital lease, a lessor must meet two additional criteria. These include (1) the collectibility of the payments required from the lessee is reasonably predictable, and (2):

A.   the lease includes an element of manufacturer or dealer profit.

B.   the lessee has the ability to meet the requirements of the guaranteed residual value.

C.   executory costs are provided for in a manner which makes their ultimate payment virtually a certainty.

D.   no important uncertainties surround the amount of unreimbursable costs yet to be incurred by the lessor under the lease.

15.   (S.O. 5) In order to properly record a direct financing lease the lessor needs to know how to calculate the lease receivable. The lease receivable in a direct financing lease is best defined as:

A.   the amount of funds the lessor has tied up in the asset which is the subject of the direct financing lease.

B.   the difference between the lease payments receivable and the fair market value of the leased property.

C.   the present value of minimum lease payments.

D.   the total book value of the asset less any accumulated depreciation recorded by the lessor prior to the lease agreement.

16.   (S.O. 7) With respect to the computation of minimum lease payments by the lessee, how are the following items handled in the computation?

	Guaranteed Residual Value	**Unguaranteed Residual Value**
A.	Included	Excluded
B.	Included	Included
C.	Excluded	Included
D.	Excluded	Excluded

17.   (S.O. 7) If the residual value of a leased asset is guaranteed by a third party:

A.   it is treated by the lessee as no residual value.

B.   the third party is also liable for any lease payments not paid by the lessee.

C.   the net investment to be recovered by the lessor is reduced.

D.   it is treated by the lessee as an additional payment and by the lessor as realized at the end of the lease term.

Use the following information for questions 18 and 19.

Davies Co. leased a machine to Callaghan Co. Assume the lease payments were made on the basis that the residual value was guaranteed and Davies gets to recognize all the profits, and at the end of the lease term, before the lessee transfers the asset to the lessor, the leased asset and obligation accounts have the following balances:

Leased equipment under capital lease	$250,000
Less accumulated depreciation--capital lease	240,000
	$ 10,000
Interest payable	$ 950
Obligations under capital leases	9,050
	$10,000

_____ 18. (S.O. 7) If, at the end of the lease, the fair market value of the residual value is $5,500, what gain or loss should Davies record?

    A. $5,500 gain.
    B. $4,500 loss.
    C. $4,050 loss.
    D. $4,450 gain.

_____ 19. (S.O. 7) If, at the end of the lease, the fair market value of the residual value is $10,500, what gain or loss should Davies record?

    A. $ 500 gain.
    B. $ 500 loss.
    C. $3,050 loss.
    D. $1,450 gain.

_____ 20. (S.O. 8) The primary difference between a direct financing lease and a sales-type lease is the:
    A.   manner in which rental receipts are recorded as rental income.
    B.   amount of the depreciation recorded each year by the lessor.
    C.   recognition of the manufacturer's or dealer's profit at the inception of the lease.
    D.   allocation of initial direct costs by the lessor to periods benefited by the lease arrangements.

_____ 21. (S.O. 8) Debbie Company leased equipment to the Trant Company on July 1, 2010, for a ten-year period expiring June 30, 2020. Equal annual payments under the lease are $50,000 and are due on July 1 of each year. The first payment was made on July 1, 2010. The rate of interest contemplated by Debbie and Trant is 9%. The cash selling price of the equipment is $350,000 and the cost of the equipment on Debbie's accounting records was $310,000. Assuming that the lease is appropriately recorded as a sale for accounting purposes by Debbie, what is the amount of profit on the sale and the interest income that Debbie would record for the year ended December 31, 2010?

    A. $0 and $0
    B. $40,000 and $13,500
    C. $40,000 and $27,000
    D. $40,000 and $31,500

_____ *22. (S.O. 11) In a sale-leaseback transaction, the seller-lessee retains the right to substantially all of the remaining use of the equipment sold. The profit on the sale should be deferred and subsequently amortized by the lessee when the lease is classified as a(n):

	Capital Lease	Operating Lease
A.	No	Yes
B.	No	No
C.	Yes	No
D.	Yes	Yes

_____ *23. (S.O. 11) On January 1, 2010, Cihla Airlines sold an airplane to an unaffiliated company for $400,000. The airplane had a book value of $360,000 and a remaining useful life of 8 years. That same day, Cihla leased back the airplane at $5,000 per month for 4 years with no option to renew the lease or repurchase the airplane. Cihla's rent expense for this airplane for the year ended December 31, 2010 should be:
   A. $ -0-.
   B. $12,000.
   C. $15,000.
   D. $60,000.

_____ *24. (S.O. 11) Any gain or loss resulting from a sale-leaseback where the lease is an operating lease must be:

   A.   taken into income on the date of the sale-leaseback agreement.
   B.   deferred and amortized in proportion to the rental payments over the period of time the asset is expected to be used by the lessee.
   C.   deferred and amortized in proportion to the rental payments over the economic life of the asset.
   D.   deferred and not taken into income until the lease agreement has terminated.

REVIEW EXERCISES

1.   (S.O. 2 and 4) List the criteria that must be met before a lease arrangement is accounted for:

a.   As a capital lease by the lessee.
b.   As a direct financing lease by the lessor.

a.

_____

_____

_____

_____

_____

_____

_____

_____

_____

_____

b.

_____

_____

_____

_____

_____

_____

_____

_____

_____

_____

2. (S.O. 5) The following is a lease amortization schedule for a direct financing lease of equipment by Chikahisa Company (lessor).

Chikahisa Company
Lease Amortization Schedule

Date	Annual Lease Payment	Interest on Lease Receivable	Lease Receivable Recovery	Lease Receivable
1-1-10				$120,000.00
12-31-10	$36,230.50	$9,600.00	$ 26,630.50	93,369.50
12-31-11	36,230.50	7,469.56	28,760.94	64,608.56
12-31-12	36,230.50	5,168.68	31,061.82	33,546.74
12-31-13	36,230.50	2,683.76	33,546.74	
	$144,922.00	$24,922.00	$120,000.00	

Instructions:
Prepare journal entries for:

a. the initial recording of the lease by the lessor,
b. the receipt of the first year's lease payment,
c. the interest income earned during the first year.

General Journal			J1
Date	Account Title	Debit	Credit
	Lease recievable	120,000.00	
	Equipment		120,000.00
	Cash	36,230.50	
	interest rev		1,600.00
	Lease recievable		26,630.50
	uncarned interest rev	9,600.00	
	interest rov		9,600.00

3. (S.O. 2) Using the lease amortization schedule presented in exercise 2 as a basis, prepare the journal entries the lessee would make (assuming the capital lease method) for:

a. the initial recording of the lease by the lessee,
b. the lease payment on 12/31/11, and
c. the purchase of the equipment by the lessee on 12/31/13, for $10,000 (accumulated depreciation equals $120,000).

General Journal			J1
Date	Account Title	Debit	Credit

4.   (S.O. 2) Prepare a lease amortization schedule for the lease agreement signed by Freter Company (lessee) on January 1, 2011. The agreement is for seven years, requiring annual rental payments of $42,000, payable at the beginning of each lease year (January 1). The executory costs associated with the lease are the responsibility of Freter Company, which has an incremental borrowing rate of 12%. Freter Company is unaware of the implicit rate computed by the lessor. At the conclusion of the lease Freter Company has the option to buy the equipment for $1.00.

Freter Company
Lease Amortization Schedule
(Annuity Due Basis)

Date	Annual Lease Payment	Interest (12%) on Lease Liability	Reduction of Lease Liability	Balance of Lease Liability
1/1/11	42,000			214,679
1/1/11	42,000	0	42,000	172,679
1/1/12	42,000	20,721	21,279	151,400
1/1/13	42,000	18,168	23,832	127,568
1/1/14	42,000			
1/1/15	42,000			
1/1/16	42,000			
1/1/17	42,000			

5.   (S. 0. 5 and 7) Hom Leasing Company agrees to lease equipment to Golden Corporation on January 1, 2010. The following information relates to the lease agreement.

1.   The term of the lease is seven years with no renewal option and the equipment has an estimated economic life of seven years.

2.   The cost of the equipment is $280,000, and the fair value of the asset on 1/1/10 is also $280,000.

3.   At the end of the lease term the asset reverts to the lessor. At the end of the lease term the asset is expected to have a residual value of $52,000, none of which is guaranteed.

4.   Golden Corporation assumes responsibility for all executory costs.

5.   The lease agreements requires equal annual rental payments, beginning on January 1, 2010.

6.   The collectibility of the lease payments is reasonably predictable and there are no important uncertainties surrounding the amount of costs yet to be incurred by the lessor.

Instructions:

a.   Assuming the lessor desires a 12% rate of return on its investment, calculate the amount of the annual rental payment required. Round to the nearest dollar.

b.   Prepare an amortization schedule for the lessor for the lease term.

c.   Prepare the journal entries the lessor would make in 2010 and 2011 related to the lease arrangement. Assume that Hom Company has a December 31 year end.

a.

_____
_____
_____
_____
_____
_____
_____

b.   Hom Leasing Company
                              Lease Amortization Schedule

Date	Annual Lease Payment Plus URV	Interest on Lease Receivable	Net Lease Receivable	Balance of Lease Receivable
1/1/10				280,000.00
1/1/10	50,178	X	50,178	229,822
1/1/11	50,178	27,579	22,599	207,223
1/1/12	50,178	24,867	25,311	181,912
1/1/13	50,178	21,829	28,349	153,563
1/1/14	50,178	2,		
1/1/15	50,178			
1/1/16	50,178			
12/31/16	52,000			

c.

	General Journal		J1
Date	Account Title	Debit	Credit
1/1/10	Lease recievable	280,000	
	equipment		280,000
	Cash	50,178	
	Lease recievable		50,178
12/31/10	interest recievable	27,579	
	interest revenue		27,579
1/1/11	Cash	50,178	
	Lease recievable		22,599
	interest recievable		27,579
	interest recievable	24,867	
	interest rev. - leases		24,867

SOLUTIONS TO REVIEW QUESTIONS AND EXERCISES

TRUE-FALSE

1. (F)   A lease is a contractual agreement conveying the rights to use property from one party to another. A lease does not by definition transfer ownership. Such arrangements can be written into a lease agreement, but the transfer of ownership is not a part of all lease agreements.

2. (T)

3. (F)   An operating lease refers to a lease arrangement that has all the characteristics of a rental agreement. When a lease is an operating lease, rent expense accrues day by day to the lessee as the property is used. The lessee assigns rent to the periods benefiting from the use of the asset and ignores any commitments to make future payments. A lessor accounts for an operating lease by recording each rental receipt as rental revenue for the use of the item which is still carried on its books as an asset.

4. (F)   The size of rental payments depends on a number of issues that are determined by the lessee and lessor. The fact that a lease is accounted for as a capital lease or as an operating lease does not have an impact on the size of the annual rental payments.

5. (T)

6. (T)

7.   (T)

8. (F)   The leased asset recorded on the books of a lessee is recorded at the lower of (a) the present value of the minimum lease payments excluding any executory cost, or (b) the fair market value of the leased asset at the inception of the lease.

9. (T)

10. (F)   Although the amount capitalized as an asset and the amount recorded as an obligation at the inception of the lease are computed at the same present value, the amortization of the asset and the discharge of the obligation are independent accounting processes during the term of the lease. They need not be written off over the same number of accounting periods.

11. (T)

12. (F)   The distinction for the lessor between a direct financing lease and a sales-type lease is the presence or absence of a manufacturer's or dealer's profit (or loss). A sales-type lease involves manufacturer's or dealer's profit, and a direct financing lease does not. The lessor is not required to be a manufacturer or dealer to account for a lease as a sales-type lease.

13. (F)   All leases that do not qualify as direct financing or sales-type leases are classified and accounted for by the lessors as operating leases.

14. (T)

15.   (T)

16.   (F)   Because the actual residual value cannot be known until the lease expires, the residual value is only an estimated amount.

17.   (F)   When the lessor accounts for the minimum lease payments, the lessor works on the assumption that the residual value will be realized at the end of the lease term whether guaranteed or unguaranteed.

18.   (T)

19.   (T)

20.   (T)

21.   (T)

22.   (T)

*23.   (T)

*24.   (F)   Any profit or loss experienced by the seller-lessee from the sale of the assets that are leased back under a capital lease should be deferred and amortized over the lease term in proportion to the amortization of the leased asset.

*25.   (F)   Leasebacks in which the present value of the rental payments are 10% or less of the fair market value of the asset are defined as minor leasebacks. Minor leasebacks are not considered financing transactions and the transaction is considered a sale (with full gain or loss recognition).

MULTIPLE CHOICE

1.   (A)   A lease is a contractual agreement between a lessor and a lessee that conveys to the lessee the right to use specific property (real or personal), owned by the lessor, for a specific period of time in return for stipulated and generally periodic cash payments. An essential element of the lease agreement is that the lessor conveys less than the total interest in the property. There are no sinking fund or lease term requirements that must be met for a lease to exist. Also, leased property need not be held for sale prior to the lease agreement.

2.   (C)   A lease arrangement does not improve financial ratios. When a capital lease is involved, an asset is recorded but so is a corresponding liability. This transaction will actually result in a negative impact on most ratios of the lessee.

3.   (C)   The lessee and the lessor treat the lease rental payments in a capital lease as consisting of interest and principal.

4. (D)   Alternative A meets the 75% of the economic life test. Alternative B meets the 90% of the fair value of the leased property test. Alternative C appears to be a bargain purchase option. Thus, these situations all describe a capital lease arrangement because they meet one of the four capital lease criteria. Alternative D has no relationship to the four capital lease criteria and is most likely an operating lease arrangement.

5   (D)   The FASB takes the position that if the inception of the lease occurs during the last 25% of the life of the asset, the economic life test cannot be used as a basis to classify a lease as a capital lease. The length of the lease is not a consideration, nor is the intent to exercise any bargain purchase option. Even if the leased property is to revert to the lessor, the economic life test is invalid as long as the asset is in the last 25% of its economic life.

6. (A)   The present value of the cost of the leased asset is not a part of the specific computation of the minimum lease payments. Minimum lease payments include the items identified in alternatives B, C, and D as well as the guaranteed residual value.

7. (D)   The one exception to the lessee using its incremental borrowing rate is when the lessor's implicit rate is known and it is less than the lessee's incremental rate; then the implicit rate must be used. The purpose for this exception concerns the fact that the implicit rate is generally more realistic. Also, use of the implicit rate, when it is lower, will help ensure that the lessee does not use an artificially high incremental rate to avoid capitalization under the 90% rule.

8. (B)   A bargain purchase option allows the lessee to purchase the leased property for a future price that is substantially lower than the property's expected future price. If a bargain purchase option exists, the lessee must increase the present value of the minimum lease payments by the present value of the option price. The certainty of exercise at lease inception is not a necessary condition for increasing the present value of the minimum lease payments. The existence of a bargain purchase option is sufficient.

9. (B)   The amount of interest expense would be calculated by multiplying the lease obligation (present value of minimum lease payments) by the effective interest rate of 10%, which is $7,582 ($75,816 X 10%). Because the lease agreement transfers ownership of the asset to the lessee, depreciation of the leased equipment is based on the economic life of the asset. Therefore, using the straight-line method, the depreciation expense for the year would be $10,831 ($75,816/7).

10. (B)   After the 2010 payment, the new lease obligation is $63,398. This is calculated by subtracting the difference between the annual lease payment ($20,000) and the amount of interest expense ($7,582) of $12,418 from the previous lease obligation of $75,816. The 2011 interest expense is therefore $6,340 (10% of $63,398), and depreciation expense is again $10,831 ($75,816/7).

11. (C)   The rent expense resulting from an operating lease is charged against income in a manner consistent with the matching concept. Thus, rent expense is charged against income in the period(s) benefiting from the use of the leased asset.

12. (B)   Because the capital lease treatment records the asset and the related debt on the lessee's financial statements, these items will both increase as a result of a capital lease. However, with total assets being greater the return on assets will decrease as the leasing arrangement does not provide an additional source of revenue to the lessee.

13. (C)

Fair market value of leased machine	$250,000
Less present value of the residual value	-0-
Amount to be recovered by lessor	$250,000

Six beginning-of-the-year lease payments to yield 12% return ($250,000/4.60478 = $54,291.41) (Table 6-5)

14. (D)   The two additional requirements for the lessor to account for a lease as a capital lease are there to be sure that the lessor has really transferred the risks and rewards of ownership. If collectibility of payments is not predictable or if performance by the lessor is incomplete, then it is inappropriate to remove the leased asset from the lessor's books and accounting for the lease as an operating lease is more appropriate.

15. (C)   The lease receivable is the present value of the minimum lease payments.

16. (A)   Whether the estimated residual value is guaranteed or unguaranteed is of accounting consequence to the lessee. The accounting difference is that the minimum lease payments, the basis for capitalization, includes the guaranteed residual value but excludes the unguaranteed residual value. A guaranteed residual value affects the lessee's computation of minimum lease payments and, therefore, the amounts capitalized as a leased asset and a lease obligation.

17. (D)   The residual value is the estimated fair market value of a leased asset at the end of the lease term. A guaranteed residual value occurs when a lessee or another third party agrees to make up any deficiency below a stated amount that the lessor realizes at the end of the lease term. If the residual value is guaranteed by a third party, it is treated by the lessee as an additional payment and by the lessor as realized at the end of the lease term.

18. (B)   If, at the end of the lease, the fair market value of the residual value is less than $10,000, Davies Co. will have to record a loss. Because the fair market value was only $5,500, Davies Co. will record a $4,500 loss ($10,000 - $5,500).

19. (A)   If, at the end of the lease, the fair market value of the residual value is greater than $10,000, Davies Co. will have to record a gain. Because the fair market value was $10,500, Davies Co. will record a $500 gain ($10,500 - $10,000).

20. (C)   The manner in which rental receipts are recorded, the amount of depreciation recorded, and the allocation of initial direct costs are not primary differences in applying the financing method to a direct financing lease or a sales-type lease. The primary difference is in recognition of the manufacturer's or dealer's profit at the inception of the lease.

21.   (B)   Under a sales-type lease, the amount of profit on the sale is the difference between the sales price of the asset and the cost of the asset. For Debbie Company the amount of the profit is thus $40,000 ($350,000 - $310,000). The amount of the interest income is calculated by multiplying the net investment by the effective interest rate (and then pro-rating to the portion of the year). In this case, the net investment at December 31, 2010, was $300,000 ($350,000 - $50,000) and the effective interest rate is 9% to obtain $27,000. However, because only a half a year has passed, only half of the $27,000, or $13,500, should be considered earned.

*22.   (D)   Any profit related to a sale-leaseback transaction in which the seller-lessee retains the right to substantially all of the remaining use of the equipment sold shall be deferred and amortized in proportion to the amortization of the leased asset, if a capital lease, or in proportion to the related gross rental charged to expense over the lease term, if an operating lease. It is important to note that losses are recognized immediately for either a capital or operating lease.

*23.   (C)   This lease is an operating lease to Cihla because there is no option to renew or repurchase the airplane, the lease term of 4 years is less than 75% of the estimated life of the aircraft (8 x 75 % = 6) and the present value of the lease payments is less than 90% of the fair value of the airplane (the lease payments without calculating present value are $240,000 ($5,000 x 12 x 4), which is less than 90% of the fair value of the plane of $360,000 (90% x $400,000). Therefore, Cihla accounts for the transaction as a sale and the lease as an operating lease. The rent expense for the year is therefore $15,000 [($5,000 x 12) ÷ 4].

*24.   (B)   Profit or loss in a sale-leaseback situation should be deferred and amortized. If the lease is a capital lease the profit or loss should be deferred and amortized over the lease term in proportion to the amortization of the leased assets. In an operating lease, the profit or loss should be deferred and amortized in proportion to the rental payments over the period of time the assets are expected to be used by the lessee.

REVIEW EXERCISES

1.   a.   The lessee should account for a lease arrangement as a capital lease if at the date of the lease agreement the lease meets **one or more** of the following four criteria:

        (1)   The lease transfers ownership of the property to the lessee.

        (2)   The lease contains a bargain purchase option.

        (3)   The lease term is equal to 75% or more of the estimated economic life of the lease property.

        (4)   The present value of the minimum lease payments (excluding executory costs) equals or exceeds 90% of the fair value of the leased property.

    b.   The lessor should account for a lease as a direct financing lease if it meets **one or more** of the criteria noted in "a" above and **both** of the following criteria:

        (1)   Collectibility of the payments required from the lessee is reasonably predictable.

        (2)   No important uncertainties surround the amount of unreimbursable costs yet to be incurred by the lessor under the lease.

2.	a.	Lease Receivable	120,000.00	
		Equipment		120,000.00
	b.	Cash	36,230.50	
		Lease Receivable		26,630.50
		Interest Revenue		9,600.00
	c.	Interest income earned during the first year:		
		Unearned Interest Revenue--Leases	9,600.00	
		Interest Revenue--Leases		9,600.00
3.	a.	Initial recording by lessee:		
		Leased Equipment Under Capital Leases	120,000.00	
		Obligations Under Capital Leases		120,000.00
	b.	Lease payment on 12-31-11		
		Interest Expense	7,469.56	
		Obligations Under Capital Leases	28,760.94	
		Cash		36,230.50
	c.	Equipment purchase on 12-31-10		
		Equipment	130,000.00	
		Accumulated Depreciation--Capital Lease	120,000.00	
		Leased Equipment Under Capital Leases		120,000.00
		Accumulated Depreciation--Equipment		120,000.00
		Cash		10,000.00

4.
Freter Company
Lease Amortization Schedule
(Annuity Due Basis)

Date	Annual Lease Payment (a)	Interest (12%) on Unpaid Obligation (b)	Reduction of Lease Obligation (c)	Balance of Lease Obligation (d)
1/1/11				$214,679
1/1/11	$42,000	-0-	$42,000	172,679
1/1/12	42,000	20,721	21,279	151,400
1/1/13	42,000	18,168	23,832	127,568
1/1/14	42,000	15,308	26,692	100,876
1/1/15	42,000	12,105	29,895	70,981
1/1/16	42,000	8,518	33,482	37,499
1/1/17	42,000	4,501*	37,499	-0-

*Rounded

(a)   Annual rental payment.
(b)   12% of the preceding balance of (d) for 1/1/11; since this is an annuity due, no time has elapsed at the date of the first payment and no interest has accrued.
(c)   (a) minus (b).
(d)   1/1/11 amount is computed by multiplying $42,000 (annual lease payment) by 5.11141 (present value of annuity due of seven periods at 12% from Table 6-5). Remaining amounts in column (d) are computed by subtracting (c) from the previous amount in column (d).

5.   a.
Fair market value of leased asset	$280,000
Less: Present value of unguaranteed residual value of	
$52,000 X .45235 (present value of 1 at 12% for 7 periods)	23,522
Amount to be recovered through lease payments	$256,478
Seven periodic lease payments: $256,478/5.11141*	$ 50,178

*(Present value of annuity due of 1 for 7 periods at 12%)

b.
Hom Leasing Company
Lease Amortization Schedule

Date	Annual Lease Payment Plus URV	Interest on Lease Receivable	Lease Receivable Recovery	Balance of Lease Receivable
1/1/10				$280,000
1/1/10	$50,178		$50,178	229,822
1/1/11	50,178	$27,579	22,599	207,223
1/1/12	50,178	24,867	25,311	181,912
1/1/13	50,178	21,829	28,349	153,563
1/1/14	50,178	18,428	31,750	121,813
1/1/15	50,178	14,618	35,560	86,253
1/1/16	50,178	10,350	39,828	46,425
12/31/16	52,000	5,575*	46,425	-0-
	$403,246	$123,246	$280,000	

*($4 rounding error)

c.

January 1, 2010

Lease Receivable	280,000	
Equipment		280,000
Cash	50,178	
Lease Receivable		50,178

December 31, 2010

Interest Receivable	27,579	
Interest Revenue		27,579

January 1, 2011

Cash	50,178	
Lease Receivable		22,599
Interest Receivable		27,579

December 31, 2011

Interest Receivable	24,867	
Interest Revenue—Leases		24,867

22

Accounting Changes and
Error Analysis

CHAPTER STUDY OBJECTIVES

1. Identify the types of accounting changes.

2. Describe the accounting for changes in accounting principles.

3. Understand how to account for retrospective accounting changes.

4. Understand how to account for impracticable changes.

5. Describe the accounting for changes in estimates.

6. Identify changes in a reporting entity.

7. Describe the accounting for correction of errors.

8. Identify economic motives for changing accounting methods.

9. Analyze the effect of errors.

*10. Make the computations and prepare the entries necessary to record a change from or to the equity method of accounting.

CHAPTER REVIEW

1.   Chapter 22 discusses the different procedures used to report accounting changes and error corrections. The use of estimates in accounting as well as the uncertainty that surrounds many of the events accountants attempt to measure may make adjustments to the financial reporting process necessary.   The accurate reporting of these adjustments in a manner that facilitates analysis and understanding of financial statements is the focus of this chapter.

Types of Accounting Changes

2.   (S.O. 1) The FASB has standardized the manner in which accounting changes are reported. The three types of accounting changes are as follows:

   a. **Change in Accounting Principle.** A change from one generally accepted accounting principle to another one.

   b. **Change in Accounting Estimate.** A change that occurs as the result of new information or additional experience. An example is a change in the estimate of the useful lives of depreciable assets.

   c. **Change in Reporting Entity.** A change from reporting as one type of entity to another type of entity, for example, changing specific subsidiaries comprising the group of companies for which consolidated financial statements are prepared.

  *   *Note: All asterisked (*) items relate to material contained in the Appendix to the chapter.*

Errors in Financial Statements

3.   Errors result from mathematical mistakes, mistakes in applying accounting principles, or oversight or misuse of facts that existed when preparing financial statements.

Changes in Accounting Principle

4.   (S.O. 2) A change in accounting principle is not considered to result from the adoption of a new principle in recognition of events that have occurred for the first time or that were previously immaterial. For example, implementing a credit sales policy when one had not previously existed is not considered a change in accounting principle. Also, a change from an accounting principle that is not acceptable to a principle that reflects GAAP is considered **a correction of an error.** Thus, only those changes from one GAAP to another GAAP are defined as a change in accounting principle. Also, an enterprise wishing to change from one GAAP to another GAAP must demonstrate that the new principle provides more useful financial information.

5.   Three approaches are suggested for recording the effect of changes in accounting principles: (a) **currently,** (b) **retrospectively,** and (c) **prospectively.** The FASB requires that companies use the retrospective approach.

6.   Treating a change in accounting principle currently requires computation of the cumulative effect of the change on financial statements in the current year's income statement as an irregular item. Advocates of this method contend that investor confidence is lost by a retroactive adjustment of financial statements for prior periods.

7.   **Retrospective Application** refers to the application of a different accounting principle to recast previously issued financial statements as if the new principle had always been used. The company shows any cumulative effect of the change as an adjustment to beginning retained earnings of the earliest year presented.

8.   **Prospective** treatment of a change in accounting principle requires no change in previously reported results. Opening balances are not adjusted and no attempt is made to compensate for prior events. Advocates of this position contend that financial statements based on acceptable accounting principles are final since management cannot change prior periods by subsequently adopting a new principle.

Retrospective Changes

9.   (S.O. 3) A retrospective adjustment of the financial statements presented is made by recasting the statements of prior years on a basis consistent with the newly adopted principle. Any part of the cumulative effect attributable to years prior to those presented is treated as an adjustment of beginning retained earnings of the earliest year presented.

10.   When a company makes a change in accounting principle, the FASB takes the position that all **direct effects** should be presented retrospectively, but **indirect effects** should not be shown retrospectely. The indirect effects are reported only in the current period.

11.   When a company cannot determine the prior period effects using every reasonable effort to do so, it is considered **impracticable** and the company should not use retrospective application. If any one of the following conditions exists, a company should not use retrospective application (a) The company cannot determine the effects of the retrospective application; (b) Retrospective application requires assumptions about management's intent in a prior period or (c) Retrospective application requires significant estimates for a prior period and the company cannot objectively verify the necessary information to develop these estimates.

Changes in Estimates

12.   (S.O. 5) The FASB requires that **changes in estimates** (for example, uncollectible receivables, useful lives, and salvage values of assets) should be handled prospectively. Opening balances are not adjusted and no attempt is made to "catch up" for prior periods. The effects of all changes in estimates are accounted for in **(a)** the period of change if the change affects that period only or **(b)** the period of change and future periods if the change affects both.

13.   For example (ignoring taxes), if an asset with a cost of $250,000 and no salvage value was originally depreciated on a straight-line basis for the first 7 years of its 25 year useful life, the book value of the asset at the end of year 7 would be $180,000 ($250,000 - $70,000). If the estimated useful life was revised at the end of year 7, and the asset was assumed to have a remaining useful life of 9 years, the following journal entry would be made for depreciation at the end of year 8:

Depreciation Expense...	20,000*	
Accumulated Depreciation		20,000
*($180,000/9)		

Whenever it is impossible to determine whether a change in principle or a change in estimate has occurred, the change should be considered a change in estimate. Also, some problems arise in differentiating between a change in an estimate and a correction of an error. The general rule is that careful estimates that later prove to be incorrect should be considered changes in estimates.

Change in an Entity

14.   (S.O.6) Reporting a **change in an entity** requires restating the financial statements of all prior periods presented to show the financial information for the new reporting entity for all periods. The financial statements of the year in which the change in reporting entity is made should describe the nature of the change and the reason for it.

Corrections of Errors

15.   (S.O.7) The FASB requires that corrections of errors be **(a)** treated as prior period adjustments, **(b)** recorded in the year in which the error was discovered, and **(c)** reported in the financial statements as an adjustment to the beginning balance of retained earnings. If comparative statements are presented, the prior statements affected should be restated to correct for the error.

16.   The text includes a Summary of Accounting Changes and Corrections of Errors. This summary indicates the accounting to be accorded an accounting change or an error correction along with the financial statement presentation and disclosure requirements to be considered. This summary is an effective way to review the major concepts and to assess your understanding of the manner in which accounting changes and errors should be handled in the financial statements.

Motivations for Change of Accounting Method

17. (S.O.8) Managers might have varying motives for reporting income numbers. Research shows some of these reasons involve political costs, capital structure, bonus payments, and to smooth earnings. To counter these pressures, the FASB has declared they will assess proposed standards from a position of neutrality.

Error Analysis

18. (S.O.9) Errors occurring in the accounting process can result from mathematical mistakes, bad faith accounting estimates, misapplication of accounting principles, as well as numerous other causes. As indicated earlier, the profession requires that errors be treated as prior period adjustments and be reported in the current year as adjustments to the beginning balance of Retained Earnings.

19. **Counterbalancing errors** are errors that occur in one period and correct themselves in the next period. **Noncounterbalancing** errors take longer than two periods to correct themselves and sometimes may exist until the item in error is no longer a part of the entity's financial statements. In the case of counterbalancing errors found at the end of the first period, the necessity for preparing a correcting journal entry depends on whether or not the books have been closed. If the books have been closed, no correcting entry is needed. Noncounterbalancing errors should always be corrected if discovered before they correct themselves, even if the books have been closed. The following indicates the accounting treatment for counterbalancing errors based on whether or not the books are closed.

1.   **The books have been closed.**

   a.   If the error has already counterbalanced, no entry is necessary.
   b.   If the error has not yet counterbalanced, an entry is necessary to adjust the beginning balance of Retained Earnings.

2.   **The books have not been closed.**

   a.   If the error has already counterbalanced and we are in the second year, an entry is necessary to correct the current period and to adjust the beginning balance of Retained Earnings.
   b.   If the error is not yet counterbalanced, an entry is necessary to adjust the beginning balance of Retained Earnings and correct the current period.

20. Some examples of counterbalancing and noncounterbalancing errors are presented here:

Counterbalancing Errors

   a.   Failure to record accrued revenues or expenses.
   b.   Failure to record prepaid revenues or expenses.
   c.   Overstatement or understatement of purchases.
   d.   Overstatement or understatement of ending inventory.

Noncounterbalancing Errors

   a.   Failure to record depreciation.
   b.   Recording a depreciable asset as an expense.
   c.   Recording the purchase of land as an expense.
   d.   Recording the discount on bonds as interest expense in the year of issue.

21.   To demonstrate a counterbalancing error assume a building owner received a rent payment for the 2011 rent of $24,000 on December 31, 2010. The following entry was made on 12/31/10 and no adjustment was recorded:

Cash	24,000	
Rent Revenue		24,000

This would cause Rent Revenue to be overstated in 2010. If the error was found in 2011, the following entry would be made assuming the books had not been closed for 2011:

Retained Earnings	24,000	
Rent Revenue		24,000

This entry would reduce Retained Earnings for the overstatement of Rent Revenue in 2010 and properly state the Rent Revenue account for 2011. If this error were discovered after the books were closed in 2011, no entry would be made because the error is counterbalanced.

22.   In situations where a great many errors are encountered, use of a work sheet, as demonstrated in the text, can facilitate analysis and ultimate correction of account balances. When numerous accounting errors are encountered, it is important to have an organized approach in deciding on the account balances in need of adjustment.   The work sheet provides the organization necessary to provide an orderly approach to error correction. Review of the comprehensive illustration on error correction at the end of the chapter will benefit the student's understanding of the work sheet and the suggested approach to error analysis and correction.

Change from the Equity Method

*23. (S.O.10) If the investor level of influence or ownership falls below that necessary for continued use of the equity method, a change must be made to the fair value method. The earnings or losses that were previously recognized by the investor under the equity method should remain as part of the carrying amount of the investment with no retroactive restatement to the new method.

Change to the Equity Method

*24. When converting to the equity method, a retroactive adjustment is necessary. Such a change involves adjusting retroactively the carrying amount of the investment, results of current and prior operations, and retained earnings of the investor as if the equity method had been in effect during all of the previous periods in which this investment was held.

GLOSSARY

Change in accounting estimate.
A change that occurs as the result of new information or as additional experience is acquired.

Change in accounting principle.
A change from one generally accepted accounting principle to another generally accepted accounting principle.

Change in reporting entity.
A change from reporting as one type of entity to another type of entity.

Counterbalancing errors.
Errors that will be offset or corrected over two periods.

Current adjustment.
The cumulative effect of the use of the new method on the financial statements at the beginning of the period is computed and is reported in the current year's income statement as an irregular item.

Errors in financial statements.
Errors occur as a result of mathematical mistakes, mistakes in the application of accounting principles, or oversight or misuse of facts that existed at the time financial statements were prepared.

Noncounterbalancing errors.
Errors that are not offset in the next accounting period.

Pro-forma statements.
Supplementary statements that are shown on an "as if" basis.

Prospective adjustment.
Previously reported results remain; no change is made. Opening balances are not adjusted, and no attempt is made to allocate charges or credits for prior events.

Retrospective adjustment.
The cumulative effect of the use of the new method on the financial statements at the beginning of the period is computed and the prior years' financial statements are recast on a basis consistent with the newly adopted principle.

CHAPTER OUTLINE

Fill in the outline presented below.

(S.O. 1) Types of Accounting Changes

   Change in Accounting Principle

   Change in Accounting Estimate

   Change in Reporting Entity

   Errors in Financial Statements

(S.O. 2) Changes in Accounting Principle

(S.O. 3) Retrospective-Effect Type Accounting Change

(S.O. 4) Impracticability

(S.O. 5) Changes in Accounting Estimate

Chapter Outline *(continued)*

(S.O. 6) Reporting a Change in Entity

(S.O. 7) Reporting a Correction of an Error

(S.O. 8) Motivations for Change

(S.O. 9) Error Analysis

Counterbalancing errors

Noncounterbalancing errors

*(S.O. 10) Changing From the Equity Method

Changing to the Equity Method

REVIEW QUESTIONS AND EXERCISES

TRUE-FALSE

Indicate whether each of the following is true (T) or false (F) in the space provided.

_____ 1. (S.O. 1) Accounting alternatives diminish the comparability of financial information between periods and between companies. They also obscure useful historical trend data.

_____ 2. (S.O. 2) A change in accounting principle results when a company adopts a new principle in recognition of events that were previously immaterial.

_____ 3. (S.O. 2) A change in accounting principle results when a company changes from one GAAP to another GAAP.

_____ 4. (S.O. 2) Instituting a policy whereby customers can now purchase merchandise on account, when in the past only cash sales were accepted, is evidence that a change in accounting principle has occurred.

_____ 5. (S.O. 2) If the previously used accounting principle was **not** acceptable, a change to a generally accepted accounting principle is considered a change in principle.

_____ 6. (S.O. 2) The FASB requires companies to use the prospective (in the future) approach for reporting changes in accounting principles.

_____ 7. (S.O. 3) When a company changes an accounting principle under the retrospective approach it adjusts its financial statements for each prior period presented.

_____ 8. (S.O. 3) When a company changes an accounting principle it should **not** adjust any assets or liabilities.

_____ 9. (S.O. 3)   When a company changes an accounting principle, one of the disclosure requirements is to show the cumulative effect of the change on retained earnings as of the beginning of the earliest period presented.

_____ 10. (S.O. 3) The FASB takes the position that companies should retrospectively apply the indirect effects of a change in accounting principle.

_____ 11. (S.O. 4) Companies should use retrospective application if the company cannot determine the effects of the retrospective application.

_____ 12. (S.O. 4) If it becomes impracticable to use retrospective application for a change in accounting principle, a company should prospectively apply the new accounting principle.

_____ 13. (S.O. 5) Changes in estimates must be handled prospectively.

_____ 14. (S.O. 5) If a change in an accounting estimate affects current net income by an amount equal to or greater than 1% of net income, the change should be handled retroactively.

_____ 15. (S.O. 5) Whenever it is impossible to determine whether a change in principle or a change in estimate has occurred, the change should be considered a change in estimate.

_____ 16.   (S.O.5) When it is impossible to differentiate between a change in estimate and correction of an error, companies should consider careful estimates that later prove to be incorrect as a correction of an error.

_____ 17.   (S.O.6) When a company makes changes that result in different reporting entities, the company should report the change by changing the financial statements of all prior periods presented and the revised statements should show the financial information for the new reporting entity for all periods.

_____ 18.   (S.O.7) A change from an accounting principle that is **not** generally accepted to an accounting principle that is acceptable should be treated as an accounting error.

_____ 19.   (S.O. 7) GAAP requires that corrections of errors be handled prospectively and shown in the current operating section of the income statement in the year the correction is made.

_____ 20.   (S.O. 7) Counterbalancing errors are two separate errors that offset one another in the same accounting period.

_____ 21.   (S.O. 7) Recording the purchase of land as an expense is an example of a noncounter-balancing error.

_____ 22.   (S.O. 9) If accrued wages are overlooked at the end of the accounting period, expenses and liabilities will be understated and net income will be overstated.

_____ 23.   (S.O. 9) If a counterbalancing error is discovered after the books are closed in the second year, no correcting entry is needed.

_____ 24.   (S.O. 9) An understatement in ending inventory will result in a corresponding understatement of net income.

_____ *25.   (S.O. 10) If an investor's level of influence has changed requiring the investor to change from the equity method to the fair value method, a retroactive adjustment is necessary.

MULTIPLE CHOICE

Select the best answer for each of the following items and enter the corresponding letter in the space provided.

_____ 1. (S.O. 1) Which of the following financial statement characteristics is adversely affected by accounting changes?

  A. Usefulness.
  B. Consistency.
  C. Timeliness.
  D. Relevance.

_____ 2. (S.O. 2) A change in accounting principle is evidenced by:

  A. a change from the historical cost principle to current value accounting.
  B. adopting the allowance method in estimating bad debts expense when a credit sales policy is instituted.
  C. changing the basis of inventory pricing from weighted-average cost to LIFO.
  D. a change from current value accounting to the historical cost principle.

_____ 3. (S.O. 2) Which of the following is **not** a change in accounting principle?

  A. A change from completed-contracts to percentage-of-completion.
  B. A change from FIFO to average cost.
  C. Using a different method of depreciation for new plant assets.
  D. A change from LIFO to FIFO for inventory valuation.

_____ 4. (S.O. 2) Schoen Company experienced a change in accounting principle which it accounted for in the following manner: opening balances were **not** adjusted and no attempt was made to allocate charges or credits for prior events. This method of recording an accounting change is known as handling the change:

  A. prospectively.
  B. currently.
  C. retrospectively.
  D. haphazardly.

_____ 5. (S.O. 2) A company that reports changes retrospectively would:

  A. report the cumulative effect in the current year's income statement as an irregular item.
  B. not change any prior-year financial statements.
  C. make changes prospectively.
  D. show any cumulative effect of the change as an adjustment to beginning retained earnings of the earliest year presented.

_____ 6. (S.O. 2) According to the FASB, which approach is required for reporting changes in an accounting principle?

     A.   Currently
     B.   Retrospectively
     C.   Prospectively
     D.   Futuristically

Questions 7, 8, and 9 are based on the following information:

In 2011, Skaggs Co., changed from FIFO to average cost for recording its inventory. The following information shows the differences in income for Skaggs since it began business in 2006.

Net Income

Year	FIFO	Average Cost
2006	35,000	33,000
2007	63,000	67,000
2008	74,000	75,000
2009	79,000	78,000
2010	93,000	94,000
2011	87,500	89,000

_____ 7. (S.O. 3) What journal entry should Skaggs report at the beginning of 2008?

A.	No entry is necessary		
B.	Inventory	2,000	
	Retained Earnings		2,000
C.	Retained Earnings	2,000	
	Inventory		2,000
D.	Retained Earnings	4,000	
	Inventory		4,000

_____ 8. (S.O. 3) What journal entry should Skaggs report at the beginning of 2011?

A.	Retained Earnings	3,000	
	Inventory		3,000
B.	Retained Earnings	4,500	
	Inventory		4,500
C.	Inventory	3,000	
	Retained Earnings		3,000
D.	Inventory	4,500	
	Retained Earnings		4,500

_____ 9. (S.O. 3) If Skaggs presents comparative statements for 2009, 2010 and 2011, then it should:
   A. Change the beginning balance of retained earnings at January 1, 2006 by showing a decrease of $2,000.
   B. Change the beginning balance of retained earnings at January 1, 2007 by showing a decrease of $2,000.
   C. Change the beginning balance of retained earnings at January 1, 2008 by showing an increase of $2,000.
   D. Change the beginning balance of retained earnings at January 1, 2009 by showing an increase of $3,000.

_____ 10. (S.O. 3) Which of the following is **not** considered a direct effect of a change in accounting principle?

   A. An employee profit-sharing plan based on net income when a company uses the percentage-of-completion method.
   B. The inventory balance as a result of a change in the inventory valuation method.
   C. An impairment adjustment resulting from applying the lower-of-cost-or-market-test to the adjusted inventory balance.
   D. Deferred income tax effects of an impairment adjustment resulting from applying the lower-of-cost-or-market test to the adjusted inventory balance.

_____ 11. (S.O. 3) Weaver Company changes from the LIFO method to the FIFO method in 2011. The increase in pre-tax income as a result of the difference in the two methods prior to 2009 is $ 100,000 and for the year 2009 is $40,000 and for the year 2010 is $30,000. The estimated tax effect is 40%. The entry to record the change at the beginning of 2010 should include.

   A. A debit to Deferred Tax Liability of $68,000.
   B. A credit to Deferred Tax Liability of $68,000.
   C. A debit to Deferred Tax Liability of $56,000.
   D. A credit to Deferred Tax Liability of $56,000.

_____ 12. (S.O. 3) In 2010 the Flynn Company has changed from the percentage-of-completion method to the completed-contract method for long-term construction contracts. The difference in pre-tax income prior to 2010 is a decrease of $60,000 and for 2010 is a decrease of $20,000. The estimated tax effect is 40%. The journal entry made by Flynn Company should include a:
   A. Debit to Deferred Tax Liability of $24,000.
   B. Credit to Deferred Tax Liability of $32,000.
   C. Debit to Deferred Tax Liability of $32,000.
   D. Credit to Deferred Tax Liability of $24,000.

_____   13.   (S.O. 4) Which of the following is a condition in which retrospective application is **not** impracticable?
    A.   The company cannot determine the effects of retrospective application.
    B.   Retrospective application requires assumptions about management's intent in a prior period.
    C.   The company has changed auditors.
    D.   Retrospective application requires significant estimates for a prior period, and the company cannot objectively verify the necessary information to develop these estimates.

_____   14.   (S.O.5) Which of the following is **not** a part of applying the current and prospective approach in accounting for a change in an estimate?

    A.   Report current and future financial statements on a new basis.
    B.   Restate prior period financial statements.
    C.   Disclose in the year of change the effect on net income and earnings per share data for that period only.
    D.   Make no adjustments to current period opening balances for purposes of catch-up.

_____   15.   (S.O. 6) Changing specific subsidiaries that constitute the group of companies for which consolidated financial statements are prepared is an example of a:
    A.   change in accounting estimate.
    B.   change in accounting principle.
    C.   change in segment reporting.
    D.   change in reporting entity.

_____   16.   (S.O. 6) Tang Corporation has a change in accounting that requires Tang to restate the financial statements of all prior periods presented and disclose in the year of change the effect on net income and earnings per share data for all prior periods presented.   This change is most likely the result of a:
    A.   change in depreciation methods.
    B.   change in accounting estimate.
    C.   change in reporting entity.
    D.   change in estimated recoverable mineral reserves.

_____   17.   (S.O. 7) Julie Company has accounted for its inventory using the NIFO (next-in, first-out) inventory method for the past two years. During the current year they changed to the FIFO inventory method at the insistence of their public accountant. The effect of this change should be reported, net of applicable income taxes, in the current:

    A.   income statement after income from continuing operations and before extraordinary items.
    B.   retained earnings statement after net income but before dividends.
    C.   income statement after extraordinary items.
    D.   retained earnings statement as an adjustment of the opening balance.

_____   18.   (S.O. 7)   The general rule for differentiating between a change in an estimate and a correction of an error is:

   A.   based on the materiality of the amounts involved. Material items are handled as a correction of an error, whereas immaterial amounts are considered a change in an estimate.
   B.   if a generally accepted accounting principle is involved, it's usually a change in an estimate.
   C.   if a generally accepted accounting principle is involved, it's usually a correction of an error.
   D.   a careful estimate that later proves to be incorrect should be considered a change in an estimate.

Questions 19, 20, and 21 are based on the following information:

Martin Marty, Inc., is a calendar-year corporation. Its financial statements for the years ended 12/31/10 and 12/31/11 contained the following errors:

	2010	**2011**
Ending inventory	$5,000 overstatement	$8,000 understatement
Depreciation expense	$2,000 understatement	$4,000 overstatement

_____   19.   (S.O. 7)   Assume that the 2010 errors were not corrected and that no errors occurred in 2009. By what amount will 2010 income before income taxes be overstated or understated?

   A. $3,000 overstatement.
   B. $7,000 overstatement.
   C. $3,000 understatement.
   D. $7,000 understatement.

_____   20.   (S.O. 7)   Assume that no correcting entries were made at 12/31/10, or 12/31/11. Ignoring income taxes, by how much will retained earnings at 12/31/11 be overstated or understated?

   A. $7,000 overstatement.
   B. $8,000 overstatement.
   C. $3,000 understatement.
   D. $10,000 understatement.

_____   21.   (S.O. 7)   Assume that no correcting entries were made at 12/31/10 or 12/31/11 and that no additional errors occurred in 2012. By how much will 2012 income before income taxes be overstated or understated?

   A. $7,000 overstatement.
   B. $8,000 overstatement.
   C. $3,000 understatement.
   D. $10,000 understatement.

_____   22.   (S.O. 9) On December 31, 2010, accrued wages in the amount of $6,500 were **not** recognized by Shwenk Company. What effect would this error have on the following account balances at 12/31/10?

	Expenses	Retained Earnings	Liabilities	Assets
A.	No Effect	Overstate	Overstate	No Effect
B.	Overstate	Understate	No Effect	Overstate
C.	Understate	Overstate	Understate	No Effect
D.	No Effect	Overstate	No Effect	Understate

_____   23.   (S.O. 9) The December 31, 2010, physical inventory of Dunn Company appropriately included $4,500 of merchandise inventory that was **not** recorded as a purchase until January, 2011. What effect will this error have on the following account balances at 12/31/10?

	COGS	Liabilities	Retained Earnings	Assets
A.	Overstate	Overstate	Understate	Understate
B.	No Effect	Understate	Understate	Understate
C.	Understate	No Effect	Overstate	Overstate
D.	Understate	Understate	Overstate	No Effect

Use the following information for questions 24 and 25.

Kielty Company purchased machinery that cost $300,000 on January 1, 2008. The entire cost was recorded as an expense. The machinery has a nine-year life and a $12,000 residual value. Kielty uses the straight-line method to account for depreciation expense. The error was discovered on December 10, 2010. Ignore income tax considerations.

_____   24.   (S.O. 9) Kielty's income statement for the year ended December 31, 2010, should show that cumulative effect of this error in the amount of:
      A. $236,000.
      B. $224,000.
      C. $221,333.
      D. $ -0-.

_____   25.   (S.O. 9) Before the correction was made and before the books were closed on December 31, 2010, retained earnings was understated by:
      A. $300,000.
      B. $236,000.
      C. $224,000.
      D. $221,333.

REVIEW EXERCISES

1.   (S.O. 3) De Lacey Co. began operations on January 1, 2008, and uses the average cost method of pricing inventory. Management is going to change to the FIFO method for 2011. The following information is available for the years 2008-2011.

Net Income

	Average Cost Method	FIFO Method
2008	$135,000	$138,000
2009	142,000	147,000
2010	163,000	167,000
2011	172,000	177,000

Instructions
(ignore all tax effects):
a.   Prepare the journal entry necessary to record a change from the average cost method to the FIFO method in 2011.
b.   Determine net income to be reported for 2008, 2009, and 2010, after giving effect to the change in accounting principle.

a.

08	135,000	138,000	3,000
09	148,000	147,000	6,000
10	163,000	167,000	4,000
begin of 11	440,000	452,000	12,000
11	172,000	177,000	5,000

General Journal			J1
Date	**Account Title**	**Debit**	**Credit**
	Inventory	12,000	
	retained earnings		12,000

b.

2. (S. O. 1) Match the items listed on the left with the appropriate description listed on the right.

Item	Description
_____ 1. Changing the companies included in combined financial statements	A. Change in an accounting principle
_____ 2. Change from the cash basis of accounting to the accrual basis	B. Change in an accounting estimate
_____ 3. Change from LIFO to FIFO	C. Change in reporting entity
_____ 4. Change from sum-of-the-years'-digits to straight-line depreciation	D. Correction of an error
_____ 5. Change to consolidated financial statements from statements of individual companies	
_____ 6. Change in the percentage applied in the determination of bad debts, resulting from new market research study	
_____ 7. Change from the current value approach to the historical cost approach in accounting for plant assets	
_____ 8. Change to the "full cost" method of accounting by an oil company	
_____ 9. Change from FIFO to weighted-average cost	
_____ 10. Change in the salvage value of machinery due to an increase in the price of scrap metal	

3.   (S.O. 7)   A three-year fire insurance policy beginning on September 1, 2008, was erroneously debited to the Land account when the $720 premium was paid. During 2010 the company sold all its land, reducing the Land account to a zero balance. Using the amount recorded in the Land account, the company suffered a $400 loss on the sale.

720   160
            240
            320

loss on sale   400
gain on sale   320

Instructions:
Prepare two correcting entries

a.   assuming that the books have not been closed in 2010 and
b.   assuming that the books have been closed for 2010.

a.

General Journal			J1
Date	Account Title	Debit	Credit
	prepaid insurance	160	
	insurance exp	240	
	retained earnings	320	
	loss on sale of land		406
	gain on sale of land		320

b.

General Journal			J1
Date	Account Title	Debit	Credit
	prepaid insurance	160	
	retained earnings		160

4.   (S.O.7) Wolochuck Company is in the process of having its financial statements audited for the first time as of 12/31/10. The Company is in its 5th year of operations and has always relied on its bookkeeper to prepare annual financial statements. The auditor has found the following incorrect or overlooked items that occurred over the past 5 years.

a.   Wolochuck purchased a machine on June 30, 2007 at a cost of $45,000. The machine has a salvage value of $3,000 and a useful life of 6 years. The bookkeeper recorded straight-line depreciation during each year, but failed to consider the salvage value.

b.   During 2010, Wolochuck changed from the straight-line method of depreciation for its building to the double-declining method.   The auditor provided the following computations which present depreciation on both bases:

	2010	2009	2008
Straight-line	$36,000	$36,000	$36,000
Declining-balance	$47,360	$59,200	$74,000

c.   The physical inventory count on December 31, 2009, improperly excluded merchandise costing $20,000 that had been temporarily stored in a public warehouse. Wolochuck uses a periodic inventory system.

d.   A $18,000 insurance premium paid on October 1, 2009, for a policy that expires on September 30, 2012. The premium was charged to insurance expense when paid.

e.   Accrued wages of $3,500 were not recorded on December 31, 2008.

f.   The auditor discovered that a sale of land on February 20, 2008 resulted in a gain of $5,000. The land was purchased in 2002 for $27,000. When the bookkeeper recorded the sale in 2008 the gain was credited to common stock.

g.   An advance payment for rent was received on January 1, 2009. The payment was for $36,000 and covers 4 years of rent for a warehouse owned by Wolochuck. When the cash payment was received the bookkeeper recorded the following entry:

| Cash | 36,000 | |
| Rent Payable | | 36,000 |

The Rent Payable account has not been altered since its original recording.

Instructions:
Prepare the journal entries necessary at 12/31/10 to correct the books for the items found by the auditor. Assume the books have not been closed for 2010. Ignore income tax considerations.

	General Journal		J1
Date	Account Title	Debit	Credit

SOLUTIONS TO REVIEW QUESTIONS AND EXERCISES

TRUE-FALSE

1. (T)

2. (F)   Adoption of a new principle in recognition of events that were previously immaterial is not an accounting change, but should be treated as a correction of an error.

3. (T)

4. (F)   This is not a change in an accounting principle but rather a new transaction that results in the use of a principle not previously required.

5. (F)   If the previously used accounting principle was not acceptable, a change to a generally accepted accounting principle is considered a correction of an error.

6. (F)   The FASB requires companies to use the retrospective approach for reporting changes in accounting principles.

7. (T)

8. (F)   When a company changes an accounting principle it adjusts the carrying amounts of assets and liabilities as of the beginning of the first year presented.

9. (T)

10. (F)   The FASB takes the position that companies should not change prior-period amounts for indirect effects of a change in accounting principle.

11. (F)   Companies should not use retrospective application if the company cannot determine the effects of the retrospective application.

12. (T)

13. (T)

14. (F)   Changes in accounting estimates must be handled prospectively, that is, no changes should be made in previously reported results. Opening balances are not adjusted and no attempt is made to catch-up for prior periods.

15. (T)

16. (F)   When it is impossible to differentiate between a change in estimate and correction of an error, companies should consider careful estimates that later prove to be incorrect as a change in estimate.

17. (T)

18. (T)

19.   (F)   The profession requires that corrections of errors be treated as prior period adjustments, be recorded in the year in which the error was discovered, and be reported in the financial statements as an adjustment to the beginning balance of retained earnings. If comparative statements are presented, the prior statements affected should be restated to correct for the error.

20.   (F)   Counterbalancing errors are errors that will offset or correct themselves over two periods. For example, the failure to record accrued wages in period one will cause (1) net income to be overstated, (2) accrued wages payable to be understated, and (3) wages expense to be understated. If no attempt is made to correct this error, then in period two net income will be understated, accrued wages payable will be correct, and wages expense will be overstated. The net effect of this error for the two years (at the end of the second year) is that net income, accrued wages payable, and wages expense will be correct.

21.   (T)

22.   (T)

23.   (T)

24.   (T)

*25.   (F)   If an investor's level of influence has changed requiring the investor to change from the equity method to the fair value method, the earnings or losses that were previously recognized by the investor under the equity method should remain as part of the carrying amount of the investment with no retroactive restatement to the new method.

MULTIPLE CHOICE

1.   (B)   While the characteristics of usefulness and relevance may be enhanced by changes in accounting, the characteristic of consistency is adversely affected. Consistent financial statements and historical 5 and 10 year summaries particularly can be distorted by changes in accounting. When changes in accounting occur, proper treatment and full disclosure should enable readers of financial statements to comprehend and assess the effects of such changes. The timeliness of financial statements should be unaffected by accounting changes.

2.   (C)   Because current value accounting is not GAAP, alternatives A and D cannot be correct. A change in accounting principle is defined as a change from one GAAP to another GAAP. Alternative B is incorrect because adopting a principle for a new transaction does not constitute a change in accounting principle.

3.   (C)   When a company uses a different method of depreciation for new plant assets, this is not considered a change in accounting principle. A, B, and D are all considered changes in accounting principle.

4.   (A)   The company has handled its accounting change prospectively. This method is required to be used for changes in accounting estimates. When a change is handled currently, the cumulative effect of the use of the new method on the financial statements at the beginning of the period is computed. This adjustment is then reported in the current year's income statement as an irregular item. A retrospective adjustment of the financial statements is made by recasting the financial statements of prior years on a basis consistent with the newly adopted principle and any cumulative effect of the change as an adjustment to beginning retained earnings of the earliest year presented. There is no haphazard treatment advocated for accounting changes.

5.   (D)   A company that reports changes retrospectively would adjust prior years' statements on a basis consistent with the newly adopted principle. In addition the company should show any cumulative effect of the change as an adjustment to beginning retained earnings of the earliest year presented.

6.   (B)   The FASB requires that companies use the retrospective approach for reporting changes in accounting principles.

7.   (A)   A journal entry is necessary only for the current year to update the accounts to their corrected status. No journal entries are made in the books for previous years.

8.   (C)   To adjust the financial records for the change from FIFO to average cost, previous year differences are accumulated as follows:

Net Income

Year	FIFO	Average Cost	Difference in Income
2006	$ 35,000	$ 33,000	$ (2,000)
2007	63,000	67,000	4,000
2008	74,000	75,000	1,000
2009	74,000	78,000	(1,000)
2010	93,000	94,000	1,000
Total at beginning of 2011			$ 3,000

Therefore the journal entry for Skaggs should be as follows:

Inventory	3,000	
Retained Earnings		3,000

9.   (D)   If a company changes accounting principles it must change the beginning balance of retained earnings of the earliest year presented. Since Skaggs is presenting comparative statements for 2009, 2010 and 2011, it must change the beginning balance of retained earnings at January 1, 2009. The cumulative effect of the prior years is calculated as follows:

Net Income

Year	FIFO	Average Cost	Difference in Cost
2006	$35,000	$33,000	$(2,000)
2007	63,000	67,000	4,000
2008	74,000	75,000	1,000
Total at beginning of 2009			$3,000

10. (A) An employee profit sharing plan based on net income when a company uses the percentage-of-completion method is considered an indirect effect of a change in accounting principle. All the other answers are considered direct effects.

11. (D) The change in accounting principles from LIFO to FIFO would result in a direct effect adjustment to deferred taxes. Because income increased, there would be a 40% increase in Deferred Tax Liability which is done with a credit entry. The amount is calculated based on the sum of the prior years of $100,000 and $40,000 multiplied by 40%.

12. (A) The change in accounting principles from percentage-of-completion method to completed-contract method for long-term construction contracts would result in a direct effect adjustment to deferred taxes. Because income decreased, there would be a 40% decrease in Deferred Tax Liability which is done with a debit entry. The amount is calculated by multiplying the difference in pre-tax income prior to 2010 by 40%.

13. (C) Retrospective application is still practicable even though a company has changed auditors. All the other answers would make retrospective application impracticable.

14. (B) Restating prior period financial statements is a part of the application of the retroactive approach. That approach is not appropriate for changes in accounting estimates. Alternatives A, C, and D represent the appropriate treatment for the current and prospective approach as applied to accounting for a change in an estimate.

15. (D) This is an example of a change in the reporting entity. This occurs when a company makes a change from reporting as one type of entity to another type of entity. This type of change should be reported by restating the financial statements of all prior periods presented to show the financial information for the new reporting entity for all periods.

16. (C) The question describes most closely the accounting and disclosure requirements necessary for a change in reporting entity. Alternatives A, B and D are all changes in according estimates and do not require the disclosures indicated in the question.

17. (D) When a company changes from an accounting principle that is not generally accepted (NIFO) to one that is generally accepted (FIFO), the change should be handled as a correction of an error. In considering this change as a correction of an error, it should be handled as a prior period adjustment. Thus, the cumulative effect at the beginning of the period of change is entered directly as an adjustment to the opening balance of retained earnings.

18. (D) Distinguishing between a change in an estimate and a correction of an error is not necessarily determined by a GAAP being involved. Also, materiality is not one of the criteria to be used in differentiating between a change in an estimate and a correction of an error. The best basis for differentiating between a change in one estimate and a correction of an error is to follow the general rule that "careful estimates that later prove to be incorrect should be considered a change in an estimate."

19. (B)   **Effect on**

	2010 Income
Ending inventory $5,000 overstatement............................	$5,000 - over
Depreciation expense $2,000 understatement....................	2,000 - over
Net effect..	$7,000 - over

20. (D)

	Effect on 2008 Retained Earnings
2010 Ending inventory	
$5,000 overstatement	-0-*
2011 Ending inventory	
$8,000 understatement	8,000 - under
2010 Depreciation expense	
$2,000 understatement	2,000 - over
2011 Depreciation expense	
$4,000 overstatement	4,000 - under
Net effect..	$10,000 - under

*This is an example of a counterbalancing error. This error overstates income by $5,000 in 2010 and understates income by $5,000 in 2011. Thus, at the end of 2011, there is no effect on retained earnings. If the $8,000 inventory error is not corrected, it will correct itself at the end of 2012. The depreciation errors are noncounterbalancing and will cause retained earnings to be in error until specifically corrected.

21. (B)

	Effect on 2012 Net Income
2011 Ending inventory	
$8,000 understatement	$8,000 - over
Net effect...	$8,000 - over

The 2010 and 2011 depreciation expense errors do not affect 2009 net income.

22. (C)   A failure to record accrued wages is a failure to make the following journal entry:

Wages Expense	6,500	
Wages Payable		6,500

Thus, the expenses would be understated and the liabilities would be understated. The retained earnings would be overstated because the expense was not recorded. Assets would be unaffected by the failure to record this entry.

23. (D)   The merchandise was correctly counted in the physical inventory and thus ending inventory and total assets are properly stated. The fact that the purchase was not recorded understates liabilities because accounts payable was not credited. Also, with the purchase not being recorded, the amount of merchandise available for sale is understated and results in an understatement of cost of goods sold. The understatement of cost of goods sold causes both net income and retained earnings to be overstated.

24. (D)   The profession requires that corrections of errors be treated as prior period of adjustments, be recorded in the year in which the error was discovered, and be reported in the financial statements as an adjustment to the beginning balance of retained earnings. Therefore, Kielty's income statement for the year ended December 31, 2010 will not be affected.

25. (B)   Corrections of errors are treated as prior period adjustments and are reported in the financial statements as an adjustment to the beginning balance of retained earnings. The company should have taken $32,000 for each year [($300,000 - $12,000) /9 = $32,000]. Therefore, $64,000 ($32,000 x 2) should have been taken as depreciation expense and $300,000 should not have been recorded as an expense; therefore, the net effect is that retained earning was understated by $236,000 ($300,000 - $64,000).

REVIEW EXERCISES

1.   The following analysis is first performed:

Net Income

Year	Average cost	FIFO	Difference in Income
2008	$ 135,000	$138,000	$3,000
2009	142,000	147,000	5,000
2010	163,000	167,000	4,000
Total at beginning of 2011	$440,000	$452,000	$12,000
Total in 2011	$172,000	$177,000	$ 5,000

a.   The entry to record the change to the FIFO method at the beginning of 2011 is as follows:

Inventory	12,000	
Retained Earnings		12,000

b.   The net incomes to be reported for 2008, 2009 and 2010 after giving effect to the change in accounting principle should be $138,000, $147,000 and $167,000, respectively.

2.   1.   C   6.   B
     2.   D   7.   D
     3.   A   8.   A
     4.   B   9.   A
     5.   C   10. B

3.   a.

Prepaid Insurance*	160	
Insurance Expense	240	
Retained Earnings	320	
Loss on Sale of Land		400
Gain on Sale of Land		320

*Land account was overstated by $720, so the $400 loss is actually a $320 gain. As of 12/31/10, $560 (28/36) of the prepaid insurance has expired. $240 of this amount is an expense for 2010, with the remainder taken directly to Retained Earnings. The unexpired portion of the prepaid insurance is recorded as an asset (Prepaid Insurance, $160).

     b.

Prepaid Insurance	160	
Retained Earnings		160

4.   a.   Accumulated Depreciation   1,750
            Depreciation Expense...   500
            Retained Earnings..   1,250

	2007-2009	2010
Depreciation Taken	$18,750	$7,500
Depreciation (Correct)	$17,500	$7,000
	$ 1,250	$ 500

   b.   Cumulative Effect of Change in Accounting Principle.   61,200*
            Accumulated Depreciation   61,200

        *($59,200 - $36,000) + ($74,000 - $36,000)

            Depreciation Expense.................................   47,360
            Accumulated Depreciation   47,360

   c.   Inventory (beginning)....................................   20,000
            Retained Earnings..   20,000

   d.   Insurance Expense   6,000
            Prepaid Insurance   10,500
            Retained Earnings..   16,500

   e.   No entry, this counterbalancing error has counterbalanced as of the end of 2009.

   f.   Common Stock   5,000
            Retained Earnings..   5,000

   g.   Rent Payable...   36,000
            Unearned Rent Revenue......................................   18,000
            Rent Revenue   9,000
            Retained Earnings..   9,000

23

Statement of Cash Flows

CHAPTER STUDY OBJECTIVES

1. Describe the purpose of the statement of cash flows.

2. Identify the major classifications of cash flows.

3. Differentiate between net income and net cash flows from operating activities.

4. Contrast the direct and indirect methods of calculating net cash flow from operating activities.

5. Determine net cash flows from investing and financing activities.

6. Prepare a statement of cash flows.

7. Identify sources of information for a statement of cash flows.

8. Identify special problems in preparing a statement of cash flows.

9. Explain the use of a work sheet in preparing a statement of cash flows.

CHAPTER REVIEW

1. Corporate investors and potential investors seek information about the financial position, results of operations, and cash flow. Chapter 23 describes the significance of the statement of cash flows and all aspects of its preparation. Numerous examples are included which assist in an understanding of how the statement is prepared and presented.

Purpose of the Statement of Cash Flows

2. (S.O. 1) The information in a statement of cash flows should help investors, creditors, and others to assess: (1) the entity's ability to generate future cash flows; (2) the entity's ability to pay dividends and meet obligations; (3) the reasons for the difference between net income and net cash flow from operating activities; and (4) the cash and noncash investing and financing transactions during the period.

Classification of Cash Flows

3.   (S.O. 2) The statement of cash flows classifies cash receipts and cash payments by **operating, investing,** and **financing** activities. **Operating activities** include all transactions and events that are not investing and financing activities. Operating activities include cash effects of **transactions that enter into the determination of net income,** such as cash receipts from the sales of goods and services and cash payments to suppliers and employees for acquisitions of inventory and expenses. **Investing activities** include **(a)** making and collecting loans and **(b)** acquiring and disposing of investments and productive long-lived assets. **Financing activities** involve liability and owners' equity items and include **(a)** obtaining cash from creditors and repaying the amounts borrowed and **(b)** obtaining capital from owners and providing them with a return on, and return of, their investment.

4.   The typical cash receipts and cash payments of a business entity classified according to operating, investing, and financing activities are shown below.

> **Operating Activities**
>   Cash inflows
>   From sale of goods or services.
>   From returns on loans (interest) and on equity securities (dividends).
>   Cash outflows
>   To suppliers for inventory.
>   To employees for services.
>   To government for taxes.
>   To lenders for interest.
>   To others for expenses.
> **Investing Activities**
>   Cash inflows
>   From sale of property, plant, and equipment.
>   From sale of debt or equity securities of other entities.
>   From collection of principal on loans to other entities.
>   Cash outflows
>   To purchase property, plant, and equipment.
>   To purchase debt or equity securities of other entities.
>   To make loans to other entities.
> **Financing Activities**
>   Cash inflows
>   From sale of equity securities.
>   From issuance of debt (bonds and notes).
>   Cash outflows
>   To shareholders as dividends.
>   To redeem long-term debt or reacquire capital stock.

It should be noted that (1) operating activities involve income determination items, **(2)** investing activities involve cash flows generally resulting from changes in long-term asset items, and **(3)** financing activities involve cash flows generally resulting from changes in long-term liability and stockholders' equity items.

5.   Some cash flows relating to investing or financing activities are classified as operating activities. For example, receipts of investment income (interest and dividends) and payments of interest to lenders are classified as operating activities. Conversely, some cash flows relating to operating activities are classified as investing or financing activities. For example, the cash received from the sale of property, plant, and equipment at a gain, although reported in the income statement, is classified as an investing activity, and the effect of the related gain would not be included in net cash flow from operating activities. Likewise a gain or loss on the payment of debt would generally be part of the cash outflow related to the repayment of the amount borrowed and, therefore, is a financing activity.

Steps in Preparation

6.   The information used to prepare the statement of cash flows generally comes from three major sources: (a) **comparative balance sheets,** (b) **the current income statement,** and (c) **selected transaction data.** Actual preparation of the statement of cash flows involves three steps:

    (1)   **Determine the change in cash.** This procedure is straightforward because the difference between the beginning and ending cash balance can be easily computed from an examination of the comparative balance sheets.

    (2)   **Determine the net cash flow from operating activities.** This procedure is complex; it involves analyzing not only the current year's income statement but also comparative balance sheets as well as selected transaction data.

    (3)   **Determine cash flows from investing and financing activities.** All other changes in the balance sheet accounts must be analyzed to determine their effect on cash.

7.   (S.O. 3) To compute net cash flows from operating activities it is necessary to report revenues and expenses on a cash basis. This is done by eliminating the effects of income statement transactions that did not result in a corresponding increase or decrease in cash. The conversion of accrual-based net income to net cash flow from operating activities may be done through either the **direct method** or **the indirect method.**

Direct and Indirect Methods

8.   (S.O. 4) Under the **direct method** (also called the income statement method) cash revenues and expenses are determined. The difference between these two amounts represents net cash flows from operating activities. In essence, the direct method results in the presentation of a cash basis income statement. Under the **indirect method** (also called the reconciliation method), computation of net cash flows from operating activities begins with net income. This accrual based amount is then converted to net cash provided by operating activities by adding back noncash expenses and charges and deducting noncash revenues. For example, an increase in accounts receivable during the year means that sales for the year increased receivables without a corresponding increase in cash. Thus, the increase in accounts receivable must be deducted from net income to arrive at cash provided by operations. Similarly, if an entry was made at the end of the year for accrued wages, the wages expense would increase without a corresponding decrease in cash. Thus, the increase in accrued wages would have to be added back to net income to arrive at cash provided by operations.

9.   The accounting profession encourages the use of the direct method when preparing the statement of cash flows, use of the indirect method is also permitted. However, if the direct method is used the FASB requires that a reconciliation of net income to net cash flow from operating activities shall be provided in a separate schedule. Therefore, under either method, the indirect (reconciliation) approach must be presented. The text book includes **three comprehensive illustrations** which provide a detailed explanation of the preparation and presentation of the statement of cash flows. Each illustration should be studied prior to attempting the assigned problem material.

10.   Both the direct method and the indirect method have distinct advantages which should be considered when deciding on the method to be used in presenting the statement of cash flows. The principal advantage of the direct method is that it shows operating cash receipts and payments. Supporters contend that this is useful in estimating future cash flows and in assessing an entity's ability to **(a)** generate sufficient cash flow from operations for the payment of debt, **(b)** reinvest in its operations, and **(c)** make distributions to owners. Proponents of the indirect method cite the fact that it focuses on the difference between net income and net cash flow from operations as its principal advantage. Also, supporters of the indirect method contend that users are more familiar with the method and it is less costly to present the statement of cash flows using this method.

Direct Method Disclosures

11.   (S.O. 7) Minimum disclosure requirements for companies which use the direct method include the following.

Receipts
a.   Cash collected from customers.
b.   Interest and dividends received.
c   Other operating cash receipts, if any.

Payments
a.   Cash paid to suppliers and employees for goods and services.
b.   Interest paid.
c.   Income taxes paid.
d.   Other operating cash payments, if any.

Use of the indirect method requires separate disclosure of changes in inventory, receivables, and payables relating to operating activities. Such disclosures are required for the purpose of aiding users in approximating the direct method.

Indirect Method Disclosures

12. The schedule shown below presents the common types of adjustments that are made to net income to arrive at net cash flow provided by operating activities under the indirect method.

Additions to Net Income
Depreciation expense.
Amortization of intangibles and deferred charges.
Amortization of bond discount.
Increase in deferred income tax liability.
Loss on investment in common stock using equity method.
Loss on sale of plant assets.
Decrease in receivables.
Decrease in inventories.
Decrease in prepaid expenses.
Increase in accounts payable.
Increase in accrued liabilities.

Deductions from Net Income
Amortization of bond premium.
Decrease in deferred income tax liability.
Income on investment in common stock using equity method.
Gain on sale of plant assets.
Increase in receivables.
Increase in inventories.
Increase in prepaid expenses.
Decrease in accounts payable.
Decrease in accrued liabilities.

Special Problems

13. (S.O. 8) Nine items, described as special problems related to preparing the statement of cash flows, are presented in the text material. These items relate to various aspects of the statement of cash flows and should be understood for accurate preparation of the statement.

(a) **Adjustments similar to depreciation** - depreciation expense is added back to net income to arrive at net cash provided by operating activities. Likewise, amortization of intangible assets and amortization of deferred costs are also added back to net income.

(b) **Accounts receivable (net)** - an increase in the Allowance for Doubtful Accounts should be added back to net income to arrive at net cash provided by operating activities. This is due to the fact that the increase in the allowance results in a charge to bad debts expense (a noncash expense).

(c) **Other working capital changes** - some changes in working capital, although they affect cash, do not affect net income. Generally, these are investing or financing activities of a current nature such as the purchase of short-term investments (trading and available-for-sale securities).

(d) **Net losses -** if an enterprise reports a net loss instead of net income, the net loss must be adjusted for those items that do not result in a cash inflow or outflow. As a result of such adjustments, the net loss may turn out to be a positive cash flow from operating activities.

(e) **Gains -** because a gain on the sale of plant assets is reported in the statement of cash flows as part of the cash proceeds from the sale of the assets under investing activities, the gain is deducted from net income to avoid double counting.

(f) **Stock options –** for share-based compensation plans, companies are required to use the fair value method to determine compensation cost. Compensation expense is recorded during the period(s) in which an employee performs the service if a company has a stock option plan. This expense is recorded by debiting compensation expense and crediting a stockholders' equity account. Thus, net income has to be increased by the amount of compensation expense in computing net cash provided by operating activities.

(g) **Postretirement benefit costs -** the difference between the pension expense recorded during the period and the amount of cash funded for the pension plan must be an adjustment to net income in arriving at net cash provided by operating activities.

(h) **Extraordinary items -** cash flows from extraordinary transactions and other events whose effects are included in net income, but which are not related to operations, should be reported as either investing or financing activities.

(i) **Significant noncash transactions -** significant noncash investing and financing activities (such as purchasing an asset by assuming long-term debt), if material in amount, should be disclosed in a separate schedule or narrative disclosure. These items are not to be incorporated in the statement of cash flows.

Worksheet and T-Account Approach

14. (S.O. 9) Near the end of Chapter 24 a **comprehensive illustration** of the statement of cash flows is presented. This illustration includes an explanation of how a work sheet can be used in preparing the statement.

GLOSSARY

Cash equivalents.	Short-term, highly liquid investments that are both: (a) readily convertible to known amounts of cash and (b) so near their maturity that they present insignificant risk of changes in interest rates.
Direct method (also called the income statement method).	A method of presenting the statement of cash flows which reports cash receipts and cash disbursements from operating activities.

Financing activities.
Activities that involve liability and stockholders' equity items and include (a) obtaining cash from creditors and repaying the amounts borrowed and (b) obtaining capital from owners and providing them with a return on, and a return of, their investment.

Indirect method (also called the reconciliation method).
A method of presenting the statement of cash flows that starts with net income and converts it to net cash provided by operating activities.

Investing activities.
Activities that involve long-term assets and include (a) making and collecting loans and (b) acquiring and disposing of investments and productive long-lived assets.

Operating activities.
The cash effects of transactions that enter into the determination of net income, such as cash receipts from sales of goods and services and cash payments to suppliers and employees for acquisitions of inventory and expenses.

Significant noncash transactions.
Investing or financing activities that do not involve cash and are material in amount, such as refinancing of long-term debt.

Statement of cash flows.
A financial statement that reflects an entity's cash receipts classified by major sources and its cash payments classified by major uses.

CHAPTER OUTLINE

Fill in the outline presented below.

(S.O. 1) Purpose of the Statement of Cash Flows

(S.O. 2) Classification of Cash Flows

Operating Activities

Investing Activities

Chapter Outline *(continued)*

        Financing Activities

(S.O. 4) The Direct Method

        The Indirect Method

(S.O. 7) Sources of Information for the Statement of Cash Flows

        Direct vs. Indirect Method

(S.O. 8) Special Problems in Statement Preparation

        Adjustments Similar to Depreciation

        Accounts Receivable (net)

        Other Working Capital Changes

        Net Losses

        Gains

Chapter Outline *(continued)*

Stock Options

Postretirement Benefit Costs

Irregular Items

Significant Noncash Transactions

(S.O. 9) Use of a Work Sheet

REVIEW QUESTIONS AND EXERCISES

TRUE-FALSE

Indicate whether each of the following is true (T) or false (F) in the space provided.

_____ 1. (S.O. 1) The information in a statement of cash flows should help investors, creditors, and others to assess the reasons for the difference between net income and net cash flow from operating activities.

_____ 2. (S.O. 2) Operating activities as defined by GAAP, involve the cash effects of transactions that enter into the determination of net income.

_____ 3. (S.O. 2) The statement of cash flows provides information **not** available from other financial statements.

_____ 4. (S.O. 2) Financing activities include (a) making and collecting loans and (b) acquiring and disposing of investments and productive long-lived assets.

_____ 5. (S.O. 2) The cash received from the sale of property, plant, and equipment at a gain, although reported in the income statement, is classified as an investing activity.

_____ 6. (S.O. 2) To prepare the statement of cash flows, only comparative balance sheets and a current income statement are needed.

_____ 7. (S.O. 2) Determining net cash provided by operating activities involves analysis of the income statement alone as it is the statement that reflects the amount of cash generated from operations as well as the amount of cash used to conduct the operations.

_____ 8. (S.O. 2) If a cash inflow and a cash outflow result from similar type transactions, such as the purchase and sale of property, plant, and equipment or the issuance and repayment of debt, they may be shown as a net amount from the two transactions in the statement of cash flows.

_____ 9. (S.O. 2) Unlike the other financial statements, the statement of cash flows is **not** prepared from the adjusted trial balance.

_____ 10. (S.O. 2) The redemption of bonds would be classified as an investing activity.

_____ 11. (S.O. 4) The conversion of net income to net cash provided by operating activities may be accomplished using either the direct method or the indirect method.

_____ 12. (S.O. 4) As its name implies, the indirect method is **not** directly involved with the computation of accrual based net income because it results in the presentation of a condensed cash basis income statement.

_____ 13. (S.O. 4) When computing net cash provided by operating activities under the indirect method, an increase in accounts receivable (net) during the year must be added to accrual based net income because more sales were made then those reflected in the income statement.

_____ 14. (S.O. 4) When the direct method is used in determining cash provided by operating activities, users of the statement of cash flows are unable to reconcile the net income to the net cash provided by operations because this is only provided when the indirect method is used.

_____ 15. (S.O. 5) Because the payment of cash dividends reduces both cash and retained earnings by a similar amount, this transaction has no effect on the statement of cash flows.

_____ 16. (S.O. 6) If a company records a loss on the sale of equipment, the amount of the loss must be added back to net income to determine the proper amount of net cash provided by operating activities.

_____ 17. (S.O. 7) The amortization of a bond premium should be handled in the same manner as depreciation of a plant asset, that is, added to net income when determining net cash provided by operating activities.

_____ 18. (S.O. 7) When a repair to equipment is debited to accumulated depreciation because it extends the asset's useful life, the transaction is considered neither an increase nor a decrease in cash for the period.

_____ 19. (S.O. 7) When accounts payable increase during a period, cost of goods sold on an accrual basis is lower than cost of goods sold on a cash basis.

_____ 20. (S.O. 7) The direct method is more consistent with the objective of the statement of cash flows because it shows operating cash receipts and payments where the indirect method does not.

_____ 21. (S.O. 7) The principal advantage of the indirect method is that it focuses on the difference between net income and net cash provided by operating activities, thus providing a useful link between the statement of cash flows, the income statement, and the balance sheet.

_____ 22. (S.O. 8) Stock dividends, stock splits, and appropriations are classified as financing activities.

_____ 23. (S.O. 8) Some changes in working capital, although they affect cash, do **not** affect net income.

_____ 24. (S.O. 8) Cash flows from extraordinary transactions and other events whose effects are included in net income, but which are **not** related to operations, should be reported either as investing activities or as financing activities.

_____ 25. (S.O. 9) The reconciling items in the work sheet are **not** entered in any journal or posted to any account.

MULTIPLE CHOICE

Select the best response for each of the following items and place the corresponding letter in the space provided.

_____ 1. (S.O. 1) Which of the following is **not** one of the benefits investors and creditors can expect as a result of the presentation of the statement of cash flows?

A. Assess the enterprise's ability to meet its obligations, its ability to pay dividends, and its need for external financing.

B. Assess the effects on an enterprise's financial position of both its cash and noncash investing and financing transactions during a period.

C. Assess the enterprise's ability to expand its operating facilities through the issuance of long-term debt.

D. Assess the reasons for differences between net income and associated cash receipts and payments.

_____ 2. (S.O. 1) Of the following questions, which one would **not** be answered by the statement of cash flows?

A. Where did the cash come from during the period?

B. What was the cash used for during the period?

C. Were all the cash expenditures of benefit to the company during the period?

D. What was the change in the cash balance during the period?

_____ 3. (S.O. 2) The basis recommended by the FASB for the statement of cash flows is "cash and cash equivalents." As described by GAAP, cash equivalents are:

A. All current assets that have no realization problems associated with them.

B. Short-term, highly liquid investments that are both readily convertible to known amounts of cash, and so near their maturity that they present insignificant risk of changes in interest rates.

C. All cash and near cash items that will be turned into cash within one operating period or one year, whichever is shorter.

D. All cash and investments in short-term securities that have a maturity of three months or less from the date of the financial statements.

_____ 4. (S.O. 2) In general, financing activities as used in the statement of cash flows refer to:

A. liability and owners' equity items and include (a) obtaining cash from creditors and repaying the amounts borrowed and (b) obtaining capital from owners and providing them with a return on, and a return of, their investment.

B. transactions involving long-term assets and include (a) making and collecting loans and (b) acquiring and disposing of investments and productive long-lived assets.

C. only debt transactions that result from long-term borrowings from financial institutions.

D. the cash effect of transactions that enter into the determination of net income and, thus, help finance the operations of the business through the generation of cash.

5. (S.O. 2) The cash received from the sale of property, plant, and equipment at no gain or loss is classified as what type of activity on the statement of cash flows?

	Investing	Financing	Operating
A.	Yes	Yes	No
B.	No	No	Yes
C.	No	Yes	No
D.	Yes	No	No

6. (S.O. 2) Which of the following activities is classified as an investing activity on the statement of cash flows?

   A.   Cash received from the sale of goods and services.
   B.   Cash paid to suppliers for inventory.
   C.   Cash paid to lenders for interest.
   D.   Cash received from the sale of property, plant, and equipment.

7. (S.O. 2) In a statement of cash flows, the cash flows from investing activities section should report:
   A.   the issuance of common stock in exchange for legal services.
   B.   a stock split.
   C.   the assignment of accounts receivable.
   D.   a payment of dividends.

8. (S.O. 2) The first step in the preparation of the statement of cash flow requires the use of information included in which comparative financial statements?

   A.   Statements of Cash Flows.
   B.   Balance Sheets.
   C.   Income Statements.
   D.   Statements of Retained Earnings.

9. (S.O. 3) To arrive at net cash provided by operating activities, it is necessary to report revenues and expenses on a cash basis. This is done by:
   A.   re-recording all income statement transactions that directly affect cash in a separate cash flow journal.
   B.   estimating the percentage of income statement transactions that were originally reported on a cash basis and projecting this amount to the entire array of income statement transactions.
   C.   eliminating the effects of income statement transactions that did not result in a corresponding increase or decrease in cash.
   D.   eliminating all transactions that have no current or future effect on cash, such as depreciation, from the net income computation.

_____ 10. (S.O. 4) The method used to compute net cash provided by operating activities that adjusts net income for items that affected reported net income but did **not** affect cash is known as the:

    A.   Indirect method.
    B.   Direct method.
    C.   Adjustment method.
    D.   Income statement method.

_____ 11. (S.O. 6) The amortization of bond premium on long-term debt should be presented in a statement of cash flows (using the indirect method for operating activities) as a(n):

    A.   Addition to net income.
    B.   Deduction from net income.
    C.   Investing activity.
    D.   Financing activity.

_____ 12. (S.O. 6) Schroeder Company uses the indirect method in computing net cash provided by operating activities. How would reported net income be adjusted for the following items?

	Loss on Sale of Machinery	Increase in Inventories
A.	Added To	Deducted From
B.	Deducted From	Added To
C.	Added To	Added To
D.	Deducted From	Deducted From

_____ 13. (S.O. 6) Crabbe Company reported $80,000 of selling and administrative expenses on its income statement for the past year. The Company had depreciation expense and an increase in prepaid expenses associated with the selling and administrative expense for the year. Assuming use of the direct method, how would these items be handled in converting the accrual based selling and administrative expense to the cash basis?

	Depreciation	Increase in Prepaid Expenses
A.	Deducted From	Deducted From
B.	Added To	Added To
C.	Deducted From	Added To
D.	Added To	Deducted From

_____ 14. (S.O. 6) During 2010, Greta Company earned net income of $128,000 which included depreciation expense of $26,000. In addition, the Company experienced the following changes in the account balances listed below:

Increases

Accounts payable $15,000
Inventory 12,000

Decreases

Accounts receivable .... $ 4,000
Prepaid expenses 11,000
Accrued liabilities 8,000

Based upon this information what amount will be shown for net cash provided by operating activities for 2010.

A. $ 89,000.
B. $ 95,000.
C. $155,000.
D. $164,000.

_____ 15. (S.O. 6) When preparing a statement of cash flows, an increase in accounts receivable during the period would cause which one of the following adjustments in determining cash flows from operating activities?

	Direct Method	**Indirect Method**
A.	Increase	Decrease
B.	Decrease	Increase
C.	Increase	Increase
D.	Decrease	Decrease

_____ 16. (S.O. 6) Cashman Company reported net income after taxes of $85,000 for the year ended 12/31/10. Included in the computation of net income were: depreciation expense, $15,000; amortization of a patent, $8,000; income from an investment in common stock of Linda Inc., accounted for under the equity method, $12,000; and amortization of a bond premium, $3,000. Cashman also paid a $20,000 dividend during the year. The net cash provided by operating activities would be reported at:

A. $57,000.
B. $73,000.
C. $77,000.
D. $93,000.

_____ 17. (S.O. 6) In its first year of operations Trumbo Company reported net income of $257,000. Total sales, all on account, amounted to $486,000, and collections of receivables during the year totaled $396,500. Trumbo uses the allowance method in accounting for bad debts expense and during the year recorded bad debts expense of $21,000. Based on these facts alone, what is the net cash provided by operating activities?

   A. $146,500
   B. $188,500
   C. $236,000
   D. $325,500

Questions 18 through 21 are based on the data shown below related to the statement of cash flows for Jeannie Western Stores, Inc.:

Jeannie Western Stores, Inc.
Comparative Balance Sheets

	December 31, 2009	December 31, 2010
Assets		
Current Assets:		
Cash	$ 180,000	$ 230,000
Accounts Receivable (net)	360,000	520,000
Merchandise Inventory	420,000	650,000
Prepaid Expense	105,000	117,000
Total Current Assets	1,065,000	1,517,000
Long-Term Investments		75,000
Fixed Assets:		
Property, Plant & Equipment	480,000	730,000
Accumulated Depreciation	(90,000)	(150,000)
Total Fixed Assets	390,000	580,000
Total Assets	$1,455,000	$2,172,000
Equities		
Current Liabilities:		
Accounts Payable	$ 365,000	$ 425,000
Accrued Expenses	94,000	103,000
Dividends Payable		67,000
Total Current Liabilities	459,000	595,000
Long-Term Notes Payable		275,000
Owners' Equity:		
Common Stock	800,000	1,000,000
Retained Earnings	196,000	302,000
Total Equities	$1,455,000	$2,172,000

Jeannie Western Stores, Inc.
Comparative Income Statements

	December 31, 2009	2010
Net Credit Sales	$1,251,000	$2,340,000
Cost of Goods Sold	627,000	1,305,000
Gross Profit	624,000	1,035,000
Expenses (including Income Tax)	458,000	862,000
Net Income	$ 166,000	$ 173,000

Additional Information:

a. Accounts receivable and accounts payable relate to merchandise held for sale in the normal course of business. The allowance for bad debts was the same at the end of 2010 and 2009, and no receivables were charged against the allowance. Accounts payable are recorded net of any discount and are always paid within the discount period.

b. The proceeds from the note payable was used to finance the acquisition of property, plant, and equipment. Capital stock was sold to provide additional working capital.

18. (S.O. 7) What amount of cash was paid on accounts payable to suppliers during 2010?

    A. $1,245,000
    B. $1,365,000
    C. $1,475,000
    D. $1,535,000

19. (S.O. 7) What amount of cash was collected from 2010 accounts receivable?

    A. $1,090,000
    B. $2,180,000
    C. $2,340,000
    D. $2,500,000

20. (S.O. 7) The amount to be shown on the cash flow statement as cash outflows from investing activities would total what amount?

    A. $(325,000)
    B. $(265,000)
    C. $(250,000)
    D. $(75,000)

21. (S.O. 7) The amount to be shown on the cash flow statement as inflows from financing activities would total what amount?

    A. $136,000
    B. $200,000
    C. $275,000
    D. $475,000

_____ 22. (S.O. 7) During 2010, Osborn Corporation, which uses the allowance method of accounting for doubtful accounts, recorded a provision for bad debt expense of $75,000 and in addition it wrote off, as uncollectible, accounts receivable of $23,000. As a result of these transactions, net cash provided by operating activities would be calculated (indirect method) by adjusting net income with a(n):

     A. $23,000 increase.
     B. $52,000 increase.
     C. $52,000 decrease.
     D. $75,000 increase.

Use the following information for questions 23 and 24.

Hyasaki Company provided the following information on selected transactions during 2010:

Purchase of land by issuing bonds	$200,000
Proceeds from sale of equipment	300,000
Proceeds from issuing bonds	600,000
Purchases of inventories	800,000
Purchases of treasury stock	400,000
Loans made to affiliated corporations	500,000
Dividends paid to preferred stockholders	100,000
Proceeds from issuing preferred stock	700,000

_____ 23. (S.O. 8) The net cash provided (used) by investing activities during 2010 is:

     A. $300,000
     B. $100,000
     C. $(200,000)
     D. $(400,000)

_____ 24. (S.O. 8) The net cash provided (used) by financing activities during 2010 is:

     A. $800,000
     B. $500,000
     C. $300,000
     D. $(1,100,000)

_____ 25. (S.O. 8) How should significant noncash transactions (purchase of equipment in exchange for common stock) be reported in the statement of cash flows according to GAAP?

     A.   They should be incorporated in the statement of cash flows in a section labeled, "Significant Noncash Transactions."
     B.   Such transactions should be incorporated in the section (operating, financing, or investing) that is most representative of the major component of the transaction.
     C.   These noncash transactions are not to be incorporated in the statement of cash flows. They may be summarized in a separate schedule at the bottom of the statement or appear in a separate supplementary schedule to the financials.
     D.   They should be handled in a manner consistent with the transactions that affect cash flows.

REVIEW EXERCISES

1.   (S.O. 4) Presented below is the income statement for the year ended December 31, 2010, for the Fiala Wahoo Company. Also presented are the changes in selected balance sheet accounts between 12/31/09 and 12/31/10.   None of the items included in the income statement meet the requirements for extraordinary items.

Fiala Wahoo Company
Income Statement
For the Year Ended December 31, 2010

Sales		$850,000
Cost of Sales		420,000
Gross Profit		$430,000
Operating Expenses:		
Salaries	$105,000	
Depreciation	36,000	
Rent	48,000	
Utilities	7,000	
Amortization of intangibles	15,000	211,000
Operating Income		$219,000
Other Income:		
Gain on Sale of Machinery	$ 18,000	
Other Expenses:		
Interest on Bonds (net of $1,200 premium amortization)	4,800	
Loss on Sale of Building	2,000	
Net Other Income and Expenses		11,200
Income before Income Taxes		$230,200
Federal and State Income Taxes		97,400
Net Income		$132,800

Selected Balance Sheet Data

Increases		**Decreases**	
Inventory	$76,000	Accounts Receivable	$69,000
Prepaid Expenses	19,000	Accrued Liabilities	9,000
Accounts Payable	54,000		

Instructions:

On the basis of the information presented, compute the net cash provided by operating activities using the indirect method.

net income   132,800

adjustments

depreciation exp	36,000
amort of intangibles	16,000
amort of premium	(1,200)
Gain on sale of machine	(18,000)
Loss on sale of building	2,000
increase in inventory	(76,000)
increase in prep. exp	(19,000)
increase in A/P	54,000
decrease in Receivables	69,000
decrease in Liability	(9,000)

52,800

185,600

2.   (S.O.6) Comparative balance sheets of the Kamria Corporation, along with an income statement, and additional information for the years ended December 31, 2009 and 2010, are presented below.

Balance Sheets

	2009	2010	
Cash	$ 10,000	$ 15,000	+ 5,000
Accounts Receivable	20,000	33,000	+ 13,000
Inventory	40,000	50,000	+10,000
Building	60,000	65,000	+ 5,000
Accumulated Depreciation	(12,000)	(16,000)	– 4,000
Total Assets	$118,000	$147,000	
Accounts Payable	$ 20,000	$ 25,000	+ 5,000
Common Stock	80,000	100,000	+20,000
Retained Earnings	18,000	22,000	+4,000
Total Equities	$118,000	$147,000	

Income Statement for 2010

Sales		$100,000
Cost of Sales		65,000
Gross Profit		$ 35,000
Operating Expenses:		
Depreciation	$ 4,000	
Other	17,000	21,000
Net Income		$ 14,000

Additional Information:

a.   Net income and a cash dividend account for the change in retained earnings.
b.   Common stock was issued for cash during 2010.

Instructions:
On the basis of the information presented, prepare a statement of cash flows using the (a) indirect method, and (b) direct method.

a.   Indirect Method

net income   14,000

adj

dec.   depreciation   4,000

inc.   recievables   (13,000)

inc   payables   5,000

inc.   inventory   (10,000)   14,000

net cash flow from operating   0

Investing

Building   (5,000)

net cash flow from investing   (5,000)

Financing

Sale of Common stock   20,000

dividends   (10,000)   10,000

Net increase in Cash   5,000

Cash at 1/1/10   10,000

Cash at 12/31/10   15,000

b.   Direct Method

3.   (S.O.6) Comparative balance sheets at December 31, 2009 and 2010, for the Morse Company are shown below.

Balance Sheets

	2009	2010	
Cash	$ 62,000	$ 98,000	
Accounts Receivable	74,000	79,000	
Inventory	118,000	124,000	
Prepaid Expenses	5,000	6,000	
Land	-	86,000	
Plant Assets	224,000	279,000	
Accumulated Depreciation	(86,000)	(80,000)	6,000
Franchise	32,000	24,000	
Total Assets	$429,000	$616,000	
Accounts Payable	41,000	53,000	
Notes Payable	63,000	58,000	
Bonds Payable	-	129,000	
Common Stock	250,000	275,000	+25,000
Additional Paid-in Capital	46,000	56,000	+ 10,000
Retained Earnings	29,000	45,000	+ 16,00
Total Equities	$429,000	$616,000	

Additional Information:

(1)   A fully depreciated plant asset, which originally cost $20,000 and had no salvage value, was sold for $1,000.

(2)   Bonds payable were issued at par value. Two-thirds of the bonds were exchanged for land; the remaining one-third was issued for cash.

(3)   Common stock was sold for cash.

(4)   The only entries in the Retained Earnings account are for dividends paid in the amount of $10,000 and for the net income for the year.

(5)   Normal depreciation expense was recorded during the year and the franchise was amortized.

(6)   The income statement for the year is as follows:

Sales	$186,000
Cost of sales	102,000
Gross Profit	84,000
Operating expenses	59,000
Income before gain	25,000
Gain on sale of plant asset	1,000
Net Income	$ 26,000

Instructions:

a. Prepare a statement of cash flows using the indirect method.
b. Prepare a statement of cash flows using the direct method.

a.   Indirect Method

_____

_____

_____

_____

_____

_____

_____

_____

_____

_____

_____

_____

_____

_____

_____

_____

_____

_____

_____

_____

_____

_____

_____

_____

b.   Direct Method

4.   (S.O.6) Presented below are data taken from the records of Geimer Company.

	December 31, 2009	December 31, 2010
Cash	$ 10,000	$17,000
Accounts Receivable (net)	36,000	41,000
Inventory	66,000	74,000
Prepaid Expenses	6,000	11,000
Land	124,000	72,000
Plant Assets	225,000	376,000
Accumulated Depreciation	(60,000)	(40,000)
	$407,000	$551,000
Accounts Payable	$43,000	$44,000
Accrued Liabilities	5,000	12,000
Bonds Payable	-0-	100,000
Common Stock	300,000	300,000
Retained Earnings	59,000	95,000
	$407,000	$551,000

Additional Data:

1. Land carried at a cost of $52,000 on 12/31/09, was sold in 2010 for $39,000. The loss (not extraordinary) was incorrectly charged directly to retained earnings.
2. Plant assets with a cost of $50,000 that were 60% depreciated were sold during 2010 for $15,000. The loss (not extraordinary) was reported on the income statement.
3. Net income as reported on the income statement for 2010 amounted to $63,000.
4. Cash dividends were paid during 2010. The entry to record the dividend included a debit to retained earnings and a credit to cash.
5. Depreciation expense for the year was $10,000.
6. Plant assets were purchased during the year. The seller accepted $100,000 in bonds and the remainder in cash.

Instructions:
Prepare a statement of cash flows using the **indirect method** for the year ended,
December 31, 2010.

5.   (S.O.6) Comparative balance sheet accounts of Sullivan Company are presented below:

Sullivan Company
Comparative Balance Sheet Accounts
December 31, 2009 and 2010

Debit Balances	2009	2010
Cash	$38,750	$50,000
Accounts Receivable	65,000	72,500
Merchandise Inventory	29,000	35,000
Long-Term Investments	42,500	27,250
Equipment	23,750	35,000
Buildings	61,250	72,500
Land	12,500	12,500
Total	$272,750	$304,750

Credit Balances	2009	2010
Allowance for Bad Debts	4,000	4,750
Accumulated Depreciation - Equipment	7,250	10,625
Accumulated Depreciation - Building	14,000	18,500
Accounts Payable	29,750	35,000
Accrued Payables	5,125	5,875
Long-Term Notes Payable	35,000	31,000
Common Stock	130,000	155,000
Retained Earnings	47,625	44,000
Total	$272,750	$304,750

Additional Data (ignore taxes):

1. Net income for the year is $69,000.
2. Cash dividends declared during the year $47,625.
3. A stock dividend was declared during the year. This resulted in retained earnings of $25,000 being capitalized.
4. Investments that cost $17,250 were sold for $26,000.
5. Equipment that cost $5,000, and was one-fourth depreciated, was sold for $2,000.

Sullivan's 2010 income statement is as follows (ignore taxes):

Sales		$630,000
Less Cost of Goods Sold		398,500
Gross profit		231,500
Less operating expenses		169,500*
Income from operations		62,000
Other:		
Gain on sale of investments	$ 8,750	
Loss on sale of equipment	(1,750)	7,000
Net income		$ 69,000

*(includes $9,125 of depreciation and $1,000 bad debts expense)

Instructions:

a. Compute net cash provided by operating activities using the direct method.

b. Prepare a statement of cash flows using the indirect method.

a.

_____

_____

_____

_____

_____

_____

_____

_____

_____

_____

_____

_____

_____

_____

_____

_____

b.

SOLUTIONS TO REVIEW QUESTIONS AND EXERCISES

TRUE-FALSE

1. (T)

2. (T)

3. (T)

4. (F)   This is the definition of investing activities.

5. (T)

6. (F)   To prepare the statement of cash flows, comparative balance sheets, the current income statement, and selected transaction data are needed.

7. (F)   Determining net cash provided by operating activities involves analyzing not only the current year's income statement but also comparative balance sheets as well as selected transaction data.

8. (F)   Individual inflows and outflows from investing and financing activities are reported separately. Thus, cash outflow from the purchase of property, plant, and equipment is reported separately from the cash inflow from the sale of property, plant, and equipment.

9. (T)

10. (F)   The redemption of bonds would be classified as a financing activity.

11. (T)

12. (F)   It is the direct method that results in the presentation of a condensed cash basis income statement.

13. (F)   When accounts receivable increase during the year, revenues on an accrual basis are higher than revenues on a cash basis because goods sold on account are reported as revenues. In other words, sales for the period led to increased revenue, but not all of those sales resulted in an increase in cash.

14. (F)   If the direct method of reporting net cash provided by operating activities is used, the FASB requires that the reconciliation of net income to net cash provided by operating activities be provided in a separate schedule.

15. (F)   The payment of dividends obviously has an impact on the statement of cash flows as it is an outflow of cash. Dividends are reported as an outflow in the financing activities section of the statement of cash flows.

16. (T)

17. (F)   The amortization of bond premium reduces the amount of interest expense reported on the income statement, but it does not reduce the amount of cash flowing out of the business. Thus, the amount of bond amortization must be deducted from net income to arrive at cash provided by operating activities.

18. (F)   The debit to accumulated depreciation as a result of an equipment repair is most likely offset by a credit to cash. Thus, such a transaction would cause a decrease in cash and be shown as an outflow on the statement of cash flows.

19. (F)   Cost of goods sold is the same under either basis. Even if items for which cash has not been expended are eliminated from the computation, the amount of cost of goods sold remains the same.

20. (T)

21. (T)

22. (F)   Stock dividends, stock splits, and appropriations are significant noncash transactions that generally are not reported in conjunction with the statement of cash flows.

23. (T)

24. (T)

25. (T)

MULTIPLE CHOICE

1. (C)   Alternatives (A), (B), and (D) are examples of the information an investor or creditor derives from use of the statement of cash flows. Alternative (C) requires a greater amount of in-depth information that is not available in the statement of cash flows alone.

2. (C)   The statement of cash flows, like the balance sheet and income statement, reflects the results of transactions entered into by the entity during the preceding year. The statement of cash flows could include the results of some cash flow transactions that were of great benefit and some that were of little benefit. The purpose of the statement is to reflect cash inflows and cash outflows, not to evaluate the benefits derived from the transactions. A great deal of additional information would have to be included in the statement of cash flows for a reader to evaluate the benefit of each cash receipt or expenditure recorded.

3. (B)   Alternative (B) is the definition of "cash and cash equivalents" .The definition also includes the requirement that only investments with original maturities of three months or less qualify as cash equivalents.

4.   (A)   Liability and owners' equity items which include borrowing money from creditors and owners and repaying the borrowings along with a return on the borrowings represent financing activities.   Alternative B refers to investing activities as defined by the statement of cash flows, and alternative D is a partial explanation of operating activities.

5.   (D)   The cash received from the sale of property, plant, and equipment at no gain or loss is classified as an investing activity.

6.   (D)   Investing activities include (a) making and collecting loans and (b) acquiring and disposing of investments and productive assets. Thus, the cash received from the sale of property, plant, and equipment represents the disposal of productive assets.

7.   (C)   In a statement of cash flows, an assignment of accounts receivable is classified as an investing activity. The issuance of common stock in exchange for legal services and a stock split (A and B) are noncash transactions that would not be reported on the statement of cash flows. A payment of dividends (D) is classified as a financing activity.

8.   (B)   The first step in the preparation of the statement of cash flows is to compute the change in cash. The change can be determined by a comparison of comparative balance sheets which would show the beginning and ending cash balances.

9.   (C)   By eliminating the effects of income statement transactions that did not result in a corresponding increase or decrease in cash, the accrual based net income is changed to a cash basis.   This procedure includes items that have no impact on cash, like depreciation, and items that have a future impact on cash, like sales on account.

10.   (A)   The question reflects the definition of the indirect method.

11.   (B)   When a bond premium exists the amortization causes the bond interest expense reported on the income statement to be smaller than the interest paid or becoming payable. Thus, because the cash outflow is larger than the deduction in arriving at net income, a deduction from net income is necessary to determine cash provided by operating activities under the indirect approach.

12.   (A)   A loss on the sale of machinery is a deduction from net income without a corresponding outflow of cash from operations. Thus, the loss would be added back to net income in computing net cash provided by operating activities. The increase in inventories indicates that cost of goods sold on an accrual basis would be less than it would have been if it were computed on a cash basis. In converting to the cash basis, the increase in inventory would be subtracted from net income to arrive at net cash provided by operating activities.

13.   (C)   The noncash depreciation charge should be deducted from the selling and administrative expense in converting it to the cash basis. The increase in the prepaid expense would be added to selling and administrative expense as it represents a cash outflow that was not charged to an expense account.

14. (D)

Net income	$128,000
Increase in accounts payable	15,000
Increase in inventory	(12,000)
Depreciation expense	26,000
Decrease in accounts receivable	4,000
Decrease in prepaid expenses	11,000
Decrease in accrued liabilities	(8,000)
Net cash provided by operating activities	$164,000

15. (D)   An increase in accounts receivable during the period would indicate that the amount of cash received during the period was less than the amount of sales reported as earned; therefore, under both the direct and indirect methods, there would be an adjustment decreasing the cash flows from operating activities.

16. (D)

Net income	$ 85,000
Depreciation expense	15,000
Amortization of patent	8,000
Amortization of bond premium	(3,000)
Investment income	(12,000)
Net cash provided by operating activities	$ 93,000

17. (B)

Increase in receivables (sales)	$486,000
Decrease in receivables (collections)	396,500
Net increase in receivables	$ 89,500

Net income	$257,000
Increase in receivables	(89,500)
Bad debts expense	21,000
Cash flow from operations	$188,500

18. (C)   The following "T" account analysis shows the amounts that need to be determined in answering this question:

Accounts Payable

Payments	?	365,000	Beginning Balance
		?	Purchases
		425,000	Ending Balance

An analysis of Cost of Goods Sold is required to determine the purchases:

Beginning Inventory	$ 420,000
Plus Purchases	?
Less Ending Inventory	(650,000)
Cost of Goods Sold	$1,305,000

Thus, purchases are equal to:

$1,305,000 - $420,000 + $650,000 = $1,535,000

Now substituting the amount for purchases in the "T" account above, cash payments on accounts payable are:

$365,000 + $1,535,000 - $425,000 = $1,475,000

19.   (B)   The following "T" account analysis shows the amount that needs to be determined in answering this question:

Accounts Payable

Beginning Balance	360,000		
Net Credit Sales	2,340,000	?	Cash Collections
Ending Balance	520,000		

The computation of cash collections is:

$360,000 + $2,340,000 - $520,000 = $2,180,000

20.   (A)   The items shown on Jeannie's balance sheet that reflect investing activities are the increases in:

Long-Term Investments	$ (75,000)
Property, Plant & Equipment	(250,000)
Cash Outflows From Investing	$(325,000)

21.   (D)   The items shown on Jeannie's balance sheet that reflect cash inflows from financing activities are:

Proceeds From Long-Term Note	$275,000
Proceeds From Issuance of Common Stock	200,000
Cash Inflows From Financing	$475,000

22.   (D)   The provision for bad debt expense is a noncash transaction that had decreased the amount of net income (or increased the amount of net loss) by $75,000. The write-off of the uncollectible accounts receivable did not affect net income (loss) or cash flow. Thus, to reflect the net cash provided by operating activities, $75,000 should be added back to net income.

23.   (C)   The net cash used by investing activities during 2010 of $(200,000) is the result of the proceeds from the sale of equipment, $300,000, and the loans made to affiliated corporations, $(500,000).

24. (A) The net cash provided by financing activities during 2010 of $800,000 is the result of the proceeds from issuing bonds, $600,000, the purchase of the treasury stock, $(400,000), the payment of dividends to preferred stockholders $(100,000) and the proceeds from issuing preferred stock, $700,000.

25. (C) According to GAAP, significant noncash transactions are not included in the statement of cash flows. The FASB indicates that such transactions can be summarized at the bottom of the statement of cash flows or appear in a separate schedule as a part of the financial statements.

REVIEW EXERCISES

1.

Fiala Wahoo Company
Statement of Cash Flows
For the Year End December 31, 2010

Cash flows from operating activities		
Net income		$132,800
Adjustments to reconcile net income to net cash provided by operating activities:		
Depreciation expense	$36,000	
Amortization of intangibles	15,000	
Gain on sale of machinery	(18,000)	
Amortization of premium	(1,200)	
Loss on sale of building	2,000	
Increase in inventory	(76,000)	
Increase in prepaid expenses	(19,000)	
Increase in accounts payable	54,000	
Decrease in accounts receivable	69,000	
Decrease in accrued liabilities	(9,000)	52,800
Net cash provided by operating activities		$185,600

2a. **Indirect Method**

Kamria Corporation
Statement of Cash Flows
For the Year Ended December 31, 2010

Cash flows from operating activities		
Net income		$ 14,000
Adjustments to reconcile net income to net cash		
provided by operating activities:		
Depreciation expense	$ 4,000	
Increase in receivables	(13,000)	
Increase in inventory	(10,000)	
Increase in payables	5,000	(14,000)
Net cash provided by operating activities		-0-
Cash flows from investing activities		
Purchase of building		(5,000)
Cash flows from financing activities		
Sale of common stock	20,000	
Payment of dividends	(10,000)	10,000
Net increase in cash		$5,000
Cash, January 1, 2010		10,000
Cash, December 31, 2010		$ 15,000

2b. **Direct Method**

Kamria Corporation
Statement of Cash Flows
For the Year Ended December 31, 2010

Cash flows from operating activities		
Cash received from customers (a)		$87,000
Cash paid to suppliers (b)	$70,000	
Other expenses	17,000	
Cash disbursed for operations		(87,000)
Net cash provided by operating activities		-0-
Cash flows from investing activities		
Purchase of building		(5,000)
Cash flows from investing activities		
Sale of common. stock	20,000	
Payment of dividends	(10,000)	10,000
Net increase in cash		$ 5,000
Cash, January 1, 2010		10,000
Cash, December 31, 2010		$15,000

(a) $100,000 − 13,000 = $87,000   *A/R*

(b) $65,000 + 10,000 − 5,000 = $70,000

Cost of Sales

3a. **Indirect Method**

Morse Company
Statement of Cash Flows
For the Year Ended December 31, 2010

Cash flows from operating activities		
Net income		$26,000
Adjustments to reconcile net income to net cash		
provided by operating activities		
Depreciation expense (a)	$14,000	
Amortization of franchise	8,000	
Gain on sale of plant assets	(1,000)	
Increase in receivables	(5,000)	
Increase in inventory	(6,000)	
Increase in prepaid expenses	(1,000)	
Increase in accounts payable	12,000	21,000
Net cash provided by operating activities		47,000
Cash flows from investing activities		
Sale of plant asset	1,000	
Purchase of plant asset	(75,000)	
Net cash used by investing activities	55,000 + 20,000	(74,000)
Cash flows from financing activities		
Sale of common stock	35,000	
Sale of bonds (129,000 x 1/3)	43,000	
Payment of dividends	(10,000)	
Payment of notes payable	(5,000)	
Net cash provided by financing activities		63,000
Net increase in cash		$36,000
Cash, January 1, 2010		62,000
Cash, December 31, 2010		$98,000
Noncash investing and financing activities		
Purchase of land through issuance of bonds		$86,000

(a) $86,000 – $20,000 + **14,000** = $80,000

6,000

3b. Direct Method

Morse Company
Statement of Cash Flows
For the Year Ended December, 31, 2010

Cash flows from operating activities		
Cash received from customers (a)		$181,000
Cash paid to suppliers (b)	$96,000	
Operating expenses (c)	38,000	(134,000)
Net cash provided by operating activities		47,000
Cash flows from investing activities		
Sale of plant assets	1,000	
Purchase of plant assets	(75,000)	
Net cash used by investing activities		(74,000)
Cash flows from financing activities		
Sale of common stock	35,000	
Sale of bonds (129,000 x 1/3)	43,000	
Payment of dividends	(10,000)	
Payment of note payable	(5,000)	
Net cash provided by financing activities		63,000
Net increase in cash		$36,000
Cash, January 1, 2010		62,000
Cash, December 31, 2010		$98,000
Noncash investing and financing activities		
Purchase of land through issuance of bonds		$86,000

(a) $186,000 – $5,000 = $181,000
(b) $102,000 + $6,000 – $12,000 = $96,000
(c) $59,000 – $14,000 – $8,000 + $1,000 = $38,000

4.

Geimer Company
Statement of Cash Flows
For the Year Ended December 31, 2010

Cash flow from operating activities

Net income (a)		$50,000
Adjustments to reconcile net income to net cash provided by operating activities		
Depreciation expense	$10,000	
Loss on sale of land	13,000	
Loss on sale of plant assets	5,000	
Increase on receivables	(5,000)	
Increase in inventory	(8,000)	
Increase in prepaid expenses	(5,000)	
Increase in payables	1,000	
Increase in accruals	7,000	18,000
Net cash provided by operating activities		$68,000
Cash flows from investing activities		
Sale of land	39,000	
Sale of plant assets	15,000	
Purchase of plant assets	(101,000)	
Net cash used by investing activities		(47,000)
Cash flows from financing activities		
Payment of dividend		(14,000)
Net increase in cash		$ 7,000
Cash, January 1, 2010		10,000
Cash, December 31, 2010		$17,000
Noncash investing and financing activities		
Purchase of plant assets through issuance of bonds		$100,000

(a) $63,000 – 13,000 = $50,000

5a.

Net Cash Provided by Operating Activities

Cash collected from revenue (1)		$622,250
Cash payments for inventory (2)	$399,250	
Cash payment for expenses (3)	158,625	(557,875)
Net cash provided by operating activities		$ 64,375

(1)   (Sales) less (Increase in Receivables) less (Net Change in Allowance)
       $630,000 – $7,500 – $250 = $622,250

(2)   (Cost of Goods Sold) plus (Increase in Inventory) less (Increase in Accounts Payable)
       $398,500 + $6,000 – $5,250 = $399,250

(3)   (Operating Expenses) less (Depreciation Expense) less (Increase in Accrued Wages) less (Bad Debts Expense) $169,500 – $9,125 – $750 – $1,000 = $158,625

5b.

Sullivan Company
Statement of Cash Flows
For the Year Ended December 31, 2010

Cash Flows from Operating Activities		
Net Income		$69,000
Adjustments to Arrive at Net Cash Provided by Operations:		
Depreciation Expense	$ 9,125	
Gain on Sale of Investments	(8,750)	
Loss on Sale of Equipment	1,750	
Increase in Receivables (Net)	(6,750)	
Increase in Inventory	(6,000)	
Increase in Accounts Payable	5,250	
Increase in Accrued Payables	750	(4,625)
Net Cash Provided by Operating Activities Operations		64,375
Cash Flow from Investing Activities		
Purchase of Investments	(2,000)	
Purchase of Equipment	(16,250)	
Addition to Building	(11,250)	
Sale of Investment	26,000	
Sale of Equipment	2,000	(1,500)
Cash Flows from Financing Activities		
Reduction in Long-Term Notes	(4,000)	
Cash Dividend Paid	(47,625)	(51,625)
Net Increase in Cash		11,250
Cash Balance January 1, 2010		38,750
Cash Balance December 31, 2010		$ 50,000
Noncash investing and financing activities		
Stock Dividend Declared		$25,000

24

Full Disclosure in Financial Reporting

CHAPTER STUDY OBJECTIVES

1. Review the full disclosure principle and describe implementation problems.

2. Explain the use of notes in financial statement preparation.

3. Describe the disclosure requirements for major business segments.

4. Describe the accounting problems associated with interim reporting.

5. Identify the major disclosures found in the auditor's report.

6. Understand management's responsibilities for financials.

7. Identify issues related to financial forecasts and projections.

8. Describe the profession's response to fraudulent financial reporting.

*9. Understand the approach to financial statement analysis.

*10. Identify major analytic ratios and describe their calculation.

*11. Explain the limitations of ratio analysis.

*12. Describe techniques of comparative analysis.

*13. Describe the techniques of percentage analysis.

*14. Describe the current international accounting environment.

CHAPTER REVIEW

1. Chapter 24 addresses the topic of financial statement disclosure. Accountants and business executives are fully aware of the importance of full disclosure when presenting financial statements. However, determining what constitutes full disclosure in financial reporting is not an easy task. Thus, the purpose of this chapter is to review present disclosure requirements and gain insight into future trends in this area. Chapter 24 presents basic financial statement analysis. This information is presented in Appendix 24A. In addition, there is a discussion on the international accounting environment included in Appendix 24B.

Note: *All asterisked (*) items relate to material contained in the Appendices to the chapter.*

2.   (S.O. 1) Recent trends in financial reporting reflect an increase in the amount of disclosure found in financial statements. This increased disclosure is a result of the efforts of the SEC and the FASB. The pronouncements issued by these organizations include many disclosure requirements that are designed to improve the financial reporting process. Numerous reasons can be cited for this increased emphasis on disclosure requirements. Some of the more significant reasons include **(a)** the complexity of the business environment, **(b)** the necessity for timely financial information, and **(c)** the use of accounting as a control and monitoring device.

Notes to Financial Statements

3.   (S.O. 2) Notes are an integral part of the financial statements of a business enterprise. Although they are normally drafted in somewhat technical language, notes are the accountant's means of amplifying or explaining the items presented in the main body of the statements. Many of the note disclosures which are common in financial accounting are discussed and presented throughout the text. The more common note disclosures are as follows:

a.   **Significant Accounting Policies.** This information is designed to inform the statement reader of the accounting methods used in preparing the information included in the financial statements. Accounting policies of a given entity are the specific accounting principles and methods currently employed and considered most appropriate in the circumstances to present fairly the financial statements of the enterprise.

b.   **Inventory.** The basis upon which inventory amounts are stated (lower of cost or market) and the method used in determining cost (LIFO, FIFO, average cost, etc.) should also be reported.

c.   **Property, Plant and Equipment.** The basis of valuation for property, plant, and equipment should be stated (usually historical cost). Pledges, liens, and other commitments related to these assets should be disclosed.

d.   **Creditor Claims.** A liability may have numerous covenants that are not conveniently disclosed in the liability section of the balance sheet. To avoid a cumbersome presentation in the body of the balance sheet, this additional information is disclosed in the notes.

e.   **Equity Holders' Claims.** The rights of various equity security issues along with certain unique features that may apply to certain issues are commonly disclosed in notes to the financial statements.

f.   **Contingencies and Commitments.** Because many contingent gains or losses are not properly included in the accounts, their disclosure in the notes provides relevant information to financial statement users. These contingencies may take a variety of forms such as litigation, debt , and other guarantees, possible tax assessments, renegotiation of government contracts, sales of receivables with recourse, and so on.

g   **Fair Values.** Companies that have assets or liabilities measured at fair value must disclose both the cost and the fair value of all financial instruments in the notes to the financial statements.

h.   **Deferred Taxes, Pensions, and Leases.** Extensive disclosures are required in these three areas. A careful reading of the notes to the financial statements provides information as to off-balance sheet commitments, future financing needs, and the quality of a company's earnings.

i.   **Changes in Accounting Principles.** Either in the summary of significant accounting policies or in the other notes, changes in accounting principles (as well as material changes in estimates and corrections of errors) are discussed.

Special Transactions

4.   In some instances a corporation is faced with a sensitive issue that requires disclosure in the financial statements. Examples of items that can be characterized as sensitive have been identified in the *Statements on Auditing Standards* issued by the Auditing Standards Board of the AICPA. These include: **related party transactions, errors and irregularities,** and **illegal acts.**   It is important for the accountant/auditor, who must determine the adequacy of the disclosure, to exercise care in balancing the rights of the company and the needs of the financial statement users.

Subsequent Events

5.   Events or transactions which occur subsequent to the balance sheet date but prior to the issuance of the financial statements should be disclosed in the financial statements.

Reporting for Diversified (Conglomerate) Companies

(S.O. 3)   With the increase in diversification within business entities, investors are seeking more information concerning the details of diversified (conglomerate) companies. Particularly, they have requested revenue and income information on the individual segments that comprise the total business income figure. Various arguments have been presented both for and against increased disclosure of disaggregated financial information.

6.   The basic reporting requirements of disaggregated information are:
  a.   Objective of Reporting Disaggregated Information.
      (1)   Better understand the enterprise's performance.
      (2)   Better assess its prospects for future net cash flows.
      (3)   Make more informed judgments about the enterprise as a whole.

  b.   Basic Principles.
      General purpose financial statements are required to include selected information on a single basis of disaggregation. The method chosen is referred to as the management approach--which is based on the way the management disaggregates the company for making operating decisions.

  c.   Identifying Operating Segments.
      An operating segment is a component of an enterprise:
      (1)   That engages in business activities from which it earns revenues and incurs expenses.
      (2)   Whose operating results are regularly reviewed by the company's chief operating decision maker to assess segment performance and allocate resources to the segment.
      (3)   For which discrete financial information is available that is generated by or based on the internal financial reporting system.
      Information about two or more operating segments may be aggregated only if the segments have the same basic characteristics in each of the following areas:
      (1)   The nature of the products or services provided.
      (2)   The technology underlying the production process.
      (3)   The type of class of customer.
      (4)   The methods of product or service distribution.
      (5)   The economic characteristics of their markets.

7.   Whether a segment is significant enough to disclose depends upon whether it satisfies one of the following tests: **(a)** its revenue is 10% or more of the combined revenue of all the enterprise's industry segments, **(b)** the absolute amount of its profit or loss is 10% or more of the greater of the combined operating profit of all operating segments that did not incur a loss or the combined loss of all operating segments that did incur a loss, or **(c)** its identifiable assets are 10% or more of the combined assets of all operating segments. In addition, the segmented results must equal or exceed 75% of the combined sales to unaffiliated customers for the entire enterprise, and an enterprise should probably not report more than 10 segments.

8.   The accounting principles to be used for segment disclosure need not be the same as the principles used to prepare the consolidated statements. Also, allocations of joint, common, or company-wide costs solely for external reporting purposes are not required. The FASB, however, does require that an enterprise report (a) general information about its operating segments, (b) segment profit and loss and related information, (c) segment assets, (d) reconciliations, (e) information about products and services and geographic areas, and (f) major customers.

Interim Reports

9.   (S.O. 4) **Interim reports** are financial reports issued by a business enterprise for a period of less than one year. The SEC requires certain companies coming under its control to file quarterly financial statements that are similar in form and content to their annual reports.

10.   The accounting profession indicates that the same accounting principles used for annual reports should be applied in preparing interim reports. However, the general approach used in preparing these reports is the subject of some debate. Two different approaches have been advocated in practice. One approach is referred to as the **discrete approach** and the other is the **integral approach.** Those advocating the discrete approach believe that each interim period should be treated as a separate accounting period. Those who favor the integral approach consider the interim report to be an integral part of the annual report. At present, many companies follow the discrete approach for certain types of expenses and the integral approach for others, because the standards employed at present are fairly flexible.

11.   The FASB has indicated that it favors the integral approach in preparing interim reports. However, certain items do not lend themselves to strict application of the guideline. As a result, unique reporting problems are encountered for such items as (a) advertising and similar costs, **(b)** expenses subject to year-end adjustments, **(c)** income taxes, **(d)** extraordinary items, **(e)** earnings per share, and **(f)** seasonality.

12.   The fact that many business entities encounter seasonal variations in their operations poses a problem in the analysis of interim reports. The greater the degree of seasonality experienced by a company, the greater the possibility for distortion. For example, a seasonal business that earns 50% of its net income in one quarter may lead the analyst to spurious conclusions. In such a situation, the analyst would be misled if the results of any one of the quarters were interpreted as representing one-fourth of the year's operating results. Thus, caution should be exercised when attempting to draw generalizations from a single interim report.

13.   Although some standards exist for interim reporting, the subject is in need of a thorough review and analysis. It is unclear as to whether the discrete, integral, or some combination of these two methods will be proposed. In addition to the problems noted in paragraphs 11 and 12, the profession continues to debate the extent of involvement an independent auditor should have with interim reports.

Auditor's Report

14. (S.O. 5) An **audit report** is issued each time an **independent** auditor performs an audit of an entity's financial statements. An audit report is essentially the expression of an opinion, by the auditor, on the **fairness** with which the financial statements present the entity's **financial position** and **results of operations.** In the audit report, the auditor must state whether the financial statements were presented in accordance with generally accepted accounting principles. Also, if such principles were not consistently applied, the auditor should make the reader aware of this fact in the audit report.

15. If an auditor arrives at the opinion that the financial statements are fairly presented, the audit report that is issued is known as an **unqualified opinion.** When an auditor is unable to express an unqualified opinion (normally as a result of scope limitation, financial statement inadequacies, or material uncertainties), he will issue either (a) **a qualified opinion,** (b) **an adverse opinion,** or (c) **disclaim an opinion.** Departures from an unqualified opinion put the financial statement reader on guard as to possible deficiencies in the presentation of the financial statements. When the auditor departs from the standard unqualified audit report, the reason for the departure must be clearly indicated in the audit report.

Other Areas in the Annual Report

16. The Securities and Exchange Commission (SEC) requires corporate management to include a disclosure in the corporate annual report referred to as **management discussion and analysis** (MD&A). This section of the annual report includes management's beliefs about favorable and unfavorable trends in liquidity, capital resources, and results of operations. Also, management is to identify significant events and uncertainties that affect these three factors. The MD&A section also must provide information concerning the effects of inflation and changing prices, if material, to the financial statements.

Management's Responsibilities

17. (S.O. 6) Companies also report on **management's responsibilities for financial statements** which includes explanation of its responsibilities for, and assessment of, the internal control system. The purposes of this report are (1) to increase the investor's understanding of the roles of management and the auditor in preparing financial statements and (2) to heighten the awareness of senior management of its responsibilities for the company's financial and internal control system.

18. Information related to the **social concerns** of a business enterprise has received a great deal of attention in recent years. Many potential investors are interested in an entity's concern for protection of the environment. In response to this concern, the SEC requires that the following types of **environmental information** be disclosed in filings with that agency.

   a. The material effects that compliance with federal, state, and local environmental protection laws may have upon capital expenditures, earnings, and competitive position.
   b. Litigation commenced or known to be contemplated against registrants by a government authority pursuant to federal, state, and local environmental regulatory provisions.
   c. All other environmental information of which the average prudent investor ought reasonably to be informed.

Financial Forecasts and Financial Projections

19. (S.O. 7) The AICPA has issued a statement on standards for the preparation of prospective financial statements. Prospective financial statements are financial statements based upon the entity's expectations about future operation. There are two types of prospective financial statements: (a) **financial forecasts** and (b) **financial projections.** A financial forecast is composed of prospective financial statements that present, to the best of the company's knowledge and belief, its expected financial position, results of operations, and cash flows. A financial projection is composed of prospective financial statements that present, to the best of the company's knowledge and belief--**given one or more hypothetical assumptions**--its expected financial position, results of operations, and cash flows.

Summary Annual Reports

20. In an effort to make financial reports more meaningful, some companies have experimented with issuing **summary annual reports (SAR).** A SAR contains a condensed financial presentation in a more readable format than that of the traditional annual report.

Fraudulent Financial Reporting

21. (S.O. 8) The **National Commission on Fraudulent Financial Reporting** defined fraudulent financial reporting as intentional or reckless conduct, whether act or omission, that results in materially misleading financial statements. Situational pressures on the company as well as individual pressures on management personnel can result in fraudulent activities which lead to fraudulent financial reporting. A weak corporate climate contributes to these situations. The Sarbanes-Oxley Act of 2002, in response to corporate fraud, raised the penalty substantially for executives who are involved in fraudulent financial reporting.

Appendix 24-A: Basic Financial Statement Analysis

*22. (S.O. 9) Appendix 24-A focuses on the methodology used in the interpretation and evaluation of the information presented in financial statements. The chapter discusses the computational aspects of the various techniques used in the analysis of financial statements as well as their meaning and significance. A variety of groups are interested in the financial progress of a business organization. These groups include creditors, stockholders, potential investors, management, governmental agencies, and labor leaders to name a few. The interests of these groups and the kind of financial information and analysis that can satisfy those interests are discussed in the chapter.

Ratio Analysis

*23. (S.O. 10) Thus far, the discussion presented in the text has been concerned with the measurement and reporting functions of accounting. Chapter 24 discusses the communication function of accounting that involves **analyzing** and **interpreting** the economic information presented in financial statements. The techniques used in the analysis of financial statement data include: (a) **ratio analysis,** (b) **comparative analysis,** (c) **percentage analysis,** and (d) **examination of related data.**

*24. Effective financial statement analysis is a skill that requires knowledge of the available techniques and extensive experience. The techniques can be learned by studying a textbook presentation on the subject. However, effective financial statement analysis requires the ability to **(a)** select the appropriate technique and (b) interpret the significance of the results obtained.

*25. Ratios can be classified as follows:

    a.   **Liquidity Ratios.** Measures of the short-run ability of the enterprise to pay its maturing obligations.

    b.   **Activity Ratios.** Measures of how effectively the enterprise is using the assets employed.

    c.   **Profitability Ratios.** Measures of the degree of success or failure of a given enterprise or division for a given period of time.

    d.   **Coverage Ratios.** Measures of the degree of protection for long-term creditors and investors.

*26. In the following paragraphs, the individual ratios included in the four classifications will be presented. The method of presentation will include: (a) **identification of the ratio,** (b) **the manner in which the ratio is computed,** and (c) **the significance of the ratio.** It is important to note that the significance of ratio analysis is dependent on a complete understanding of the circumstances surrounding the computation. For example, there are no minimum or maximum amounts that can be identified with individual ratios that are considered to be always good or always bad. Thus, the interpretation of any one ratio cannot be accomplished in a vacuum. **The proper interpretation of ratios involves trend analysis, comparisons with other ratios or industry averages, and a thorough understanding of the environment within which the entity operates.**

LIQUIDITY RATIOS

*27. The **current ratio** (Ch. 13) is the ratio of total current assets to total current liabilities. **It is computed by dividing current assets by current liabilities,** and is sometimes referred to as the working capital ratio. The significance of the current ratio concerns the company's ability to meet its maturing short-term obligations.

*28. The **acid-test ratio** (Ch. 13) relates total current liabilities to the most liquid current assets (cash, marketable securities, and net receivables). **To compute the acid-test ratio, these current assets are divided by total current liabilities.** This ratio is significant in that it focuses on the ability of a company to meet its short-term debt immediately.

*29. The **current cash debt ratio (Ch. 5) is computed by dividing net cash provided by operating activities by average current liabilities.**

ACTIVITY RATIOS

*30. The **receivables turnover ratio (Ch. 7) is computed by dividing net sales by net average receivables** (beginning plus ending divided by 2) **outstanding during the year.** This ratio provides an indication of how successful a firm is in collecting its outstanding receivables. As a general rule, the receivables turnover is acceptable if it does not exceed the time allowed for payment under the selling terms by more than 10 to 15 days.

*31. The **inventory turnover ratio (Ch. 9)** is a function of average inventory (beginning plus ending divided by 2) and cost of goods sold. **This ratio is computed by dividing cost of goods sold by average inventory.** Normally, a high inventory turnover is sought by an enterprise along with a minimum of "stock-out costs."

*32. The **asset turnover ratio (Ch. 10) is determined by dividing net sales for the period by average total assets.** This ratio indicates how efficiently the company utilizes its assets. If the turnover ratio is high, the implication is that the company is using its assets effectively to generate sales. If the asset turnover ratio is low, the company either has to use its assets more efficiently or dispose of them.

PROFITABILITY RATIOS

*33. The **profit margin on sales (Ch. 10) is computed by dividing net income by net sales for the period.** The significance of this ratio is that it indicates that amount of profit, on a percentage basis, that results from each sales dollar earned by the company.

*34. **Dividing net income by total average assets yields the rate of return on assets (Ch. 10) earned by a company.** In computing this ratio, companies sometimes use net income before the subtraction of interest charges because, they contend, interest represents a cost of securing additional assets and, therefore, should not be considered as a deduction in arriving at the amount of return on assets.

*35. The **rate of return on common stock equity (Ch. 15) is computed** by **dividing net income after interest, taxes, and preferred dividends by average common stock equity.** When the rate of return on total assets is lower than the rate of return on common stock equity, the enterprise is said to be trading on the equity at a gain. The term **"trading on the equity"** describes the practice of using borrowed money at fixed interest rates or issuing preferred stock with constant dividend rates in hopes of earning a higher rate of return on the money used than the interest or preferred dividends paid.

*36. As mentioned earlier in the text, many investors consider **earnings per share (Ch. 16)** to be the most significant statistic presented by a business entity. A discussion of the significance of earnings per share and the manner in which it is computed is presented in **Chapter 16.** Basically, earnings per share is computed by dividing net income by the weighted average number of shares of common stock outstanding. However, a complex capital structure alters this computation significantly.

*37. **Dividing the market price of a share of stock by the earnings per share yields the price earnings (P/E) ratio (Ch. 16).** The factors that affect the price earnings ratio include relative risk, stability of earnings, trends in earnings, and the market's perception of the growth potential of the stock.

*38. The **payout ratio (Ch. 16) is the ratio of cash dividends to net income.** This ratio gives investors an indication of the portion of net income a company distributes to its stockholders (adjusted for preferred dividends). If investors desire cash yield from an investment in stock, they should seek out entities with high payout ratios.

COVERAGE RATIOS

*39. The extent to which creditors are protected in the event of an entity's insolvency may be determined by the **debt to total assets ratio (Ch. 14).** This information may also be gained from the ratio of long-term debt to stockholders' equity or the ratio of stockholders' equity to long-term debt.

*40. The **times interest earned ratio (Ch. 14) is computed by dividing net income before interest charges and taxes by the interest charge.** This ratio focuses on the ability of a company to cover all its interest charges. In general, difficulty in meeting interest obligations is indicative of serious financial problems.

*41. The **cash debt coverage ratio (Ch. 5) is computed by dividing net cash provided by operating activities by average total liabilities.**

*42. The **book value per share of stock (Ch. 15)** is the amount each share would receive if a company were liquidated and the amounts reported on the balance sheet were realized. **Book value per share is computed by allocating the stockholders' equity items among the various classes of stock and then dividing the total so allocated to each class of stock by the number of shares outstanding.** This calculation loses its significance when the amounts reported on the balance sheet do not reflect the fair market value of the items.

Limitations of Ratio Analysis

*43. (S.O. 11) Ratio analysis is not without its limitations. Before placing a great deal of reliance on ratios alone, an investor must be aware of the fact that any ratio is only as sound as the financial data upon which it is built. The great variety of accounting policies relating to the computation of net income provides a good example of the reasons for exercising caution when interpreting financial ratios.

Comparative and Percentage Analysis

*44. (S.O. 12) The presentation of **comparative financial statements** affords an analyst the opportunity to determine trends and analyze the progress an entity has made over a specified period of time. The annual financial statement presentation in a corporate annual report normally includes detailed comparative financial statement for the current and preceding year along with a 5- or 10-year summary of pertinent financial data.

*45. (S.O. 13) **Percentage** or **common-size** analysis is a method frequently used to evaluate a business enterprise. This type of analysis involves reducing all the dollar amounts to a percentage of a base amount in the financial statement. All items in an income statement are frequently expressed as a percentage of sales or sometimes as a percentage of cost of sales. The items in a balance sheet are often analyzed as a percentage of total assets. **Horizontal analysis** is a form of percentage analysis that is useful in evaluating trend situations. Another approach, called **vertical analysis,** involves expressing each number on a financial statement in a given period as a percentage of some base amount.

*International Accounting Standards

*46. (S.O. 14) There is a need for one set of globalized accounting standards for the following reasons:
>   a. Multinational corporations.
>   b. Mergers and acquisitions
>   c. Information technology.
>   d. Financial markets.

*47.   The primary organization involved in developing international standards is the International Accounting Standards Board (IASB). It is privately funded and based in London. Its members currently come from nine countries. The IASB develop standards referred to as International Financial Reporting Standards (IFRS). The use of their standards are completely voluntary.

GLOSSARY

Accounting policies.
The specific accounting principles and methods currently employed and considered most appropriate to present fairly the financial statements of an enterprise.

*Acid-test ratio.
The ratio of cash, marketable securities, and net receivables to total current liabilities.

*Activity ratios.
Ratios that measure how effectively an enterprise is using the assets employed.

Adverse opinion.
There are so many material exceptions that in the auditor's judgment the financial statements taken as a whole are not presented in accordance with generally accepted accounting principles.

*Asset turnover.
Net sales divided by the average total assets during the year.

Auditor.
An accounting professional who conducts an independent examination of the accounting data presented by a business enterprise.

Auditor's report.
The auditor's expression of an opinion concerning whether financial statements are presented fairly, in all material respects, in accordance with generally accepted accounting principles.

*Book value per share.
Common stockholders' equity divided by outstanding shares.

*Cash debt coverage ratio.
Net cash provided by operating activities divided by average total liabilities.

Common costs.
Costs that are incurred for the benefit of more than one segment and whose interrelated nature prevents a completely objective division of costs among segments.

*Common-size analysis.
Reducing all the dollar amounts to a percentage of a base amount.

*Comparative analysis.
The same information is presented for two or more different dates or periods so that like items can be compared.

*Coverage ratios.
Ratios that measure the degree of protection for long-term creditors and investors.

*Current cash debt ratio.
Net cash provided by operating activities divided by average current liabilities.

*Current ratio.
The ratio of total current assets to total current liabilities.

*Debt to total assets.	Debt divided by total assets or equities.
Disclaimer of an opinion.	The auditor has gathered so little information on the financial statements that no opinion can be expressed.
Discrete approach.	Each interim period should be treated as a separate accounting period; deferrals and accruals would therefore follow the principles employed for annual reports.
Earnings per share.	Net income minus preferred dividends divided by weighted shares outstanding.
Errors.	Unintentional mistakes.
Financial forecast.	Prospective financial statements that present, to the best of the responsible party's knowledge and belief, an entity's expected financial position, results of operations, and cash flows.
Financial projection.	Prospective financial statements that present, to the best of the responsible party's knowledge and belief, given one or more hypothetical assumptions, an entity's expected financial position, results of operations, and cash flows.
Fraudulent financial reporting.	Intentional or reckless conduct, whether act or omission, that results in materially misleading financial statements.
Full disclosure principle.	Financial reporting of any financial facts significant enough to influence the judgment of an informed reader.
*Horizontal analysis.	Percentage analysis that indicates the proportionate change over a period of time.
Integral approach.	The interim report is an integral part of the annual report and deferrals and accruals should take into consideration what will happen for the entire year.
Interim reports.	Reports that cover periods of less than one year.
*International Accounting Standards Board (IASB)	The primary organization involed in developing international accounting standards.
*Inventory turnover.	Cost of goods sold divided by the average inventory during the year.
Irregularities.	Intentional distortions of financial statements.

*Liquidity ratios.	Ratios that measure an enterprise's short-run ability to pay its maturing obligations.
Management discussion and analysis (MD&A).	The section of the annual report which covers three financial aspects of the enterprise's business-liquidity, capital resources, and results of operations.
*Payout ratio.	The ratio of cash dividends to net income less preferred dividends.
*Percentage analysis.	Reducing a series of related amounts to a series of percentages of a given base.
*Price earnings (P/E) ratio.	The market price of stock divided by earnings per share.
*Profit margin on sales.	Net income divided by net sales.
*Profitability ratios.	Ratios that measure the degree of success or failure of a given enterprise or division for a given period of time.
*Rate of return on assets.	Net income divided by average total assets during the year.
*Rate of return on common stock equity.	Net income after interest, taxes, and preferred dividends divided by the average common stockholders' equity.
*Receivables turnover.	Net sales divided by the average receivables outstanding during the year.
Related party transactions.	Transactions which arise when a business enterprise engages in transactions in which one of the transacting parties has the ability to influence significantly the policies of the other, or in which a nontransacting party has the ability to influence the policies of the two transacting parties.
Qualified opinion.	The auditor's standard opinion contains an exception.
Safe harbor rule.	An SEC rule which provides protection to an enterprise that presents an erroneous forecast as long as the forecast is prepared on a reasonable basis and is disclosed in good faith.
Summary annual reports.	A report that contains a condensed financial presentation in a more readable format than that of the traditional annual report.
*Times interest earned.	Income before taxes and interest charges divided by interest charges.
Transfer pricing.	The practice of charging a price for goods "sold" between divisions or subsidiaries of a company.
Unqualified opinion (clean opinion).	The auditor's opinion that the financial statements present fairly, in all material respects, the financial position, results of operations, and cash flows of the entity in conformity with generally accepted accounting principles.

*Vertical analysis.   Percentage analysis that indicates the proportional expression of each item on a financial statement in a given period to a base figure.

CHAPTER OUTLINE

Fill in the outline presented below.

(S.O. 1) Full Disclosure Principle

(S.O. 2) Notes to the Financial Statements

Accounting Policies

Inventory

Property, Plant, and Equipment

Creditor Claims

Equity Holders' Claims

Contingencies and Commitments

Deferred Taxes, Pensions, and Leases

Changes in Accounting Policies

Chapter Outline *(continued)*

Subsequent Events

Disclosures of Special Transactions or Events

Related Party Transactions

Errors

Irregularities

Illegal Acts

(S.O. 3) Reporting Disaggregated Information

Selecting Reportable Segments

Segment Tests

Information to Be Reported

(S.O. 4) Interim Reports

Chapter Outline *(continued)*

Interim Reporting Requirements

Unique Problems of Interim Reporting

Advertising and similar costs

Expenses subject to year-end adjustment

Income taxes

Extraordinary items

Changes in accounting

Earnings per share

Seasonality

(S.O. 5) Auditor's Report

Unqualified or Clean Opinion

Qualified Opinion

Adverse Opinion

Chapter Outline *(continued)*

Disclaimer of an Opinion

Other Areas in the Annual Report

Management's Discussion and Analysis

(S.O. 6) Management's Responsibilities for Financial Statements

Social Responsibility

(S.O. 7) Financial Forecasts and Projections

Summary Annual Reports

(S.O. 8) Fraudulent Financial Reporting

*(S.O. 9) Financial Statement Analysis

*(S.O. 10) Ratio Analysis

Chapter Outline *(continued)*

*Liquidity Ratios

*Activity Ratios

*Profitability Ratios

*Coverage Ratios

*(S.O. 11) Limitations of Ratio Analysis

*Reporting Ratios—Some Issues

*(S.O. 12) Comparative Analysis

*(S.O. 13) Percentage Analysis

*(S.O. 14) International Accounting Standards

REVIEW QUESTIONS AND EXERCISES

TRUE-FALSE

Indicate whether each of the following is true (T) or false (F) in the space provided.

_____ 1. (S.O. 2) Notes are an integral part of the financial statements of a business enterprise.

_____ 2. (S.O. 2) Normally, the information disclosed in notes to financial statements is less relevant to an understanding of the financial statement than the information presented in the body of the financial statements.

_____ 3. (S.O. 2) When gain or loss contingencies exist, an enterprise will generally disclose them in notes to the balance sheet.

_____ 4. (S.O. 2) A careful reading of the notes to the financial statements provides information as to off balance sheet commitments, future financing needs, and the quality of a company's earnings.

_____ 5. (S.O. 2) Notes related to the claims of equity holders are quite rare, as this kind of information is presented in the equity section of the balance sheet directly opposite the class of security to which the information applies.

_____ 6. (S.O. 2) An executory contract refers to a contract entered into by an enterprise that must be fulfilled by an executive of the company.

_____ 7. (S.O. 2) When consolidated financial statements are presented by a business enterprise, that enterprise is required to disclose the principles of consolidation in the notes to its financial statements.

_____ 8. (S.O. 2) Accounting policies of a given entity are normally the specific accounting principles recommended by the industry in which the entity operates.

_____ 9. (S.O. 3) Segment information that is required to be reported must be prepared on the same accounting basis as that used in the enterprise's consolidated financial statements.

_____ 10. (S.O. 3) A particular segment is **not** significant enough to disclose unless its revenues exceed 10% of the revenues earned by the other segments being reported.

_____ 11. (S.O. 4) Interim financial reports prepared by a business enterprise normally include a complete set of financial statements for a period of less than one year.

_____ 12. (S.O. 4) The required approach to handling extraordinary items in interim financial reports is to charge or credit the loss or gain in the interim period that it occurs instead of attempting some arbitrary multiple-period allocation.

_____ 13.   (S.O. 4) For purposes of computing earnings per share and making the disclosures required by GAAP, each interim period should stand alone; that is, all applicable tests should be made for that single period.

_____ 14.   (S.O. 4) According to GAAP, when a company issues a quarterly income statement, that statement should represent approximately one-fourth of the total net income for the year in which the quarter exists.

_____ 15.   (S.O. 5) When an auditor examines the financial statements of a business enterprise for the purpose of expressing an opinion thereon, he or she attempts to determine whether the statements are an accurate representation of the entity's financial position and results of operations.

_____ 16.   (S.O. 5) An auditor is a professional who conducts an independent examination of the accounting data presented by the business enterprise for the purpose of expressing an opinion thereon.

_____ 17.   (S.O. 5) An adverse opinion is an indication that the financial statements do **not** present fairly the financial position and results of operations.

_____ 18.   (S.O. 6) Management is required to highlight favorable or unfavorable trends and to identify significant events and uncertainties that affect the enterprise's liquidity, capital resources, and results of operations.

_____ 19.   (S.O. 7) Companies are required to issue a summary annual report which contains a condensed financial presentation in a more readable format than that of the traditional annual report.

_____ 20.   (S.O. 8) The SEC has a safe harbor rule which allows companies to report fraudulent information as long as it was done in good faith.

_____ *21.   (S.O. 10) Rate of return on assets is computed by using as a numerator net income and as a denominator average total assets.

_____ *22.   (S.O. 10) The price earnings ratio is computed by dividing the market price of a share of common stock by the net income for the period.

_____ *23.   (S.O. 11) One limitation of ratios is that they are based on historical cost, which can lead to distortions in measuring performance.

_____ *24.   (S.O. 11) In situations where the calculations of net income includes a significant amount of estimated items, profitability ratios lose some of their credibility.

_____ *25.   (S.O. 12) The relevance of conclusions drawn from an analysis of financial ratios is enhanced when the ratios are computed from comparative financial statements.

_____ *26.   (S.O. 13) When the percentage analysis is used in connection with an income statement, the items shown on the income statement are normally expressed as a percentage of net sales.

_____ *27. (S.O. 13) Vertical analysis is the proportionate change over a period of time.

_____ *28. (S.O. 14) The International Financial Reporting Standards (IFRS) issued by the International Accounting Standards Board are **not** enforceable and therefore completely voluntary.

MULTIPLE CHOICE

Select the best answer for each of the following items and enter the corresponding letter in the space provided.

_____ 1. (S.O. 1) The full disclosure principle, as adopted by the accounting profession, is best described by which of the following?

A. All information related to an entity's business and operating objectives is required to be disclosed in the financial statements.
B. Information about each account balance appearing in the financial statements is to be included in the notes to the financial statements.
C. Enough information should be disclosed in the financial statements so a person wishing to invest in the stock of the company can make a profitable decision.
D. Disclosure of any financial facts significant enough to influence the judgment of an informed reader.

_____ 2. (S.O. 2) Which of the following questions would an analyst be **least** likely to find addressed by the notes to the financial statements?

A. What method of depreciation is used on plant assets?
B. What type of inventory method is being used to account for inventory?
C. How many separate bank accounts does the company maintain?
D. What restrictions are required by the new bond issue?

_____ 3. (S.O. 2) The disclosure of accounting policies is important to financial statement readers in determining:

A. net income for the year.
B. whether accounting policies are consistently applied from year to year.
C. the value of obsolete items included in ending inventory.
D. whether the working capital position is adequate for future operations.

_____ 4. (S.O. 2) Which of the following should be disclosed in a Summary of Significant Accounting Policies?

A. The aggregate amount of maturities and sinking fund requirements for all long-term borrowings.
B. Inventory method followed.
C. The existence of outstanding stock options.
D. Possible tax assessments.

_____ 5. (S.O. 2) If a business entity entered into certain related party transactions it would be required to disclose all of the following information **except**:

    A.   The nature of the relationship between the parties to the transactions.
    B.   The nature of any future transactions planned between the parties and the terms involved.
    C.   The dollar amount of the transactions for each of the periods for which an income statement is presented.
    D.   Amounts due from or to related parties as of the date of each balance sheet presented.

_____ 6. (S.O. 2) Which of the following describes **unintentional** mistakes?

	Errors	**Irregularities**
A.	Yes	Yes
B.	No	Yes
C.	No	No
D.	Yes	No

_____ 7. (S.O. 3) In presenting segment information, which of the following items must be reconciled to the entity's consolidated financial statements?

	Revenues	**Operating Profit (Loss)**	**Identifiable Assets**
A.	Yes	Yes	Yes
B.	No	Yes	Yes
C.	Yes	No	Yes
D.	Yes	Yes	No

_____ 8. (S.O. 3) An industry segment is regarded as significant and therefore identified as a reportable segment if it satisfies one or more quantitative tests that deal with segment revenues, income, or assets. In addition to these quantitative tests the FASB believes entities should not report too many segments so as to overwhelm users with detailed information that may not be useful. The FASB also requires that:

    A.   segment results equal or exceed 75% of the combined sales to unaffiliated customers for the entire enterprise.
    B.   a separate set of financial statements be shown for each identified segment.
    C.   any segment reporting a net loss for two consecutive years be eliminated.
    D.   the entity disclose in the notes to the financial statements each segment considered but not reported.

_____ 9. (S.O. 4) The accounting profession indicates that:

    A.   all companies that issue an annual report should issue interim financial reports.
    B.   the discrete view is the most appropriate approach to take in preparing interim financial reports.
    C.   the three basic financial statements should be presented each time an interim period is reported upon.
    D.   the same accounting principles used for the annual report should be employed for interim reports.

10.   (S.O. 4) In the first week of June 2010, Travis Company incurred advertising expenses at a cost of $300,000. These advertising costs will benefit operations for the second half of the calendar year. How should these expenses be reflected in Travis's quarterly income statements?

Three Months Ended

	3/31/10	6/30/10	9/30/10	12/31/10
A.	$75,000	$ 75,000	$ 75,000	$ 75,000
B.	$ -0-	$100,000	$100,000	$100,000
C.	$ -0-	$ -0-	$150,000	$150,000
D.	$ -0-	$ -0-	$300,000	$ -0-

11. (S.O. 5) The standard unqualified opinion issued at the conclusion of an audit by the independent public accountant contains how many paragraphs?

    A.   Two.
    B.   Three.
    C.   Four.
    D.   Five.

12. (S.O. 5) If the financial statements examined by an auditor lead the auditor to issue an opinion that contains an exception that is **not** of sufficient magnitude to invalidate the statement as a whole, the opinion is said to be:

    A.   unqualified.
    B.   qualified.
    C.   adverse.
    D.   exceptional.

13. (S.O. 5) The management discussion and analysis (MD&A) section of the annual report should focus attention on which of the following financial aspects of an enterprise's business?

	Liquidity	Capital Resources	Results of Operations
A.	No	No	Yes
B.	No	Yes	Yes
C.	Yes	Yes	Yes
D.	No	No	No

_____ 14. (S.O. 7) Which of the following best characterizes the difference between a financial forecast and a financial projection?

    A. Forecasts include a complete set of financial statements while projections include only summary financial data.

    B. A forecast is normally for a full year or more and a projection presents data for less than a year.

    C. A forecast attempts to provide information on what is expected to happen whereas a projection may provide information on what is not necessarily expected to happen.

    D. A forecast includes data which can be verified about future expectations while the data in a projection is not susceptible to verification.

_____ 15. (S.O. 7) The publication of profit projections by a business enterprise is:

    A. required by the SEC on an annual basis.

    B. recommended for all companies whose primary source of revenue changes during any one fiscal period.

    C. prohibited by the AICPA because accounting is considered to be historical in nature rather than forward-looking.

    D. encouraged by the SEC, which has issued a safe harbor rule to protect entities that present this kind of information.

_____ 16. (S.O. 8) Opportunities for fraudulent financial reporting are present in circumstances when the fraud is easy to commit and when detection is difficult. An opportunity for fraud would **least** likely arise from the following situation:

    A. Unusual or complex transactions.

    B. The absence of a Board of Directors or audit committee.

    C. Ineffective internal audit staffs.

    D. Strong internal controls.

_____*17. (S.O. 10) Durdil Company has a current ratio of 2:1. If current assets and current liabilities are both increased by $10,000, the current ratio will:

    A. increase.

    B. decrease.

    C. remain unchanged.

    D. either increase or decrease based on the total amount of current assets and current liabilities before the increase took place.

_____*18.   (S.O. 10) Information from Hardy Company's balance sheet is as follows:

Current assets
Cash	$ 150,000
Marketable securities	200,000
Accounts receivable	300,000
Inventories	350,000
Prepaid expenses	20,000
Total current assets	$1,020,000

Current liabilities
Notes payable	$ 50,000
Accounts payable	450,000
Accrued expenses	100,000
Income taxes payable	200,000
Total current liabilities	$ 800,000

What is the acid-test ratio?

A.   .4375 to 1
B.   .8125 to 1
C.   .8750 to 1
D.   1.275 to 1

_____*19.   (S.O. 10) Rosseto Company reports the following information about its sales and accounts receivable for 2010:

Sales
Net Cash Sales	$164,000
Net Credit Sales	451,000
Total sales	$615,000

Accounts Receivable
Balance 1/1/10	$ 86,000
Balance 12/31/10	78,000

What is the Rosseto Company's receivable turnover for 2010?

A.   2.0
B.   5.5
C.   7.5
D.   7.9

_____*20.   (S.O. 10) When should an average amount be used for the numerator or denominator?

A.   For an income statement item when a ratio consists of an income statement item and a balance sheet item.
B.   For a balance sheet item when a ratio consists of an income statement item and a balance sheet item.
C.   When the numerator is a balance sheet item or items.
D.   When the denominator is a balance sheet item or items.

_____*21.   (S.O. 10) Vrany Company's income statement included the following information related to its gross profit on sales.

Sales		$2,560,000
Beginning Inventory	$ 826,000	
Purchases	1,250,000	
	$2,076,000	
Less Ending Inventory	(904,000)	
Cost of Goods Sold		1,172,000
Gross Profit		$1,388,000

Vrany Company's inventory turnover is:

A.   1.296.
B.   1.355.
C.   1.419.
D.   1.605..

_____*22.   (S.O. 10) How are net sales used in the computation of each of the following ratios?

	Asset Turnover	**Profit Margin On Sales**
A.	Numerator	Denominator
B.	Denominator	Numerator
C.	Not Used	Denominator
D.	Numerator	Not Used

_____*23.   (S.O. 10) Nick Baker Company earns a 7.4% return on assets. If net income amounts to $275,000, total average assets must be:

A. $ 18,500.
B. $ 203,500.
C. $2,035,000.
D. $3,716,216.

_____*24.   (S.O. 10) Presented below is information related to Riley, Inc.:

	December 31	
	2010	**2011**
Common stock	$500,000	$600,000
Preferred stock	400,000	400,000
Retained earnings (includes net income for current year)	150,000	200,000
Net income for year	40,000	130,000

What is Riley's rate of return on common stock equity for 2011 if a $20,000 dividend was given to the preferred shareholders during 2011?

A.   22%
B.   20%
C.   13%
D.   9%

_____ *25.   (S.O. 10) Devers Company has 120,000 shares of common stock outstanding on December 31, 2010, selling at a current market price of $56 per share. If the price-earnings ratio at December 31, 2010 is 14, what amount of net income did Devers Company earn in 2010?

    A. $ 480,000.
    B. $1,680,000.
    C. $5,040,000.
    D. $6,720,000.

_____ *26.   (S.O. 10)   The times interest earned ratio includes which of the following in its computation?

	Income Before Taxes and Interest	Interest Charges	Total Debt
A.	Denominator	Numerator	Not Included
B.	Not Included	Numerator	Denominator
C.	Numerator	Not Included	Denominator
D.	Numerator	Denominator	Not Included

_____ *27.   (S.O. 11) Perhaps the most severe criticism aimed at ratio analysis is:

    A.   the difficulty involved in computing most ratios.
    B.   the extensive variety of ratios that must be computed in order to answer the same questions.
    C.   the additional financial data that must be prepared along with the financial statements so the various ratios can be computed.
    D.   the difficult problem of achieving comparability among firms in a given industry.

_____ *28.   (S.O. 12) Ratio analysis provides only a single snapshot, the analysis being for one given point or period in time. When an investment analyst wishes to concentrate on a given item to determine whether it appears to be growing or diminishing year by year and the proportion of such change to related items, they should use:

    A.   speculative analysis.
    B.   combined ratio and percentage analysis.
    C.   comparative analysis.
    D.   common place analysis.

REVIEW EXERCISES

1. Match the item on the left with the phrase on the right that most appropriately describes that item.

A. Note information
B. Accounting policy disclosure
C. Auditor's report
D. Reporting of segment information
E. Interim financial reporting
F. Social responsibility disclosures
G. Financial forecast
H. Financial projection
I. Fraudulent financial reporting
J. Management discussion and analysis

_____1. A report useful to investors that indicates, among other things, the accounting basis used by an entity to prepare its financial statements.

_____2. A report used to provide information on the profitability of a company for less than a one-year period.

_____3. Information related to environmental and ecological issues addressed by the firm.

_____4. Financial information based on a company's assumptions reflecting conditions it expects would exist in the future, given one or more hypothetical assumptions.

_____5. Information that is an integral part of the financial statements that serves as a means of amplifying or explaining the items presented in the main body of the statements.

_____6. A part of an entity's annual report that covers three aspects of the business--liquidity, capital resources, and results of operations.

_____7. Information related to the accounting methods used in the preparation of year-end financial statements.

_____8. Information based on a company's assumptions reflecting conditions it expects to exist in the future and the course of action it expects to take.

_____9. Intentional or reckless conduct, whether act or omission, that results in materially misleading financial statements.

_____10. Information related to revenue and profit breakdowns by divisional lines.

*2.   (S.0.10) The following ratios were prepared from data included in the December 31, 2010, financial statements of Williams Corporation.

Current Ratio:	3.0 to 1
Acid-test Ratio:	1.4 to 1
Current Assets to Total Assets:	.3 to 1
Owners' Equity to Total Assets:	.4 to 1
Owners' Equity to Total Debt:	2.0 to 3

If total owner's equity at December 31, 2010 amounts to $950,000, compute the following account balances (round to the nearest hundred):

a.   Current Assets   _____   d.   Working Capital   _____
b.   Quick Assets   _____   e.   Long-Term Assets   _____
c.   Current Liabilities   _____ f.   Long-Term Debt   _____

*3.   (S.O. 10) Listed below are a series of transactions and financial events. Opposite each transaction a ratio is listed which is used in financial analysis.

Transaction	Ratio	Effect
a. Purchased merchandise inventory on account.	Acid-test ratio	_____
b. Paid two-years' rent in advance.	Current ratio	_____
c. Net sales remained unchanged, while total cost of operations decreased.	Profit margin on sales	_____
d. Net income and total cash dividends were both increased by 5%.	Payout rates	_____
e. Issued 5% nonconvertible preferred stock. No dividends were paid in the first year of issue.	Earnings per share	_____
f. Bonds payable with a face value of $500,000 were converted dollar for dollar for common stock.	Debt to equity ratio	_____
g. Sold marketable securities at a price in excess of original cost.	Current ratio	_____
h. Purchased a building in exchange for a long-term mortgage.	Book value per share	_____

Instructions:
Indicate the effect (increase, decrease, or no effect) the transaction would have on the ratio listed opposite the transaction.

*4.   (S.O. 10) The following data was taken from the accounts of Wasserman Company as of December 31, 2010.

Accounts and Notes Payable	$ 46,500
Accounts Receivable (net), beginning	58,000
Accounts Receivable (net), ending	64,600
Cash	35,000
Prepaid Expenses	19,000
Purchases (net)	127,800
Inventories, beginning	81,500
Inventories, ending	92,000
Sales	388,000
Sales Returns and Allowances	20,000
Other expenses (all cash expenses)	165,800
Accrued Liabilities	9,600
Marketable Securities	15,900

On the basis of the information above determine the December 31, 2010:

a.   Amount of working capital
b.   Current ratio
c.   Acid-test ratio
d.   Receivables turnover
e.   Inventory turnover
f.   Profit margin on sales

*5.   (S.O. 10) The following data was taken from the accounts of Forman Company as of December 31, 2010.

Total Assets, 1/1/10	$1,860,000
Total Assets, 12/31/10	2,245,000
Common Shares Outstanding	
All Year (no potential dilution)	48,000
Sales	1,525,000
Cost of Goods Sold	778,000
Cash Expenses (including interest of	
$40,000 and taxes of $110,000)	327,000
Depreciation and Amortization	160,000
Market Price of Stock 12-31	45
Cash Dividends	96,000
Total Debt	1,415,000
Sales Returns	40,000

On the basis of the information shown above compute the following as of December 31, 2010.

a. Asset turnover

b. Rate of return assets

c. Earnings per share

d. Price earnings ratio

e. Payout ratio

f. Debt to total assets

g. Times interest earned

h. Book value per share

*6.   (S. 0. 10) The following comparative financial statements are for the Wetzel Company for the periods ending 12/31/09 and 12/31/10

Wetzel Company
Income Statement
For the Years Ended December 31, 2009 and 2010
(000 Omitted)

	2009	2010
Sales and Other Revenue		
Net Sales	$1,250,000	$1,740,000
Interest Revenue	60,000	75,000
Other revenue	35,000	40,000
Total Revenue	**$1,345,000**	**$1,855,000**
Costs and Other Charges		
Cost of Goods Sold	850,000	1,055,000
Depreciation & Amortization	124,000	133,000
Selling & Administrative	145,000	165,000
Interest Expense	40,000	60,000
Total Expenses	**1,159,000**	**1,413,000**
Income Before Taxes	186,000	442,000
Income Taxes	65,000	175,000
Net Income	**$ 121,000**	**$ 267,000**

Wetzel Company
Balance Sheet
December 31, 2009 and 2010
(000 Omitted)

Assets	2009	2010
Current Assets		
Cash	$ 38,000	$ 56,000
Marketable Securities	85,000	100,000
Accounts Receivable (net)	275,000	325,000
Inventories (LCM)	240,000	260,000
Total Current Assets	**638,000**	**741,000**
Investments (at cost)	**345,000**	**355,000**
Fixed Assets		
Property, Plant, & Equipment	1,500,000	2,100,000
Accumulated Depreciation	(600,000)	(700,000)
Total Fixed Assets	**900,000**	**1,400,000**
Intangibles	60,000	80,000
Total Assets	**$1,943,000**	**$2,576,000**

Liabilities and Stockholders' Equity

Current Liabilities

Accounts Payable	$125,000	$181,000
Notes Payable	250,000	275,000
Accrued Liabilities	180,000	225,000
Total Current Liabilities	**555,000**	**681,000**

Long-Term Debt

Bond Payable	**700,000**	**1,000,000**
Total Liabilities	**1,255,000**	**1,681,000**

Stockholders' Equity

Common Stock, $10 par	300,000	300,000
Additional Paid-in Capital	280,000	280,000
Retained Earnings	108,000	315,000
Total Equity	**688,000**	**895,000**
Total Debt and Equity	**$1,943,000**	**$2,576,000**

Additional Information:
Shares outstanding in 2007 = 30 million
Cash dividend paid $2 per share
Ending 2010 market price of stock = $50

Instructions:
Compute the following ratios for 2010:

a.	Current Ratio	h.	Return on Common Stock Equity
b.	Acid-Test Ratio	i.	Earnings Per Share
c.	Receivables Turnover	j.	Price Earnings Ratio
d.	Inventory Turnover	k.	Payout Ratio
e.	Asset Turnover	l.	Debt to Total Assets
f.	Profit Margin on Sales	m.	Times Interest Earned
g.	Rate of Return on Assets	n.	Book Value Per Share

SOLUTIONS TO REVIEW QUESTIONS AND EXERCISES

TRUE-FALSE

1. (T)

2. (F)   The information in the notes to financial statements and the information in the body of the financial statements are equally relevant. The notes provide a means of amplifying on the data presented in the body of the financial statements. Because of the complexity of economic events reflected in the financial statements, notes are a necessary part of full disclosure in financial reporting.

3. (T)

4. (T)

5. (F)   It is quite common to have equity notes related to contracts and senior securities outstanding that might affect the various claims of the residual equity holders. These notes are important and are by no means rare.

6. (F)   When two parties commit themselves to some undertaking on the basis of a signed contract but neither party has yet performed, the contract is executory.

7. (T)

8. (F)   The accounting policies of a given entity are the specific accounting principles and methods currently employed and considered appropriate to present fairly the financial statements of the enterprise. An entity is required, by GAAP, to include a note in its financial statements that provides information about the significant accounting policies it has adopted.

9. (F)   The accounting principles to be used for segment disclosure need not be the same as the principles used to prepare the consolidated statements.

10. (F)   There are three quantitative tests that determine whether a segment is significant enough to disclose. To be disclosed, a segment must meet either a revenue test, a profit test, or an asset test. The revenue test requires the segment's revenue to be 10% or more of the combined revenue of all the enterprise's industry segments.

11. (F)   Interim financial reports normally show summarized information on revenues, expenses, assets, liabilities, and shareholder's equity. The profession encourages but does not require companies to publish a balance sheet and a statement of cash flows.

12. (T)

13. (T)

14.   (F)   The profession has not taken a definite position on the most appropriate method to use in recognizing revenues and expenses during an interim period. Entities currently use both the discrete and integral viewpoint in the preparation of interim financial statements. Because of the vague nature of the standards for interim financial reports, it is difficult to characterize the relationship of interim financial reports and annual financial reports.

15.   (F)   This statement is made false by the use of the word *accurate*. An auditor expresses an opinion on whether the financial statements "present fairly" the financial position and results of operation. In the auditing literature the term *presents fairly* has a specific meaning.

16.   (T)

17.   (T)
18.   (T)

19.   (F)   Summary annual reports are not required. However, some companies have experimented with their issuance.

20.   (F)   The SEC does not have a safe harbor rule concerning fraudulent information. The SEC does, however, have a safe harbor rule concerning financial forecasts and projections.

*21.   (T)

*22.   (F)   The price earnings ratio is computed by dividing the market price of the stock by its earnings per share.

*23.   (T)

*24.   (T)

*25.   (T)

*26.   (T)

*27.   (F)   Vertical analysis is the proportional expression of each item on a financial statement in a given period to a base figure. Horizontal analysis indicates the proportionate change over a period of time.

*28.   (T)

MULTIPLE CHOICE

1. (D) The concept of full disclosure assumes an informed reader of the financial statements. Also, the facts being disclosed must be significant enough to influence the judgment of the reader in making an informed decision. The information that is required to be disclosed in the financial statements should help the informed reader better understand the entity's financial position, results of operations, and cash flow. Thus, some information relevant to an entity's business or operating objectives should not be disclosed because it might be considered confidential. For example, R & D considerations, secret formulas or processes, and pending marketing strategies represent information relevant to an entity's operations but beyond the requirements of full disclosure.

2. (C) Notes are the accountant's means of amplifying or explaining the items presented in the main body of the financial statements. The information in the notes is designed to increase the reader's ability to understand an entity's financial position, results of operations, and changes in financial position. Knowing the number of bank accounts a company maintains adds little if anything to one's ability to understand the financial statements.

3. (B) Financial statement users are concerned with comparability between financial statements issued in different accounting periods. In an attempt to promote comparability, the accounting profession requires consistent application of accounting principles or an explanation in the financial statements about any changes that have taken place. The disclosure of accounting policies in each year's financial statements helps readers evaluate the consistent application of accounting principles.

4. (B) The Summary of Significant Accounting Policies is a separate section of the financial statements or the initial notes that covers the accounting principles adopted and followed by the reporting entity. Answers A, C and D represent items that are to be reported in the other notes.

5. (B) Alternatives A, C, and D represent required disclosures where related party transactions are involved. There is no requirement to anticipate future transactions with parties known to be related to the entity or to make any disclosures along these lines.

6. (D) Errors are defined as unintentional mistakes. Irregularities are intentional distortions of financial statements.

7. (B) The professional standards require that the operating profit (loss) before income taxes and identifiable assets be reconciled to the consolidated financial statements.

8. (A) The reason the FASB requires the 75% rule is to prevent a company from providing limited information on only a few segments and lumping all the rest into one category.

9. (D)   GAAP makes no requirements about who would present interim reports nor does it express a preference for the discrete or integral view. Also, GAAP does not require management to present any specific financial statements for an interim period. However, GAAP does require use of the same accounting principles in interim reports as in annual financial statements.

10. (C)   The general guidelines are that costs such as advertising should be deferred in an interim period if the benefits extend beyond that period; otherwise, they should be expensed as incurred. Because the advertising expenses benefit the remainder of the calendar year, the costs should be apportioned for both periods ending 9/30/10 and 12/31/10.

11. (B)   The standard unqualified opinion issued by the independent public accountant includes three paragraphs. These paragraphs, in the order of their presentation, are known as the (1) introductory, (2) scope, and (3) opinion paragraphs. When the independent auditor issues an unqualified opinion he or she indicates that the financial statements present fairly, in all material respects, the financial position, results of operations, and cash flows of the entity in conformity with generally accepted accounting principles.

12. (B)   A qualified opinion is issued by an auditor when an item material to the financial statements or the audit examination requires mention in the financial statements. An adverse opinion is issued when the financial statements do not present fairly the financial position of the entity.

13. (C)   The management discussion and analysis (MD&A) section of the annual report covers three financial aspects of an enterprise's business--liquidity, capital resources, and results of operations. It requires management to highlight favorable or unfavorable trends and to identify significant events and uncertainties that affect these three factors.

14. (C)   Because a projection includes at least one hypothetical assumption, the data presented therein is not necessarily expected to happen. There is normally no difference in the type of information or the length of time covered by the data in forecasts or projections.

15. (D)   Profit projections are not required by the SEC nor are they prohibited by the AICPA. Also, there is no reason why a company whose primary source of revenue changes is any more likely to present profit projections. The SEC has encouraged management to present this information. The safe harbor rule provides protection to an enterprise that presents an erroneous projection as long as the projections were prepared on a reasonable basis and were disclosed in good faith.

16. (D)   An opportunity for fraud can exist from:

(1)   The absence of a Board of Directors or audit committee;
(2)   Weak or nonexistence internal accounting controls;
(3)   Unusual or complex transactions;
(4)   Accounting estimates, requiring significant subjective judgment; and
(5)   Ineffective internal audit staffs.

Strong internal accounting controls assist in preventing the opportunity for fraud.

*17. (B)   When the current ratio is positive (current assets greater than current liabilities) and both current assets and current liabilities are increased by the same amount, the new current ratio will decrease. For example, the following demonstrates the original and new current ratio based on the increase.

	Original	**New**
Current assets	$40,000	$50,000
Current liabilities	$20,000	$30,000
Current ratio	2:1	1.7:1

*18. (B)   The acid-test ratio is cash, marketable securities and net receivables divided by current liabilities which is equal to .8125 [($150,000 + $200,000 + $300,000)/$800,000].

*19. (B)   The receivables turnover is computed by dividing net credit sales by net average receivables. In the problem, average receivables equals $82,000 [($86,000 + $78,000)/2]. Thus, $451,000/$82,000 = 5.5.

*20. (B)   Although ratio analysis is not an exact science, because the income statement item represents a period of time, it is better if the balance sheet item also reflects the same period of time; otherwise, an unusual ending balance amount of the balance sheet item can distort the relationship between the income statement item and the balance sheet item.

*21. (B)   Inventory turnover: $\dfrac{\text{Cost of goods sold}}{\text{Average inventory}}$

$$\left[\dfrac{1,172,000}{\dfrac{826,000 + 904,000}{2}}\right] = 1.355$$

*22. (A)   The formula for asset turnover is: $\dfrac{\text{Net Sales}}{\text{Average Total Assets}}$

The formula for profit margin on sales is: $\dfrac{\text{Net Income}}{\text{Net Sales}}$

*23. (D) Return on assets: $\dfrac{\text{Net income}}{\text{Average total assets}}$

$$\frac{\$275,000}{\text{Average total assets}} = 7.4\%$$

$$\text{Average total assets} = \frac{\$275,000}{.074}$$

$$\text{Average total assets} = \underline{\$3,716,216}$$

*24. (B) The rate of return on common stock equity is net income of $130,000 minus preferred dividends of $20,000 divided by average common stockholders' equity of $550,000 [$500,000 + $600,000)/2] to calculate 20% ($110,000/$550,000).

*25. (A) Price earnings ratio: $\dfrac{\text{Market price of stock}}{\text{Net income} \div \text{shares outstanding}}$

$$\frac{\$56}{\text{Net income} \div 120,000} = 14$$

$$\text{Net income} \div 120,000 = 4$$

$$\text{Net income} = \underline{\$480,000}$$

*26. (D) The times interest earned ratio is computed as follows:

$$\frac{\text{Income before Taxes and Interest Charges}}{\text{Interest Charges}}$$

*27. (D) Ratio analysis is criticized because a problem does exist in achieving comparability among firms in a given industry. Achieving comparability among firms that apply different accounting procedures is difficult and requires that the analyst (a) identify basic differences existing in their accounting and (b) adjust the balances to achieve comparability.

*28. (C) The presentation of comparative financial statements affords an analyst the opportunity to determine trends and analyze the progress an entity has made over a specified period of time.

REVIEW EXERCISES

1.

1.	C	6.	J
2.	E	7.	B
3.	F	8.	G
4.	H	9.	I
5.	A	10.	D

*2.

a.	Current Assets	$712,500	d.	Working Capital	$ 475,000
b.	Quick Assets	$332,500	e.	Long-Term Assets	$1,662,500
c.	Current Liabilities	$237,500	f.	Long-Term Debt	$1,187,500

To solve this exercise, the ratios should be computed in the following order (solve for "x" in each case):

1. Owners' equity to total debt:

$$\frac{\$950,000}{x} = 2/3; x = \$1,425,000 \text{ total debt.}$$

2. Owners' equity to total assets:

$$\frac{\$950,000}{x} = .4; x = \$2,375,000 \text{ total assets.}$$

3. Current assets to total assets:

$$\frac{x}{\$2,375,000} = .3; x = \$712,500 \text{ current assets.}$$

4. Current ratio:

$$\frac{\$712,500}{x} = 3.0; x = \$237,500 \text{ current liabilities.}$$

5. Acid-test ratio:

$$\frac{x}{\$237,500} = 1.4; x = \$332,500 \text{ quick assets}$$

6. Long-term debt:
   $1,425,000 – $237,500 = $1,187,500

7. Working capital:
   $712,500 – $237,500 = $475,000

8. Long-term assets:
   $2,375,000 – $712,500 = $1,662,500

*3. a. $$\frac{\text{Cash} + \text{Marketable Securities} + \text{Net Receivables}}{\text{Current Liabilities (Increase)}} = \text{Decrease}$$

b. $$\frac{\text{Current Assets}}{\text{Current Liabilities}} = \text{No Effect}$$

c. $$\frac{\text{Net Income (Increase)}}{\text{Net Sales}} = \text{Increase}$$

d. $$\frac{\text{Cash Dividends (Increase by 5\%)}}{\text{Net Income Less Preferred Dividends (Increase by 5\%)}} = \text{No Effect}$$

e. $$\frac{\text{Net Income Minus Preferred Dividends}}{\text{Weighted Shares Outstanding}} = \text{No Effect}$$

f. $$\frac{\text{Debt (Decrease)}}{\text{Equities (Increase)}} = \text{Decrease}$$

g. $$\frac{\text{Current Assets (Increase)}}{\text{Current Liabilities}} = \text{Increase}$$

h. $$\frac{\text{Common Stockholder's Equity}}{\text{Outstanding Shares}} = \text{No Effect}$$

*4. a. Current Assets = $64,600 + $35,000 + $19,000 + $92,000 + $15,900 = $226,500
     Current Liabilities = $46,500 + $9,600 = $56,100
     Amount of Working Capital = $226,500 − $56,100 = $170,400

b. Current Ratio = $226,500 ÷ $56,100 = 4.04 to 1

c. Cash, Marketable Securities and Receivables = $115,500
    Acid-Test Ratio = $115,500 ÷ $56,100 = 2.06 to 1

d. Average Trade Receivables (Net) = ($58,000 + $64,600) ÷ 2 = $61,300
    Net Sales = $388,000 − $20,000 = $368,000
    Receivables Turnover = $368,000 ÷ $61,300 = 6 times

e. Average Inventory ($81,500 + $92,000) ÷ 2 = $86,750
    Inventory Turnover $117,300 ÷ $86,750 = 1.35 times
    *Cost of Goods Sold = ($81,500 + $127,800 − $92,000) = $117,300

f. Net Income = $368,000 - ($117,300 + $165,800) = $84,900
    Profit Margin on Sales = $84,900 ÷ $368,000 = 23%

*5.   a.   Net Sales = $1,525,000 - $40,000 = $1,485,000
          Average Total Assets = ($1,860,000 + $2,245,000) ÷ 2 = $2,052,500
          Asset Turnover = $1,485,000 ÷ $2,052,500 = .72 times

     b.   Net Income = $1,485,000 – ($778,000 + $327,000 + $160,000) = $220,000
          Rate of Return on Assets = $220,000 ÷ $2,052,500 = 10.7%

     c.   Earnings Per Share = $220,000 ÷ 48,000 = $4.58

     d.   Price-Earnings Ratio = $45 ÷ $4.58 = 9.83

     e.   Payout Ratio = $96,000 ÷ $220,000 = 43.6%

     f.   Debt to Total Assets = $1,415,000 ÷ $2,245,000 = 63%

     g.   Income Before Interest Charges and Taxes = $220,000 + $40,000 + $110,000 =
            $370,000
          Times Interest Earned = $370,000 ÷ $40,000 = 9.25 times

     h.   Common Stockholders' Equity = $2,245,000 – $1,415,000 = $830,000
          Book Value Per Share = $830,000 ÷ 48,000 = $17.29

*6.   a.   Current Ratio = $741,000 ÷ $681,000 = 1.09 times

b.   Cash, Marketable Securities and Receivables =
$56,000 + $100,000 + $325,000 = $481,000
Acid-Test Ratio = $481,000 ÷ $681,000 = .71 times,

c.   Average Trade Receivables (Net) = ($275,000 + $325,000) ÷ 2 = $300,000
Receivables Turnover = $1,740,000 ÷ $300,000 = 5.8 times or Every 63 Days
(365 ÷ 5.8)

d.   Average Inventory ($240,000 + $260,000) ÷ 2 = $250,000
Inventory Turnover = $1,055,000 ÷ $250,000 = 4.22 times or
Every 86 Days (365 ÷ 4.22)

e.   Average Total Assets = ($1,943,000 + $2,576,000) ÷ 2 = $2,259,500
Asset Turnover = $1,740,000 ÷$2,259,500 = .77 times

f.   Profit Margin on Sales = $267,000 ÷ $1,740,000 = 15.3 %

g.   Rate of Return on Assets = $267,000 ÷ $2,259,500 = 11.8%

h.   Average Common Stockholders' Equity = ($688,000 + $895,000) ÷ 2 = $791,500
Rate of Return on Common Stockholders' Equity = $267,000 ÷ $791,500 = 33.7 %

i.   Earnings Per Share = $267,000 ÷ 30,000 = $8.90

j   Price - Earnings Ratio = $50 ÷ $8.90 = 5.62

k.   Payout Ratio   (30,000 x $2) ÷ $267,000 = 22%

l..   Debt to Total Assets = $1,681,000 ÷ $2,576,000 = 65%

m.   Income Before Interest Charges and Taxes = $267,000 + $60,000 + $175,000 =
$502,000
Times Interest Earned = $502,000 ÷ $60,000 = 8.37 times

n.   Book Value Per Share = $895,000 ÷ 30,000 = $29.83

NOTES

NOTES

NOTES

NOTES

NOTES

NOTES

NOTES

NOTES

NOTES

NOTES

NOTES

NOTES

NOTES

NOTES

NOTES

NOTES

NOTES

NOTES

NOTES

NOTES